2 vol

HISTORY OF THE
STUDY OF THEOLOGY

STUDIES IN THEOLOGY

12mo, cloth. 75 cents net per vol.

NOW READY

A Critical Introduction to the New Testament
By ARTHUR SAMUEL PEAKE, D.D.

Faith and its Psychology
By the Rev. WILLIAM R. INGE, D.D.

Philosophy and Religion
By the Rev. HASTINGS RASHDALL, D.Litt. (Oxon),
D.C.L. (Durham), F.B.A.

Revelation and Inspiration
By the Rev. JAMES ORR, D.D.

Christianity and Social Questions
By the Rev. WILLIAM CUNNINGHAM, D.D., F.B.A.

Christian Thought to the Reformation
By HERBERT B. WORKMAN, D.Litt.

Protestant Thought Before Kant
By A. C. McGIFFERT, Ph.D., D.D.

An Outline of the History of Christian Thought Since Kant
By EDWARD CALDWELL MOORE, D.D.

The Christian Hope: A Study in the Doctrine of Immortality
By WILLIAM ADAMS BROWN, Ph.D., D.D.

The Theology of the Gospels
By the Rev. JAMES MOFFATT, D.D., D.Litt.

The Text and Canon of the New Testament
By ALEXANDER SOUTER, D.Litt.

A Critical Introduction to the Old Testament
By the Rev. GEORGE BUCHANAN GRAY, D.D., D.Litt.

A Handbook of Christian Apologetics
By ALFRED ERNEST GARVIE, M.A., D.D.

Gospel Origins
By the Rev. WILLIAM WEST HOLDSWORTH, M.A.

The Religious Ideas of the Old Testament
By H. WHEELER ROBINSON, M.A.

Christianity and Sin
By ROBERT MACKINTOSH, D.D.

Christianity and Ethics
By ARCHIBALD B. D. ALEXANDER, M.A., D.D.

The Environment of Early Christianity
By S. ANGUS, M.A., Ph.D.

The Holy Spirit in Thought and Experience
By T. REES, M.A.

The Doctrine of the Atonement
By J. K. MOZLEY, M.A.

History of the Study of Theology. 2 Vols.
By CHARLES AUGUSTUS BRIGGS, D.D., D.Litt.

HISTORY OF THE
STUDY OF THEOLOGY

BY

CHARLES AUGUSTUS BRIGGS

D.D., D.LITT.

Prepared for Publication by his Daughter
EMILIE GRACE BRIGGS, B.D.

VOL. II.

NEW YORK
CHARLES SCRIBNER'S SONS
1916

Published 1916

CONTENTS

PART I

THE STUDY OF THEOLOGY IN THE MIDDLE AGES

PART II

THE MODERN AGE

PART I

THE STUDY OF THEOLOGY IN THE MIDDLE AGES

CHAPTER I

THE STUDY OF THEOLOGY IN THE NINTH AND TENTH CENTURIES

1. *A palace school was established by the Franks for the training of princes and nobles; when Charlemagne appointed Alcuin as its superintendent, it rapidly became a great centre of learning.*

The palace school was founded by one of the predecessors of Charlemagne for the training of the sons of princes and nobles. As a court school it moved about with the monarch from place to place. Charlemagne himself was trained there.[1] He had some knowledge of Greek as well as Latin, and studied with the grammarian, *Peter of Pisa* ; possibly also with *Paul the Deacon* († 797), a Benedictine monk and noted Lombard scholar, who taught Greek at his court for a time, and afterwards wrote a history of the Lombards.

The school of the palace was reorganised by *Alcuin*, and became celebrated during the eight years of his superintendence. His classes were frequented by Charlemagne himself, the members of his family and

[1] *Vide* Maître, *Les Écoles épiscopales et monastiques*, pp. 34 *seq.*

many of his courtiers. The emperor sought a reform in education, and states this purpose in the introduction to the Book of Homilies, revised at his order by Paul the Deacon :

'Desirous as we are of improving the condition of the churches, we impose upon ourselves the task of reviving, with the utmost zeal, the study of letters, well-nigh extinguished through the neglect of our ancestors. We charge all our subjects, as far as they may be able, to cultivate the liberal arts, and we set them the example.'

In the year 787 Charlemagne issued the famous capitulary addressed to all the bishops and abbots in his realm :

'During past years we have often received letters from different monasteries informing us that at their sacred services the brethren offered up prayers on our behalf ; and we have observed that the thoughts contained in these letters, though in themselves most just, were expressed in uncouth language, and while pious devotion dictated the sentiments, the unlettered tongue was unable to express them aright. Hence there has arisen in our minds the fear lest, if the skill to write rightly were thus lacking, so too would the power of rightly comprehending the sacred Scriptures be far less than was fitting ; and we all know that though verbal errors be dangerous, errors of the understanding are yet more so. We exhort you, therefore, not only not to neglect the study of letters, but to apply yourselves thereto with perseverance and with that humility which is well pleasing to God ; so that you may be able to penetrate with greater ease and certainty the mysteries of the Holy Scriptures. For as these contain images, tropes, and similar figures, it is impossible to doubt that the reader will arrive far more readily at the spiritual sense according as he is the better instructed in learning. Therefore, let there be chosen for this work men who are both able and willing to learn, and also desirous of instructing others ; and let them apply themselves to the work with a zeal equalling the earnestness with which we recommend it to them.' [1]

Alcuin was the chief assistant of Charlemagne in the work of educational reform. According to the Monk of

[1] *Vide* Mullinger, *The Schools of Charles the Great*, 1877, pp. 98 *seq.*

St. Gall, 'his teaching bore such fruit among the Gauls and Franks that they approached the ancient Romans and Athenians in learning.'[1]   But the journeys of the court Alcuin found irksome, and in 790 he withdrew from the palace school.   In the following years he took an important part in the theological discussions with the Adoptionists.   Although never advanced beyond the order of deacons, he was given a seat in the Council of Frankfort (794), in view of his great reputation for learning 'in the doctrines of the Church.'   He took a leading part in the deliberations of that body, which was composed of representative bishops from all parts of the West, was presided over by papal legates, and took decisive action against Adoptionism and image worship. Five years later, at the Council of Aachen, Alcuin had what he himself calls 'a great disputation' with a leader of the Adoptionists, Felix of Urgel, and won from him a public confession of error.   In 796 Alcuin was appointed abbot of the celebrated monastery of St. Martin at Tours, and there he laboured until his death.   He was a great teacher rather than a man of learning, and his *Grammatica* gives his views on education.   While chiefly a grammarian, he made his influence felt all along the range of scholarship, and wrote text-books on grammar, rhetoric, arithmetic, astronomy and the other liberal arts, some of which have been lost.   The Monk of St. Gall declares that his familiarity with the Scriptures 'in their whole extent' was beyond that of all the other scholars of his time.   He revised the text of the Vulgate, and wrote commentaries on various parts of the Bible, including Genesis, the Psalms, the Song of Songs, John's Gospel and the Hebrews.   He made great use of the Fathers, and subordinated the literal to the allegorical sense.   His works on theology include contributions to

[1] *Vide* Thatcher and M'Neal, *Source Book for Mediæval History*, p. 52.

dogmatics, ethics, liturgics, and hagiography. His
treatise on the Trinity ' contains the germs of the later
scholastic theology.' [1] Three hundred of his letters are
extant, and also hymns, epigrams and other forms of
verse.

Two years after the retirement of Alcuin from the
school of the palace, the headship was given to *Clement
of Ireland*, who came to the court of Charlemagne from
an Irish monastery in company with *Dungal*, another
noted scholar. Clement continued in charge of the
school under the son of Charlemagne, Louis the Pious.
A monk of St. Gall writes in the ninth century :

' Two Scots from Ireland lighted with British merchants on
the coast of Gaul, men learned without compare as well in secular
as in sacred writing. . . . (Charlemagne) enjoined the one named
Clement to abide in Gaul ; to whom he entrusted youths of the
most noble, middle and lowest ranks, in goodly number. . . .
The other he despatched into Italy, and appointed him the
monastery of St. Austin beside the Ticinian city, that there such
as were willing to learn might gather unto him.' [2]

In 804, the year of Alcuin's death, Charlemagne
opened at Osnabrück a school for training in the Greek
language and literature, which was influential in promoting higher education among the clergy.

2. *Alcuin revived the monastic school of Tours, and his
great pupil Rabanus Maurus carried his principles and
methods into Germany. The pupils of Rabanus, teaching
in various monasteries in Northern and Western Europe,
greatly enhanced theological education.*

Under the care of *Alcuin* the monastery of Tours
became a great centre of scholarship. To his monks
were distributed ' the honey of the sacred writings,' ' the
wine of ancient learning,' and ' the apples of grammatical
subtlety.' [3] Students flocked to him from all parts, and

---

[1] *Vide* Hahn, 'Alcuin,' in *New Schaff-Herzog Encyclopedia.*
[2] Poole, *History of Medieval Thought*, pp. 16 seq.
[3] *Vide* Mullinger, *Schools of Charles the Great*, pp. 112 *seq.*

the Anglo-Saxons came in such numbers that a native monk is said to have cried : ' They swarm hither like bees to their hive.' Alcuin introduced a reform in the Scriptorium, saying : ' Better than the digging of vines is the penning of books.' His school became noted for the clearness of its script, and the *Caroline Minuscule* was ' accepted as the standard in the imperial schools.' [1]

The greatest scholar among the pupils of Alcuin at Tours was *Rabanus Maurus* († 856), *Primus Germaniæ Præceptor*. He was born at Mainz in 776, and was trained in the liberal arts and theology in the monasteries of Fulda and Tours. He became a favourite of Alcuin, who gave him the surname of Maurus, the chief assistant of Benedict, implying thereby that he regarded Rabanus as his own chief successor, which indeed he became. In the year that Alcuin died Rabanus returned to Fulda. He became its most famous teacher, attracting students from all parts. Princes and nobles were trained in his school, as well as monks and clerics, and no applicant was rejected on the ground of poverty. When the Council of Aachen (817) closed the doors of the monastic schools to all save the *oblati*, a second school was opened at Fulda to provide for the ' seculars,' and this example was followed in other monasteries. Special attention was given to the training of preachers and teachers, and many of the students of Fulda were called to positions of power. In the year 822 Rabanus was chosen abbot. At that time Fulda was mother-house to sixteen lesser monasteries. Rabanus added six to the number, so that his rule extended over twenty-two institutions. He undertook to build up the library at Fulda, and it prospered greatly under his care. Like Alcuin, he saw the importance of multiplying manuscripts, and twelve monks were regularly employed in the Scriptorium. After nearly forty years of service, including a rule of twenty

[1] *Vide* Putnam, *Books and their Makers in the Middle Ages*, i. p. 107.

years as abbot, Rabanus retired from Fulda to compose
his encyclopædia *De Universo*, based on the theological
part of Isidore's work. Five years later he was made
archbishop of Mainz. He took a leading part in the
synods held there in 847, 848, and 852. In the controversy over predestination he opposed Gotteschalk; in
the eucharistic controversy he opposed Radbertus. His
writings cover a wide range. From the point of view of
education the most important is his treatise *De institutione clericorum*, which was based on Augustine's
De doctrina christiana, Cassiodorus' *Institutiones*, and
Gregory's *Cura Pastoralis*. Rabanus follows Alcuin in
recommending the study of dialectic to students of
theology. It is the *disciplina disciplinarum*. It
teaches how to teach, how to discriminate, how to know
and to make others know. 'It behoves the clergy to
acquaint themselves with this most noble art.' Rabanus
strongly emphasises the importance of the study of the
Scriptures, and like Alcuin makes great use of the
Fathers in their exposition. He wrote commentaries on
many of the books of the Bible and the Apocrypha, and
thus describes the principles of Biblical exegesis :

'If any one would master the Scriptures, he must first of all
diligently find out the amount of history, allegory, anagoge and
trope there may be in the part under consideration. For there
are four senses to the Scriptures, the historical, the allegorical,
the tropological and the anagogical, which we call the daughters
of Wisdom. Through these Wisdom feeds her children. To those
who are young and beginning to learn she gives the milk of
history; to those advancing in the faith the bread of *allegory*;
those who are truly and constantly doing good, so that they
abound therein, she satisfies with the savoury repast of *tropology*;
while, finally, those who despise earthly things and ardently desire
the heavenly she fills to the full with the wine of *anagoge*.' [1]

The writings of Rabanus include works on ethics,
martyrology, Church discipline, chronology and grammar,

[1] *Vide* Schaff, *History of the Christian Church*, vol. iv. p. 719.

sermons, letters and verse of various kinds. Some of his hymns are contained in the Breviary, and to him is ascribed the great pentecostal hymn, *Veni Creator Spiritus*.

The chief pupil of Rabanus was *Walafrid Strabo* (809-849). He studied for a time at the monastery of Reichenau on Lake Constance, and then for several years at Fulda. He was subsequently chosen abbot of Reichenau, which he made a centre of theological scholarship. He was the originator of the brief commentaries on the Scripture known as *Glossa Ordinaria*. He also made contributions to liturgics and Christian archæology and biography, and wrote verse, of unusual merit, including *The Vision of Wettin*, ' an early precursor of Dante's *Divina Commedia*.' [1]

Another noted scholar of Fulda was *Servatus Lupus* (805-862), who studied with Rabanus for six years. He was trained at the monastery of Ferrières before going to Fulda, and returned there to serve first as teacher and then as abbot. He was a literary man as well as a theologian, and a lover of wisdom for its own sake. He had a passion for books, and sought them far and wide, for his own use and for the library of his monastery. He was prominent in several councils, including those of Verneuil (843) and Soissons (853), and he corresponded with most of the great men of his day, one hundred and thirty of his letters being still extant. His works include a treatise on predestination, *Liber de tribus quæstionibus*, and also several lives of saints.

Among the famous pupils of Rabanus was *Rudolphus*, his successor in the school of Fulda, who was noted as a preacher and historian. The work of Einhard, *Annales Fuldenses*, was continued by him.

The monastery of Corbie, Picardy, was for many years in charge of the brothers Adalhard and Wala,

---

[1] *Vide* Sandys, *History of Classical Scholarship*, i. p. 485.

the cousins of Charlemagne, and Alcuin's pupils in the
palace school. Among the scholars of Corbie was
Paschasius Radbertus (c. 786-865), a man noted for piety
and learning. He taught in his monastery with great
success, and many of his pupils became famous. In
844 he was made abbot, but seven years later he resigned
his office and devoted the rest of his life to study. He
was active at the Councils of Paris (846) and Quiercy
(849). Great discussion was excited by a treatise of
Radbertus, in which he expressed a gross view of the
Eucharist; but no dogmatic decision resulted at that
time. His views were opposed by an anonymous
writing, *De corpore et sanguine Domini*, usually attributed
to *Ratramnus*, himself a monk of Corbie; but by the
Synod of Vercelli (1050) to John Scottus Erigena, who
agreed with it in any case. Radbertus also wrote on
the Virgin Birth and the Christian virtues, on Matthew
and Lamentations, on the lives of Adalhard and Wala,
and lesser works.

3. *In the reign of Louis the Pious the line was drawn
strictly between the monastic and the cathedral schools.
The latter were promoted by the bishops in their several
dioceses to vie with the monastic and palace schools in
learning.*

A capitulary of the year 817 decreed that monastic
schools were thereafter to be confined to monks, and that
the secular clergy were to be educated at the episcopal
schools under a *scholasticus* appointed by the bishops.
These episcopal schools were very ancient, indeed the
most ancient of all the Christian schools; but in France
they now began to multiply, and became more vigorous
and efficient.

In 822 Louis published a capitulary calling for an
increase in the number and efficiency of the Church
schools, that there might be a suitable place and properly

qualified teachers for the training of every aspirant to clerical rank, young or old. The following year he recalled to the bishops their promise to provide a sufficient number of such schools. In 824 a council in Paris urged this duty upon every bishop.[1] The most important cathedral schools of the ninth century were those at Rheims and Orléans.

Theodulphus, bishop of Orléans († 821), followed Alcuin, and nobly supported Charlemagne in the work of educational reform. About ten years after the publication of Charlemagne's famous capitulary, Theodulphus sent to his clergy one of his own, providing free schools for ' the children of the faithful in every town and village,' and recommending study as ' a means whereby the life of the righteous is nourished, and ennobled, and the man himself fortified against temptation.' [2] Under Theodulphus and his helper Wulfin the school of Orléans flourished. It became specially noted for the work of transcription, and the manuscripts copied there were models of skill and accuracy. Theodulphus himself was a scholar of exceptional attainments. Charlemagne called upon him for an account of the ceremonies of baptism, and also for a collection of sayings from the Fathers in support of the doctrine of the *filioque*. His didactic poems were famous, and his great hymn, *Gloria, laus et honor tibi*, was sung in France on Palm Sunday up to the time of the Revolution.

The cathedral school at Rheims was for many years under the supervision of *Hincmar* († 882). He became archbishop of Rheims in 845, and used his great authority to advance the cause of learning, enriching the libraries of Rheims, and calling upon his clergy to build up the schools of the diocese.

[1] *Vide* Maître, *Les Écoles épiscopales et monastiques de l'Occident*, 1866, pp. 24 *seq.*
[2] *Vide* Mullinger, *Schools of Charles the Great*, p. 103.

Lyons and Turin were also important centres of learning at this period. *Agobard*, archbishop of Lyons (779-840), was probably born in Spain and educated at Lyons. He was widely influential as a polemic divine, and wrote against Adoptionism, verbal inspiration, image worship and popular superstitions. Of special interest are his works, *De dispensatione ecclesiasticarum rerum*, and *Comparatio utriusque regiminis ecclesiastici et politici*.

Claudius, bishop of Turin († 832), was born also in Spain, and became a pupil of Felix of Urgel, but did not imbibe Adoptionism from his master. Like Agobard, he opposed image worship, and other customs tending toward superstition. He wrote commentaries on many of the books of the Bible, chiefly in the form of *catenæ*. He was suspected of Nestorianism.

4. *An effort was made in the second quarter of the ninth century to organise public schools of a higher order under the patronage of the crown, but the plan failed because of wars.*

In 829 an assembly of the bishops at Paris petitioned the emperor, Louis the Pious, to establish three large public schools to which seculars and regulars alike might resort. These were to be higher or graduate schools. This proposal was made about three centuries before the universities of Europe were established. But war and the division of the empire prevented the carrying out of the plan.

5. *In Italy nine public schools were established in the chief cities of the North, under the influence of Irish monks, and of Charlemagne. Two Roman councils ordained that every bishopric should have its school in which the Scriptures should be taught.*

During the seventh and eighth centuries theological as well as classical education met with varied fortunes in Italy, owing to frequent wars and invasions. But in the

ninth century there was a revival of learning. In 823
Lothair I. made a decree establishing central schools in
nine important cities : Pavia, Ivrea, Turin, Cremona,
Florence, Fermo, Verona, Vicenza, and Friuli. The
head of the school at Pavia was an Irishman named
Dungal, probably the same as the companion of Clement
at the court of Charlemagne.[1] Doubtless Lothair was
stimulated to the organisation of these schools by the
influence of his grandfather Charlemagne, whose own
teachers had come from the north of Italy.

Provision for episcopal schools was made by a Roman
council under Eugene II. (825), which ordained that
every see should have its bishop's school. This decree
was emphasised by a later council under Leo IV. (850),
which also required the appointment in every diocese of
teachers to interpret the Scriptures.

6. *Erigena was made head of the palace school in 845.
He used the dialectic method in the study of theology,
translated into Latin ' Dionysius the Areopagite,' and
made much use of the Greek Fathers.*

The older monastic education of Ireland again made
its influence felt in France at the court of Charles the
Bold, grandson of Charlemagne, through *Johannes Scottus*,
also called *Erigena* (*c.* 815-875). Greek was still taught
in the Irish schools, and Erigena was a Greek scholar.
He translated ' Dionysius the Areopagite ' into Latin,
and thus introduced this famous work of Neo-Platonism
to the West. Anastasius, the papal librarian, wondered
how ' this barbarian living on the confines of the world,
who might have been deemed to be as ignorant of Greek
as he was remote from civilisation, could have proved
capable of comprehending such mysteries and translating
them into another tongue.' [2] Erigena was a student of

[1] *Vide* p. 4.
[2] *Vide* Sandys, *History of Classical Scholarship*, p. 492.

Origen and the great Cappadocians, and through him their influence also was revived in the Western Church. In exegesis he made use of the allegorical method ; but in argument he appealed to the reason, using the dialectic method instead of the traditional citation of authorities in the Positive Theology. An example of this is his treatise *De divina prœdestinatione*, written against the high-Augustinian Gotteschalk. Erigena also appealed to the Greek rather than to the Latin Fathers. These unfamiliar methods brought him into trouble with the Latin theologians of his time. His great work is *De divisione naturœ*. He claims for theology and philosophy a common source—the divine Wisdom.

7. *Alfred the Great, of England, encouraged the study of theology by his patronage and his own translations.*

Alfred († 901) was a studious youth and a scholarly king. He revived the study of theology in England, and himself undertook the work of translation. He founded new monasteries at Winchester and Athelney, and assembled learned men from all parts to teach in his schools. He also established a school at his court for the training of the sons of nobles and officials, after the model of the school of Charlemagne. He and his helpers translated Boëthius' *Consolation of Philosophy*, the *Universal History* of Orosius, the *Ecclesiastical History* of Bede, Gregory's *Pastoral Care* and Augustine's *Soliloquies*.

8. *In the middle of the ninth century appeared for the first time the Pseudo-Isidorian Decretals, which, in connection with the Donation of Constantine, greatly influenced the development of Canon Law.*

They are summarily described by Gieseler :

'These decretals consisted of admonitions, instructions, and regulations, compiled for the most part from existing ecclesiastical literature. But they are of historical importance only in consequence of the new principles of ecclesiastical law by which, developing a tendency that had arisen already in the Church amid the weakness and disunion of worldly power, they were meant to make the Church independent of the State, and to give it a self-dependent centre of protection in the Roman see.   Exaltation of the episcopal dignity; numerous definitions for the purpose of securing the clergy, and in particular the bishops, against attacks; limitation of the metropolitans, who were often very much dependent upon the civil power; elevation of the primates to be the first instruments of the popes; and in particular, an enlargement of the privileges of the Roman see; these form the chief ecclesiastical and legal contents of the *Pseudo-Isidoriana.*' [1]

These decretals were issued under a pseudonym to support the bishops in their conflicts with the metropolitans in France. They were used by the popes, and in canon law, from the time of Nicolaus I. (864) onward to the Reformation, when they were shown to be without real authority. They originated in eastern France according to some scholars,[2] in western France according to others. Müller [3] suggests Rheims; Loofs [4] and Lesne,[5] either Rheims or Le Mans; Febronius, Theiner, and others, Rome.[6] There is the same uncertainty as to the date. Müller proposes 851-2, Loofs 847-853, Lesne 847-852. Many give an earlier date. Alexander Natalis, Mabillon and others assign them to the time of Charlemagne; Febronius to 744; Theiner to the years 774-785; Eichhorn to the eighth century; [7] but these earlier dates are improbable.

The *Donation of Constantine* was composed in Rome at a much earlier time, in the middle of the eighth century.

1 *Vide* Gieseler, *Ecclesiastical History*, ii. pp. 110 *seq.*
2 So Gieseler, following Blondel, Ballerini, Spittler, and Planck.
3 Karl Müller, *Kirchengeschichte*, i. p. 365.
4 Loofs, *Grundlinien der Kirchengeschichte*, p. 68.
5 Lesne, *La hiérarchie épiscopale, provinces, métropolitains, primats en Gaule et Germanie*, pp. 186 *seq.*
6 *Vide* Gieseler, ii. p. 114, *n.* 11.
7 *Vide* Gieseler, *ibid.*

9. *The tenth century was a time of destructive invasions by barbarians. Nevertheless the monastery of Cluny was founded, and produced many famous scholars. In Germany scholarship revived under the influence of Bruno. The greatest theologian of this age was Gerbert, a prodigy of learning, who also had distinguished pupils.*

During the latter half of the ninth and the whole of the tenth century everything in Europe was in confusion, owing to the constant struggles with heathen invaders, who destroyed cities and monasteries, burned books, and killed or took captive monks and scholars. England was overrun by the Danes ; western France by the Normans ; Germany, the east and south of France, and northern Italy by the Hungarians. These laid waste the monasteries of St. Gall in Switzerland, and of Fulda in Germany. South and West Italy, Spain, and southern France were in constant peril from the Saracens, who sacked Rome in 846. And yet even in this dark period new institutions of learning were founded, especially in France and Germany.

In the year 910 William, Duke of Aquitaine, founded the monastery of Cluny, in the diocese of Mâcon, with *Berno* as its first abbot († 927). Under his successor *Odo* († 941) it became a great seat of learning, from which as a centre the influence of reform pervaded the schools at Metz, Rheims, Liége and Paris, and spread even to other lands. Odo was trained in the monastery of St. Martin at Tours, and afterwards studied the Trivium and Quadrivium in Paris with Remi of Auxerre.

Gerbert (950-1003), a monk of Aurillac, was trained in that monastery under Raimund, a pupil of Odo at Cluny. He was sent to Barcelona, Spain, and there devoted himself to study, especially to mathematics, astronomy, and music. On his return to France he taught in the schools of Tours, Fleury, Sens, and Rheims. In the latter school he acquired a reputation for extraordinary learning.

The range of his studies included medicine, which gave
rise to the suspicion that he practised the magic arts.
This did not prevent his rapid advancement in the
Church ; and he became in succession abbot of Bobbio,
archbishop of Rheims, archbishop of Ravenna, and
finally pope (999), under the name of Silvester II.

Gerbert had many distinguished pupils, among whom
may be mentioned *Richer of Rheims*, the historian
(† 1010), and *Fulbert of Chartres*,[1] the founder of that
famous school. But of all the pupils of Cluny or its
scholars, the most illustrious was *Hildebrand*, who, as
Gregory VII., became the greatest of the mediæval
popes.[2]

In Germany the cause of learning was upheld by
Bruno (925-965), son of Henry the Fowler and brother of
Otto the Great. He was educated at Utrecht, and
was entrusted by Otto with the building up of the *schola
palatina*. In 940 he was made chancellor, in 951
archicapellanus, and two years later archbishop of
Cologne. He is said to have ' restored the long ruined
fabric of the seven liberal arts.' Wherever he went, he
carried with him his library, ' as if it had been the ark of
the Lord.' Poole likens him to Alfred of England, and
ascribes to his influence the fact that ' the clergy of
Germany became marked out from the rest of Christendom no less by their education than by its fruit, their
moral excellence.' Poole cites Arnulf of Orléans as
saying ' in his famous speech before the Council of St.
Basol, near Rheims (991) : " *In Belgica et Germania . . .
summos sacerdotes dei religione admodum præstantes
inveniri.*" '[3]

10. *During the Middle Ages there was much less intellectual activity in the Greek Church than in the Latin.*

---

[1] *Vide* pp. 24 f.   [2] *Vide* pp. 17 f.
[3] *Vide* Poole, *Medieval Thought*, pp. 86 *seq.*

*In the ninth and tenth centuries the only great writers were
Photius and Suidas.*

Photius (c. 820-897), patriarch of Constantinople, led
the Greeks in their dispute with the Latin Church over
the *filioque*. He was a voluminous writer of encyclopædic learning, and is called the greatest scholar of his
time. His chief works on theology are : his *Bibliotheca*
or *Myriobiblon*, which describes two hundred and eighty
books in as many chapters ; and his *Amphilochia*, which
gives answers to three hundred questions, chiefly relating
to the Scriptures. He also wrote a lexicon, commentaries, a treatise on the Holy Spirit, a polemic against the
Paulicians, letters, poems and other minor works. Many
of his writings are extant in fragments only ; others
have been lost altogether.

Suidas is known only through his lexicon (c. 976), a
work of great learning and permanent value, which has
some of the features of an encyclopædia.

The only other writers worthy of mention are :
Œcumenius, the exegete († 999), *Simeon Metaphrastes*,
the hagiographer (c. 900), and the minor historians
Nicephorus († 829) and *Theophanes* († c. 817), belonging
to the Constantinopolitan school.[1] This age, however,
produced some of the greatest hymns of the Greek
Church.

[1] *Vide* pp. 38 f.

CHAPTER II

THE STUDY OF THEOLOGY IN THE ELEVENTH AND TWELFTH CENTURIES

THE tenth century had been a time of terrible disaster, of corruption in morals and disorders of every kind, all calling for reform. The eleventh century was a time of revival. The second period of the Middle Ages properly begins in the midst of this century, when the Hildebrandian reforms began.

1. *Hildebrand, a scholar of Cluny, of extraordinary ability in theology and law, became the great reformer of the Church of the eleventh century, whose influence has remained through all the subsequent times.*

Hildebrand (c. 1020-1085) was born in Tuscany, and received his education in Rome. He entered a Benedictine monastery on the Aventine, which was under the reforming influence of Cluny, and ' the home of its abbots on their pilgrimages to Rome.' [1]   It is said that Hildebrand spent some time at Cluny during his student years. He became the disciple and assistant of Gregory VI., accompanying him on his journeys. On the death of that pope Hildebrand retired to Cluny. In 1049 he was called to Rome as companion of Bruno, who was received there with acclamation as Pope Leo IX. Hildebrand now became a man of affairs. He had doubtless been trained in law, though where is not known. He now took up the

[1] Schaff, *History of the Christian Church*, v., Pt. i. p. 11.

work of reform begun at the Synod of Sutri (1046), and carried it on during the pontificates of Leo IX. and his successors. He himself became pope in 1073, as Gregory VII. At his election he was declared to be ' a man eminent in piety and learning, a lover of equity and justice, . . . well brought up and educated in the bosom of this mother church.' [1] In 1075 he wrote to Hugh of Cluny, in great distress, mourning the evils that existed in the Church :

' The Eastern Church, fallen from the faith, and attacked from without by the infidels. In the West, South or North, scarcely any bishops who have obtained their office regularly, or whose life and conduct correspond to their calling, and who are actuated by the love of Christ instead of worldly ambition. . . . And when I look to myself, I feel oppressed by such a burden of sin, that no other hope of salvation is left me but in the mercy of Christ alone.' [2]

As pope Hildebrand laboured for twelve, as reformer for six-and-thirty years. He transformed the papacy and the entire priesthood and hierarchy, after monastic models. Of the three vows of the regulars, enforcing chastity, obedience and poverty, two were extended by him to the secular clergy as well. There could be no more married priests, and the law of obedience of the seculars must be as strict as that of the regulars.

Gregory thereby accomplished two great reforms : he overcame simony and concubinage for a time among the clergy ; and he emancipated the Church from the dominion of the state. But he erred in straining the authority of the pope, so as to extend it beyond faith and morals into civil and social affairs, which belong to the state. He even went so far as to depose an emperor, and to put whole nations under the ban.

2. *In the eleventh century there was a great revival in the Benedictine order ; and many new monasteries were*

---

[1] *Vide* Schaff, *History of the Christian Church*, v., Pt. i. p. 25.
[2] *Ep.* ii. 49, as quoted by Schaff, *ibid.*, p. 26.

*established, the chief of which was that of Bec, in Normandy,
out of which came Lanfranc and Anselm.*

The Benedictine order gave birth in the eleventh
century to several new forms, which perpetuated themselves in the different countries. The most important of
these were established : (1) at Camaldoli in the Apen-
nines (1012), where Romuald of Ravenna founded the
Camaldolites ; (2) at Vallombrosa, near Florence (1038),
where Gualbert founded the Vallombrosans ; (3) at
Grenoble, in France (1084), where Bruno founded the
Carthusian order, which laid great stress on the gathering
and transcribing of books ; (4) at Citeaux, in France
(1098), where Robert Cluniac founded the Cistercians, the
order of St. Bernard.

Bruno († 1101) was trained at the cathedral school of
Rheims, and taught there as *scholasticus* for some twenty
years. According to Maître,[1] he lectured on the liberal
arts and theology with such distinction that the whole
of France resounded with the triumph of ' the doctor of
doctors,' and associated his name with those of Lanfranc
and Anselm.

Bernard of Clairvaux (1090-1153), the great mystic,
built up the Cistercian order, and was one of the most
influential teachers and preachers of the Mediæval
Church. He is said by his friend, John of Salisbury, to
have known ' little of secular letters ' ; yet he was ' a man
mighty in work and speech before God, as it is believed,
and before men, as is well known.'[2]   William of St.
Thierry († 1149) wrote : 'I tarried with him a few days ...
and whichever way I turned my eyes, I marvelled, and
thought I saw a new heaven and a new earth. ... One could
feel that God was in the place.'[3]   Bernard was remarkable for his knowledge of the Scriptures, and was revered

---

[1] *Vide* Maître, *Les Écoles épiscopales et monastiques*, p. 105.
[2] *Vide* Poole, *History of Medieval Thought*, p. 189.
[3] *Vita prima*, i. 7 ; *vide* Migne, clxxxii.

in his lifetime as a saint and a prophet. His writings include dogmatic, mystic, polemic, ascetic and practical treatises, also many valuable letters, sermons, and hymns. Calvin says : ' In his *De consideratione* Bernard speaks as though the very truth itself were speaking.' Luther deems him ' superior in his sermons to all the doctors, even to Augustine.' [1]

The monastery of Bec was founded in Normandy, near the mouth of the Seine (*c.* 1034), by St. Herluin, and became the most famous monastic school of France in the eleventh century. Lanfranc (*c.* 1042) and Anselm (*c.* 1060) studied there : both ruled as prior, and Anselm as abbot (1078-1093). These distinguished scholars were both Lombards, and had studied in Italy before going to Bec. *Lanfranc* († 1089) had studied law as well as the liberal arts at Pavia, according to the statement of his early biographer ; [2] and it is probable that he introduced the study of law at Bec. It is related of Lanfranc that, when he visited Alexander II., the pope rose to meet him, saying that he did so ' not because he is archbishop of Canterbury, but because I was in his school at Bec, and sat at his feet with his other pupils.' [3]

Anselm († 1109) left family and fortune to attach himself to Lanfranc, whose fame filled the West. He replaced his master, first at Bec and then at Canterbury ; and far surpassed him as a theologian. He has been called a ' second Augustine ' and ' the last of the fathers.' [4] His influence was perpetuated by his pupil, Anselm of Laon, who counted among his hearers all the learned scholars of the twelfth century. The greater number of the pupils of Bec succeeded to positions in which they were able to exercise a powerful influence

[1] *Vide* Schaff, *History of the Christian Church*, pp. 344 *n.* 2, 351.
[2] Milo Crispin, *Vita Lanfranci*, I. v. ; *vide* Migne, *P.L.*, c]. 29, 39.
[3] *Vita Lanfranci*, ap. Migne, *P.L.*, cl. 19 ; Maître, *Les Écoles épisco-pales et monastiques*, p. 124.
[4] *Vide* Poole, *Medieval Thought*, p. 104.

on theological education. In England especially the
scholars of Bec were in demand.[1]

3. *Lanfranc and Anselm became the centres of two great
theological debates, namely, those on the Eucharist and the
Atonement.*

The eucharistic controversy was a revival of the
milder one of the ninth century, which raged for a while
about Paschasius Radbertus, Ratramnus, and John
Scottus Erigena, but did not then result in a dogmatic
definition. In 1050 *Berengar of Tours* wrote a letter to
Lanfranc, then prior of Bec, sustaining (as he thought)
Erigena's views, but really going to the length of heresy
in his conception of the Eucharist as symbolic. He
was condemned under the influence of Lanfranc, first at
Rome and Vercelli (1050), then at Florence (1055) and
Rome (1059), and finally in two councils held at Rome
(1078-1079), under Gregory VII., when he was compelled
to subscribe a profession of faith defining the church
doctrine of the Eucharist.[2] The doctrine as defined
was : (*a*) that the body of Christ is really present in the
Eucharist ; (*b*) that it is the identical body that was
crucified, rose from the dead, and is enthroned in heaven ;
(*c*) that the substance of the bread and wine is converted
into the substance of the body of Christ ; (*d*) that the
Eucharist is a sacrifice, representing the sacrifice of
Christ.[3]

Anselm was the greatest theologian of his time. He
made less use of the principle of authority than his
predecessors, even Lanfranc, and made great use of
reason and logic in the discussion of Christian doctrine.
This was especially so in his great works, the *Monologium*
and the *Proslogium*, notably in *Cur deus homo ?*, in

[1] *Vide* Maître, *Les Écoles épiscopales et monastiques*, p. 125.
[2] *Vide* Denzinger, *Enchiridion Symbolorum et Definitionum*, p. 105.
[3] *Vide* Briggs, *Theological Symbolics*, pp. 132 *seq.*

which he lays the foundation for the doctrine of the
Atonement for all time.   But as this did not provoke
serious discussion, it did not occasion a definition by the
Church.   His doctrine was that the Incarnation was a
voluntary act of the Son of God ; in order that He might,
by the death of the Cross, satisfy the divine majesty and
merit the divine grace for the sinful world.   Sin was an
offence against the divine majesty according to the
feudal conception, and it involved the extreme penalty
of death.   The sinner must suffer death or render
adequate satisfaction.   Only the Son of God could do
this by rendering infinite satisfaction and earning infinite
merit.   The older undogmatic view, still represented by
Bernard, was that the devil had a claim on the sinner,
and his claim was satisfied by the death of Christ on the
Cross.[1]

4. *In the eleventh century the cathedral schools became
prominent, especially those of Laon, Chartres, and Paris.*

1. The school of Laon became celebrated through two
brothers, *Anselm* († 1117) and *Ralph* († 1138), who
attracted students from great distances, from Milan in
the south and from Bremen in the north.   Many came
over from England.   These men were the teachers of
William of Champeaux, Abélard, Alberic of Rheims,
Gilbert de la Porrée, and many other notable scholars.
After the death of Ralph the school lost its importance.
Anselm studied at Bec, and ' laid the foundation of his
reputation ' at Paris, where he taught theology (*c.* 1076).
He was made *scholasticus* of the cathedral school at Laon
(*c.* 1089) ;   and he and his brother became ' the two eyes '
of that church.[2]   John of Salisbury calls them the
' most splendid luminaries of Gaul, the glory of Laon,

---

[1] *Vide* Briggs, *Theological Symbolics*, pp. 137 *seq.*
[2] Guibert de Nogent, cited by Feret, *La Faculté de théologie de Paris
au moyen âge*, i. p. 26.

whose memory is in pleasantness and blessing.'[1] Anselm's theology has been described as ' properly only a simple and solid exposition of the Holy Scripture, supported by the authority of the holy fathers, whom he studied all his life.' Guibert de Nogent says that he ' made more good Catholics than the heterodox (teachers) of his time made heretics, " tam sincera est in Scripturarum ac fidei assertione severitas." ' He was ' the light of all France and of the Latin Church.' John of Salisbury calls him ' doctorum doctorem.' Pope Eugene III. said : ' God caused him to be born so that the Holy Scriptures might not perish.'[2] Anselm, indeed, is especially distinguished in the history of Biblical Exegesis for his *Glossa interlinearis*, which continued to be used all through the Middle Ages. He also wrote special commentaries on the Song of Songs, Matthew, and Revelation. Abélard said of Anselm : ' He kindled a fire, not to give light, but to fill the house with smoke.'[3] But Crévier's comment is :

' It is hard to restrain one's indignation, at beholding thus treated a man who, for the forty years during which he taught theology, was regarded . . . as the light and the oracle of the Latin Church ; who was called the " doctor of doctors," and in whose school were trained the great theologians, scholars, and pious prelates, who gave lustre not only to France, but to England, Germany, and Italy.'[4]

The school of Laon, as Poole remarks,[5] ' acquired a peculiar and almost unique name for the steadfast fidelity with which it maintained and handed on the pure theological tradition of the Church ' ; and while this reputation may have been ' apart from the personal weight of (these) teachers,' it was doubtless the result of their labours.

[1] *Vide* Poole, *Hist. of Medieval Thought*, p. 112.
[2] Cited by Feret, *La Faculté de théologie de Paris*, i. pp. 27, 28.
[3] Abélard, *Ep.* i. 3 ; *vide* Poole, *Hist. of Medieval Thought*, p. 144 ; Feret, *La Faculté de Théologie de Paris*, i. p. 27.
[4] Crévier. *Hist. de l'Univ. de Paris*, i. pp. 124 *seq.*
[5] Poole, *Hist. of Medieval Thought*, pp. 111 *seq.*

2. The school of Chartres gained its importance from Fulbert, a pupil of Gerbert, and from Ivo, a pupil of Lanfranc. *Fulbert* († 1028) like Gerbert added medicine to theology, philosophy, and the liberal arts ; and Chartres soon took rank with Rheims as a seat of the higher learning. In 1006 Fulbert was made bishop; but he continued to teach in the school, following what seems to have been the traditional usage of the see, whose bishops in the sixth, seventh, eleventh, and twelfth centuries are known to have presided in the school.[1]   Fulbert was still young when he began to teach at Chartres ; and he presided there as bishop for considerably over twenty-one years. In that time multitudes came under his influence. An English monk of the following century writes :

'The town of Chartres, even in our time, is full of the genius of Fulbert. It is second to no other in Gaul in the number and the learning of its scholars.' [2]

The bond which united Fulbert to his pupils, and these to one another, was very strong. Adelmann, *scholasticus* of Liége, recalls with pleasure his life as a student ' sub nostro illo venerabili Socrate.'[3]   He describes himself to Fulbert as ' vernaculus tuus,' ' alumnus tuus.'   ' To others,' he cries, ' I have shown something of myself, but to you I have disclosed the whole.'   At Fulbert's death he wrote : ' I was his companion ; I was often by his side ; I drank with avidity the words of gold, sweet as honey, that fell from his lips.'   Hildegaire, another pupil, seeking pardon for having given way to anger in his presence, wrote : ' I implore you not to refuse me the boon of your counsel and your correction.   The greatest of misfortunes for me would be to be abandoned

---

[1] *Vide* Clerval, *Les Écoles de Chartres au moyen âge, du V⁰ au XVI⁰ siècle,* pp. 29 *seq.*
[2] Cited by Clerval, *ibid.,* p. 96.
[3] *Vide* Maître, *Les Écoles épisc. et monast.,* p. 103.

by you.' The same pupil compares himself to the hart
'panting for the water-brooks' in his longing for the
teaching of his master, 'more precious than gold or
silver, than life itself.' At Fulbert's death his scholars
wrote in his epitaph :

> 'He is dead, dear to God and to man, our Father of precious
> memory, Fulbert, bishop of this holy see. He was a conspicuous
> luminary, given to the world by God, . . . a man most eloquent
> and versed in the divine sciences and in the books of the liberal
> arts. . . . He has made this church illustrious with the rays of
> his sanctity and his learning, and has wrought great things for
> his students.' [1]

William of Malmesbury describes him as 'most
eminent in holiness and philosophy.' Clerval remarks
that he was acquainted with Hebrew, and cites the
Septuagint ; and that 'if he did not know the Greek
fathers, he was familiar with the Latin.' [2] In exegesis he
avoided excess in the use of both the allegorical and the
critical methods, basing his interpretation on the
literal and historical sense, and having recourse for that
purpose to the original text. Once possessed of the
literal meaning he passed on to its moral and spiritual
application. His theology, like that of Anselm of Laon,
was Positive Theology. Fulbert also appeals to codes
of canon law and to Charlemagne's Capitularies. He
'cites numerous councils, both ancient and modern.'
Clerval suggests that there was at Chartres some study
of law. Among the pupils of Fulbert was the famous
Berengarius († 1088), who became *scholasticus* at Tours
and archdeacon of Angers, and who reintroduced the
eucharistic controversy.[3]

The school of Chartres gained new distinction under
Ivo, or St. Ives († 1116), the most famous teacher of
canon law of his times. He is described as 'a religious

[1] Cited by Clerval, *Les Écoles de Chartres*, pp. 32, 101 *seq.*
[2] *Vide* Clerval, *ibid.*, pp. 36 *seq.*, 130 *seq.*, 141 *seq.*
[3] *Vide* p. 21.

man and of great learning.' In his youth he had
studied in Paris, and had 'heard master Lanfranc, prior
of Bec, treat of secular and divine letters in that famous
school which he had at Bec.' [1] Anselm was his fellow-
student there. He became himself a teacher in that
school, and then went as abbot to St. Quentin, which
he made illustrious as a centre of learning. To theology
and the liberal arts he added the study of canon law,
and probably began here his great collections of Canons
known as the *Collectio tripartita*, *Decretum*, and *Panormia*.
Ivo had already attained to great fame as a teacher,
when he was made bishop of Chartres (*c.* 1090). He is
the last bishop of that see who is known to have taught
in the school; but shortly after his death it rose once
more into prominence, and so remained until the middle
of the twelfth century, under the brothers Theodoric and
Bernard, and their pupils Gilbert de la Porrée, William of
Conches, and Richard l'Évêque.

Bernard of Chartres († *c.* 1130) became chancellor *c.*
1119. He was called by John of Salisbury *perfectissimus
inter Platonicos seculi nostri*. He was wont to say :

'We are as dwarfs mounted on the shoulders of giants, so that
we can see more and further than they; yet not by virtue of
the keenness of our eyesight, nor through the tallness of our
stature, but because we are raised and borne aloft upon that
giant mass.' [2]

Poole remarks : 'In this reverent dependence on the
ancients lies therefore the main peculiarity of the school
of Chartres.' He adds : 'It is the choice of reading that
stands out as the salient characteristic of Bernard's
method, and marks it as aiming at a totally different
level of excellence from that which had hitherto been
deemed sufficient.' [3] Among his many noted pupils

[1] *Vide* Poole, *History of Medieval Thought*, p. 114.
[2] John of Salisbury, *Metalogicus*, iv. 35 ; iii. 4.
[3] Poole, *History of Medieval Thought*, pp. 117, 120.

Gilbert de la Porrée was the most distinguished, and succeeded him as chancellor in 1126. He was devotedly attached to Bernard, and wrote to him from Aquitaine where he ' kept school ' :

' I have one sorrow, only one, which tortures me. It is that I am constrained to remain far from the presence of a teacher so illustrious. . . . I would fain be with you always, when you explain the mysteries hidden in the treasures of knowledge. I would draw with all my might upon the limpid and inexhaustible source of your wisdom. Separated in body from your Excellence, I am united to you by ardour of desire and by the heart, which brings near what is far ; and all that God has given or will give to me, by way of endowment, virtue, knowledge, all that I am—after God I owe it to you.' [1]

Gilbert was called away to Paris ; and two other pupils of Bernard carried on his work in the school, William of Conches and Richard l'Évêque. *William* († *c.* 1154) was ' post Bernardum Carnotensem opulentissimus grammaticus.' [2]

' With him, as with Bernard, . . . grammar, dialectic, and rhetoric . . . are the first things which the philosopher must possess: "with them equipped as with arms, we ought to approach the study of philosophy," first as learned in the sciences of the *Quadrivium*, and finally in Theology. . . . But the basis of the whole is grammar : " in omni doctrina grammatica praecedit." This is the mark of the school of Chartres.' [3]

Richard l'Évêque united with William in ' perpetuating the teaching of Bernard, and thus carried on a sound and healthy tradition. . . . The general method of the school was founded on the scheme of education laid down by Quintilian.' [4] Clerval says that Chartres was the centre of a universal renaissance of learning, showing a love for profane antiquity and a passion for its writers, its poets and philosophers. Greedy for knowledge, this school

[1] *Vide* Clerval, *Les Écoles de Chartres au moyen âge*, p. 219.
[2] John of Salisbury, *Metalogicus*, i. 5 ; *vide* Clerval, *Les Écoles de Chartres au moyen âge*, p. 181.
[3] Poole, *History of Medieval Thought*, p. 125.   [4] Sandys, i. p. 539.

searched for the writings of Aristotle, of Ptolemy, and of
other Greek authors, even among the Arabs of Spain,
and enlarged the circle of culture.[1]

Other cathedrals had distinguished scholars.   Among
these may be mentioned *Hildebert* († 1134), bishop of
Le Mans, and later archbishop of Tours.   He was noted
for his letters, which were ' studied, and even learnt
by heart, as patterns of epistolary composition ' ; [2] and
also, still more, as the first Latin writer to compose a
system of doctrine.   His *Tractatus theologicus* is a
Positive Theology, using the Scriptures and the Fathers,
and among the latter especially Augustine.   But he
also uses dialectic, and indulges in a great amount of
scholastic speculation.

The work has forty-one chapters and treats of faith and its
objects (Chapters i.-iii.), the Trinity (iv.-viii.), prescience, predestination, the will and the omnipotence of God (ix.-xi.), the
incarnation and nature of Christ (xii.-xvi.), angels (xvii.-xxii.),
the creation (xxiii.-xxv.), human nature, sin and virtue (xxvi.-
xxxix.), the sacraments (xl.), the divine Law (xli.).[3]

There were other chapters, which have not been preserved.   Hildebert was the first to use the term *trans-
substantiatio*.[4]

3. The cathedral school of Notre Dame at Paris
became, in the twelfth century, the most prominent in
France, under a number of famous teachers, the first of
whom was William of Champeaux.   *William* († 1121)
studied with the philosopher Manegold, with Anselm of
Laon, and with Roscelin.   He himself taught at Paris a
crowd of students from all parts, at first in the cathedral
school, and then (*c.* 1108) in the monastic school of St.
Victor, where his influence was long felt.   ' In those

---

[1] Clerval, *Les Écoles de Chartres*, p. 272.   [2] Sandys, i. p. 551.
[3] *Vide* Flügge, *Geschichte der theologischen Wissenschaften*, iii. pp.
387 *seq.*
[4] *Vide* Harnack, *Dogmengeschichte*, p. 303 (*Grundriss der theologischen Wissenschaften*).

days,' as Poole says, ' the school followed the teacher,
not the teacher the school.' [1]   William taught rhetoric
and dialectic as well as theology ; and came into conflict with his pupil Abélard as an advocate of Realism.
But as a theologian his method was that known as
Positive Theology, the Theology of the Fathers.   He
retained the friendship of St. Bernard, and was even,
according to Fisher, ' in some sense (his) guide.' [2]   In
1113 William was called from Paris to become bishop of
Châlons.   After his departure from the cathedral school
students still continued to flock there, and it attained
new celebrity under the pupils of William.[3]

5. *The brilliant Abélard taught a multitude of students,
attracted by his new method of speculative inquiry, with
which he enriched Positive Theology.*

Abélard (1079-1142) was for a time a pupil of Roscelin
of Compiègne ; then, after visiting other schools, he went
to Paris to study with William of Champeaux.   He came
into conflict with this teacher, and overpowered him by
a skilful use of dialectic, winning for himself a great
reputation.   When William retired to the monastery of
St. Victor, Abélard sought his class-room there ; but the
old conflict was soon renewed.   In the meanwhile
Abélard also had acquired a great body of followers,
who went about with him from place to place, ' to
Corbeil, to Melun, to Provins, to Saint Denis, and into
Brittany.' [4]   At the time that William left Paris for
Châlons, Abélard went to Laon to study theology with
Anselm ; but, professing to find that famous teacher
' a barren fig-tree,' he began a rival course of lectures—
a breach of order which led to his expulsion.   Returning
to Paris he took William's place at the head of the

---

[1] Poole, *History of Medieval Thought*, p. 109.
[2] Fisher, *History of Christian Doctrine*, p. 226.
[3] *Vide* pp. 31 ff.
[4] Maître, *Les ₋coles épisc. et monast.*, p. 145.

cathedral school. Some years later he entered the
monastery of St. Denis, and students flocked to him
there also. During his several residences in Paris he
greatly increased the renown of that seat of learning,
especially when he taught in the school attached to the
collegiate church of St. Geneviève. Abélard's methods
were speculative and critical. His aim was to seek the
truth by inquiry, and not from authority. ' By doubt-
ing we are led to inquire ; by inquiry we perceive the
truth.' [1] He exposed himself to suspicions of heresy by
the boldness of his speculation, his independence of
authority, his contests with all other teachers, and his
open-minded balancing of opinions over against one
another. He took an intermediate position between
the Nominalism of Roscelin and the Realism of William,
which is known as Conceptualism, and is nearer the
position of Aristotle.

' *Universalia ante rem* is the watchword of the Realists ;
Universalia in re of the Conceptualists ; *Universalia post rem* of
the Nominalists.' [2]

As the Nominalism of Roscelin had brought him into
a dilemma between Unitarianism and Tritheism, and
caused him to be charged with the latter, so the Conceptualism of Abélard led him in the direction of Sabel-
lianism. His treatise *De unitate et trinitate divina*
brought him into trouble. Otto of Freising represents
that he was charged with having ' effaced the discrimination of the Three Persons, which the Church
held to be not mere names, but distinct things with
separate properties.' [3] All of his teachers were against
him, having been alienated by his audacious and un-
generous criticisms, by his vanity and overbearing
manners. A council was called at Soissons (1121), and

[1] Abélard, *Sic et non, proe.* 17 ; *vide* Migne, *P. L.*, clxxviii.
[2] Fleming, *Vocabulary of Philosophy*, ed. Calderwood, 1887[4], p. 284.
[3] Poole, *History of Medieval Though'*, p. 152.

he was condemned; but the general opinion was that he had been treated unfairly.

A more formidable attack was made upon him by St. Bernard. He had composed an *Introduction to Theology*, understanding by theology the doctrine of God and the Trinity, which alone he discusses. This Introduction is usually regarded as the first attempt to construct a philosophical system of doctrine. The method of Abélard was more objectionable to the traditionalists than his results. Because of his method they suspected and misrepresented his results. St. Bernard, with his immense popularity and eloquence, was a formidable opponent; and Abélard was once more condemned in 1141 by the Council of Sens. He took refuge with Peter the Venerable at Cluny, and there in the following year he died. It is said that at Cluny he 'read constantly, prayed often, gladly kept silence.' [1] According to Peter's verdict he was 'ever to be named with honour; the servant of Christ, and verily Christ's philosopher.' [2] His writings include, besides those already named, his famous *Sic et non*, a work on Ethics called *Scito te ipsum*, a commentary on Romans, *Theologia Christiana*, *Hexameron*, a treatise on Dialectics, and an autobiography, *Historia calamitatum*.

6. *The cathedral school of Paris continued to flourish under the care of distinguished teachers, the most important of whom were Gilbert de la Porrée, Robert Pulleyn, and Peter the Lombard.*

1. *Gilbert* (c. 1070-1154) was born at Poitiers, and studied in the episcopal school there, and afterwards at Chartres, Paris, and Laon. Otto of Freising, his pupil, writes:

'From his youth Gilbert placed himself under the discipline of great teachers, relying more upon their authority than upon

---

1 *Vide* article 'Abélard,' in *New Schaff-Herzog Encyclopedia*.
2 *Vide* Poole, *History of Medieval Thought*, p. 166.

his own genius. These masters were, first, Hilary of Poitiers, then Bernard of Chartres, finally the two brothers Anselm and Ralph of Laon. With them he acquired not little, but great learning, remaining under their control a long time, bringing his manners and his conduct into harmony with his knowledge.' [1]

At Paris he studied with William of Champeaux and also with Abélard. He was recalled to Chartres by Bernard, whom he served for a time as assistant and finally succeeded as chancellor. Some years later he went to teach in Paris, and then in Poitiers, where he was made bishop (1142). His chief contributions to theology are (1) commentaries on the Bible in the form of glosses, an elaboration of the *Glossa interlinearis* of his master Anselm of Laon ; (2) *De Trinitate*, a work attributed then to Boëthius, but really a collection of several writings on the subject by different persons at different periods. This treatise brought Gilbert into trouble. His tendency was towards Tritheism, although he denied it. Thus Realism had its perils in discussing the doctrine of the Trinity, as well as Nominalism and Conceptualism. Gilbert was attacked by Bernard of Clairvaux in a council held at Paris, 1147. No agreement was reached, and the council, adjourning to Rheims in the following year, became hopelessly divided, so that Gilbert escaped condemnation. It is remarkable that he seems to have retained the respect of his bitterest opponents. One of these is forced to acknowledge that ' though few were for the doctrine, very many were for the man, and did all they could to excuse and extenuate even opinions which they did not hold.' Otto of Freising, Gilbert's pupil, denies that there is any resemblance between his trial and that of Abélard.

'The case was not the same, nor the matter kindred. For Gilbert had from youth submitted himself to the teaching of great men, and trusted in their weight rather than in his own powers.'

---

[1] *Vide* Clerval, *Les Écoles de Chartres*, pp. 163 *seq.*

John of Salisbury remarks :

' It is certain that a good many things are now handled by scholars in public which, when (Gilbert) put them forward, were reckoned as profane novelties. . . . Gilbert was a man of the clearest intellect, and of the widest reading ; he had spent some sixty years in study and the exercise of literature, and was so ripe in liberal culture as to be surpassed by no one, rather it was believed that in all things he excelled all men.' [1]

His work *De sex principiis*, ' a supplement to the *Categories* of Aristotle, was accepted through the Middle Ages as second only in authority to the works of the founder of logic.' [2] An unknown writer of the time of Gilbert declares :

' He was a master most celebrated, intrepid, learned, and superior to all the other masters. He was a logician, theologian, moralist, dialectician. Of the seven arts he lacked only astronomy. . . . He might himself be called, and with reason, another Boëthius.' [3]

2. *Robert Pulleyn* († c. 1150), an Englishman, taught both at Paris and at Oxford. He was finally made a cardinal, and died in Rome. He wrote *Sententiarum theologicarum libri VIII.* A pupil of both William of Champeaux and Abélard, he unites Speculative and Positive Theology, but with special weight upon the latter.

3. The most important of these three scholars was *Peter the Lombard*, the *Magister Sententiarum* († c. 1160). He was born at Novara, Italy, early in the twelfth century, and was bishop of Paris at his death. He studied at Bologna and Rheims, and finally went to Paris, where he studied in the school of St. Victor and taught theology in the school of Notre Dame. He was not the first writer of *Sentences*. Several before him had

---

[1] For these citations *vide* Poole, *Medieval Thought*, pp. 184 *seq.*
[2] Poole, *ibid.*, p. 132.
[3] Clerval, *Les Écoles de Chartres*, p. 168.

written systems of doctrine under that title, as we have seen. There has been preserved a work of this kind by an unknown Bandinus, which so closely resembles the Lombard's work that some kind of dependence seems probable. But Peter's *Sentences* have been those on which all the Scholastics build. The work of Peter is entitled *Sententiarum libri IV*.

The first book discusses chiefly the Trinity, in forty-eight distinctions; the second the creation, in forty-four distinctions; the third the incarnation, faith and morals, in forty distinctions; the fourth the sacraments, in forty-two distinctions, and the Last Things, in eight distinctions.

This system has the merit of simplicity and of thoroughness. The theology is essentially Augustinian, although the Scriptures and the Fathers are used with freedom and skill, after the manner of Positive Theology. The method is Aristotelian, and in so far dialectical and philosophical. The combination of the dialectic method with Positive Theology is so sound, that the orthodoxy of these Sentences as well as their excellence is almost unimpeachable. They became at once, and remained for generations, the compendium, the student's textbook of doctrine. Peter was also distinguished for his contributions to Exegetical Theology. He took the *Glossa interlinearis* of Anselm as a basis, and put them in a new form, known as the *Magna glossatura*. He also wrote commentaries on the Psalms, Job, and the Epistles of Paul.

The most distinguished pupil of the Lombard was *Peter of Poitiers*, who carried on his work as teacher in Paris for forty years, succeeding Peter Comestor in the cathedral school, and dying as chancellor at the beginning of the thirteenth century. His lectures, published in part as *Sententiarum libri V.*, were based upon the *Sentences* of his master, and this did much to give them the currency they attained.

7. *The monastic school of St. Victor in Paris became an important centre of mystic theology under the three great mystic theologians, Hugh, Richard, and Walter.*

The collegiate church of St. Geneviève was reorganised in 1147, and the chapter of seculars became a body of Canons Regular. The change was disastrous to the school, which soon declined in importance. But the monastic school of St. Victor rose to eminence through several distinguished teachers, in hostility to the teachers of the cathedral school. The chief of these were, in their order, Hugh, Richard, and Walter, all mystic theologians.

1. *Hugh* (c. 1097-1141) was born in Saxony, and was trained first at Hamersleben, and then in Paris, at St. Victor's. He was especially distinguished in exegesis, and wrote an Introduction to the Scriptures entitled *De scripturis et scriptoribus sacris prænotationes*. He recognises only twenty-two books as belonging to the canon of the Old Testament, excluding the Apocrypha. He also wrote commentaries on the Pentateuch, Judges, Ruth, Kings, Psalms, Lamentations, and Joel, and sermons on Ecclesiastes and Obadiah. He was a positive theologian as well as a mystic, and wrote many dogmatic treatises, a comprehensive system of doctrine entitled *Summa sententiarum*, and *De sacramentis fidei*, also an encyclopædic work called *Eruditio didascalica*, and a commentary on Dionysius the Areopagite. He was opposed to the dialectic method. He defines the three grades of speculative mysticism as *cogitatio, meditatio,* and *contemplatio*.

2. *Richard* († 1173) was a Scot, a pupil and friend of Hugh. Dante describes him as 'in contemplation more than man.'[1] His works include six books on the Trinity, a discussion of the Incarnation, and commentaries on the Song of Songs, Ezekiel, and Revelation, as

[1] Dante, *Paradiso*, x. 132.

well as various mystic writings. He used the dialectic and allegorical methods, the latter to excess.

3. *Walter* († *c.* 1180) succeeded Richard as prior of the monastery of St. Victor. He wrote a polemic work : *Contra manifestas et damnatas etiam in conciliis hœreses, quas sophistœ Abœlardus, Lombardus, Petrus Pictavinus et Gilbertus Porretanus libris sententiarum suarum acuunt, limant, roborant*. He names these four theologians, ' the four labyrinths of France,' all possessed by the spirit of Aristotle.

8. *John of Salisbury was a broad-minded scholar. After frequenting the various great schools of learning, he became himself an able teacher in Canterbury and Chartres.*

John (*c.* 1115-1180) was born at Salisbury, and studied ' in all the schools with all the great masters,' of France and Italy as well as England.[1] He tells of going about from teacher to teacher in France, very much as students do now in German universities. John left England to study in Paris *c.* 1136. He went first to study logic with Abélard on Mount St. Geneviève, and took lessons in dialectic for two years with Alberic of Rheims and Robert of Melun at the same place. Afterwards he went for three years to Chartres, where he had for professors William of Conches, Richard l'Évêque, Pierre Hélie, and others. Then he became a teacher as well as pupil. Aristotle he studied under the guidance of an Englishman known as Adam du Petit Pont, who subsequently became bishop of St. Asaph. Having returned to Paris, he studied logic and theology with Gilbert de la Porrée, and theology alone with his successors Robert Pulleyn and Simon of Poissy. In this manner the studies of John extended over twelve years. He gives vivid descriptions of his various teachers. Abélard he calls ' the Peripatetic of Palais . . . an illustrious teacher and admired of all men.

---

[1] Clerval, *Les Écoles de Chartres*, p. 276.

At his feet I acquired the first rudiments of the dialectical art, and snatched according to the scant
measure of my wits whatever passed his lips with entire
greediness of mind.' Of Alberic and Robert of Melun
John says : ' The one was in questions subtle and large,
the other in responses lucid, short, and agreeable. . . . They
were both men of sharp intellect, and in study uncon-
querable.' Of the three years spent with ' the Grammarian of Conches' John says, 'I shall never regret that
time.' Richard l'Évêque he describes as ' a man whose
training was deficient in almost nothing, who had more
heart even than speech, more knowledge than skill,
more truth than vanity, more virtue than show.' Adam
he deems ' a man of exceeding sharp wits, and, whatever
others may think, of much learning. . . . He used to say
that he would have few hearers or none, if he propounded
dialectic with that simplicity of terms and easiness of
sentences with which it ought to be taught.' Master
Gilbert was ' too quickly removed.' Robert Pulleyn
' life and knowledge alike recommend.' Simon of Poissy
proved ' a trusty lecturer, but dull in disputation.'
John concludes :

' It seemed pleasant to me to revisit my old companions on the
Mount, whom I had left, and whom dialectic still detained, to
confer with them touching old matters of debate ; that we might
by mutual comparison measure together our several progress. I
found them as before, and where they were before ; nor did they
appear to have reached the goal in unravelling the old questions,
nor had they added one jot of a proposition. The aims that
once inspired them, inspired them still : they had progressed in
one point only ; they had unlearned moderation ; they knew
not modesty ; in such wise that one might despair of their
recovery.' [1]

John became an important man of affairs as well as
a great scholar. He was attached to the archbishop's
court at Canterbury under Theobald, Thomas à Becket,

[1] For John of Salisbury *vide* Poole, *Medieval Thought*, pp. 203 *seq.*

and Richard. He was constantly engaged in diplomatic missions, and crossed the Alps ten times. He was the most broad-minded scholar of his age, and 'for thirty years the central figure of English learning.' The last four years of his life he was bishop of Chartres. His principal work was entitled *Policraticus*, and is ' to some extent an encyclopædia of the cultivated thought of the middle of the twelfth century.' [1] In his *Metalogicus* he tells us about scholars, their methods, and the state of learning. According to Sandys,

He 'stands out as the most learned man of his time. He gives an analysis of the whole series of Aristotle's treatises on Logic. His *Metalogicus* is, in fact, the first work of the Middle Ages in which the whole of the *Organon* is turned to account, and Aristotle's own criticisms on Plato's doctrine of Ideas applied to the scholastic controversy on universals.' [2]

John also wrote *Historia pontificalis*, letters of great importance for the ecclesiastical history of the time, and commentaries on St. Paul. The Lateran Council of 1179, which decreed that every cathedral should have its teacher of theology, was attended by John.[3]

9. *In this period the Eastern Church produced few theologians of distinction. The chief seats of learning were Constantinople, Thessalonica, and Mount Athos.*

In the eleventh century the only writers of importance were the exegetes, *Theophylact*, archbishop of Achrida, Bulgaria († 1007), and *Euthymius Zigabenus*, a monk of Constantinople († 1118). Like the Western commentators they were compilers, and reproduced the expositions of the Fathers. Their exegesis is chiefly that of Chrysostom, Theodoret, and the Antiochan school.

In the twelfth century there appeared several canonists and polemic writers. *Eustathius*, archbishop of Thessa-

---

[1] Sandys, i. pp. 537 *seq.* ; Poole, *Medieval Thought*, p. 218.
[2] Sandys, i. pp. 539 *seq.*
[3] *Vide* Clerval, *Les ⌐coles de Chartres*, p. 276.

lonica († 1193), a zealous opponent of formalism, became famous both as a reformer and as a commentator on Homer. *Nicholas of Methone* († before 1166) produced important polemic works. *Theodore Balsamon* of Constantinople († 1203) wrote commentaries on the *Nomocanon* and *Syntagma*, erroneously ascribed to Photius, and a series of *Answers* and one of *Dissertations* on canon law, all of great value. *Johannes Zonaras* wrote works of importance on Church history and law, dating apparently from the first half of the twelfth century. Valuable work was done all through the Middle Ages in the Eastern monasteries, where the works of the Fathers were diligently studied, copied, and annotated. Mount Athos and Studium were the chief centres of this activity.

CHAPTER III

THE ORIGIN AND GROWTH OF THE UNIVERSITIES IN THE TWELFTH AND THIRTEENTH CENTURIES

THE study of theology, which had so greatly revived in the eleventh century, increased in public interest in the twelfth and attained its highest development in the thirteenth century, especially in the universities, and through the great scholastics, who were attached chiefly to the new mendicant orders.

1. *At the beginning of the twelfth century there was a great revival in the study of law, both civil law and canon law, favoured especially by the establishment of the University of Bologna under the famous teacher Irnerius.*

The twelfth century witnessed a great revival in the study of law, due doubtless to the conflict between the popes and the emperors, which Hildebrand had carried on with so much vigour, and which was to continue through the entire Middle Age. Both sides needed trained lawyers to maintain their cause.

The study of law had been carried on from the most ancient times in the great Italian centres, especially at Rome. When the Lombards established themselves in the north and Pavia became their chief seat of learning, it also became a school of law. So Ravenna, the seat of the exarchate, had become from the seventh century a centre for the study of law. But for the most part this branch of learning was studied under private teachers,

and the teaching and practice were closely connected
under leading lawyers, both civil and ecclesiastical.
In the eleventh century both Lombard and Roman law
were certainly taught in the school of Pavia. But
Ravenna seems to have been the chief law school in the
last half of the eleventh century.[1]

Bologna, which had long been famous as a school of
grammar and rhetoric, began in the twelfth century to
be a legal centre. The origin of the law school at Bologna
is involved in some obscurity. It first comes into
prominence with Irnerius (1100-1130), a teacher of
Roman civil law. He had been preceded by Pepo,
who lectured on the 'Old Digest.' The whole of the
Digest was probably first discussed by Irnerius. The
great increase of students of law brought about the
separation of these students from all others. All the
students began to organise themselves into guilds for
self-protection, defence and mutual assistance, dividing
themselves into four nations ; and so the schools of
Bologna became a university of students, an organisation
of students, electing their own officers. The teachers
also organised themselves for mutual protection into a
guild, and thus the University of Bologna originated.

The canon law was developing alongside of the civil
law. The Pseudo-Isidorian Decretals had given it a
great impulse in the ninth century ; and, on the basis
of these, other compilations of papal decrees were made.
In the eleventh century the chief were : the *Decretum*
of Burchard of Worms (1012-1023), the *Collectio canonum*
of Anselm of Lucca († 1086), the *Liber canonum* of
Cardinal Deusdedit († 1086-1087). In the first part of the
twelfth century the *Panormia* of Ivo of Chartres († *c.*
1116), and the *Decretum*, probably by the same author,
were the most complete collections. They were the
basis of the *Decretum* of Gratian, which became the great

[1] *Vide* Rashdall, *Universities of Europe in the Middle Ages*, i. p. 107.

text-book for canon law, the basis for all mediæval canonists. The proper title of Gratian's compilation is : *Concordantia discordantium Canonum.* It was probably published in 1142.[1] Gratian was a Camaldulensian monk and a teacher of canon law at Bologna. Roland Bandinelli, a cotemporary of Gratian, a teacher of theology at Bologna and afterwards Pope Alexander III., also wrote a *Summa* of canon law, which has been preserved.

As Rashdall says :

' Bologna was absorbed with the questions about Investiture, about the relations of Papacy and Empire, Church and State, Feudalism and civic liberty, while the schools of France were distracted by questions about the Unity of Intellect, about Transubstantiation, about the reality of Universals.' [2]

In the thirteenth century the canon law developed still further in five books of Decretals, published by Gregory IX., to which *Liber Sextus* was added by Boniface VIII. The *Corpus juris canonici* was completed by adding the *Clementines* of Clement V., published in 1317, and the *Extravagants*, extending down to the time of Sixtus IV. ' The Decretum (of Gratian) was a text-book : the Decretals were a Code.' Rashdall says :

' At all periods of the Middle Age it was the Canonists who filled the most important sees in Christendom. . . . It was chiefly through the Canon Law that the Civil Law transformed the jurisprudence of nearly the whole of continental Europe.' [3]

2. *The University of Paris grew out of the cathedral school, owing to the great increase of professors and students in the middle of the twelfth century, but was not fully organised until the thirteenth century.*

The chancellor of the cathedral of Paris had the sole authority to license teachers. As the teachers grew in

[1] Schulte, *Geschichte der Quellen und Literatur des Canonischen Rechts,* i. p. 48 ; Rashdall, i. p. 132.
[2] Rashdall, i. pp. 139 *seq.*   [3] *Ibid.,* i. pp. 142 *seq.*

number, there was not room for them all in the cathedral
precincts ; therefore some were licensed to teach on the
little bridge connecting the cathedral isle with the mainland to the south, and also on the mainland, the students
residing wherever they could.   The teachers gradually
came together in a guild or association, somewhere about
the middle of the twelfth century (1150-1170).[1]   After
a teacher was licensed by the chancellor he was initiated
into the association of masters.   There arose an inevitable conflict of jurisdiction between the chancellor
and the association of teachers ; and out of this conflict,
early in the thirteenth century, the organisation of the
university was born.   Apparently this conflict arose
after the death of the great teacher, Peter of Poitiers
(† 1205), when he was succeeded by weaker men.   The
teachers appealed to the pope against the chancellor,
and the pope gradually defined the relative jurisdiction
of each party.

The situation in Paris was complicated by the rise and
suppression of a dangerous heresy.   At the beginning of
this century the Arabian version of Aristotle made its
appearance in the schools of Paris in a roundabout way,
through the Arabs, Moors and Jews ; and, indeed, in
the pantheistic form of Avicenna († 1037) and Averroès
(† c. 1198).   This originated an outbreak of speculation
in Paris, under the lead of Simon de Tournai, Almaric of
Bena († 1205-1207), and David de Dinant († after 1215).
In 1209 a synod of Paris began to suppress their followers
by a bloody persecution.   Some were burned at the
stake, others imprisoned, and the works of Aristotle
upon natural philosophy and his commentaries were
prohibited by the council.   This intellectual movement
was cotemporary with the outbreak of the Albigenses
in the south of France, who were also suppressed by
the most severe measures.

[1] Rashdall, i. p. 294.

In 1215 Cardinal Robert de Courçon made for the university a code of statutes, a sort of constitution ; but the association of teachers was allowed to make statutes (such as we call *by-laws*) within a limited sphere. These statutes contained a prohibition of the physical and metaphysical works of Aristotle. Gregory IX. renewed this prohibition in 1231, with the reservation : ' until they shall have been examined and purged from all heresy.' [1] This reservation was due to the influence of the more correct and pure translations of Aristotle directly from the Greek, which began to make their way, especially in Italy, immediately after the conquest of Constantinople by the Latins in 1204. The difference between the real Aristotle and his Arabian interpreters now gradually became evident. In the meantime (*c.* 1219-1221) the masters of arts were organised into four nations, as were the students at Bologna. Over each of the nations a proctor presided, and over the whole body a rector. These officials are clearly discriminated for the first time in a document of the year 1245. The four faculties of Arts, Theology, Law, and Medicine were distinguished, and all in operation ; but the most important in Paris were those of Arts and Theology. The four faculties are recognised in the earliest corporate act of the university, a deed of 1221.[2] The chancellor of the cathedral was virtually the head of the theological faculty, although not himself a member of the faculty. The headship of the whole university was in the rector of the faculty of arts. By a bull of Pope Gregory IX., *Parens scientiarum*, the university received, in 1231, a charter of privilege, called by Denifle its *Magna Charta*.[3]

3. *The University of Oxford originated in the latter part of the twelfth century, probably through students and*

---

[1] Rashdall, i. p. 358.   [2] *Ibid.*, p. 324.
[3] *Ibid.*, p. 339.

professors from Paris ; the University of Cambridge soon after, by a migration from Oxford.

The English universities of Oxford and Cambridge had an obscure origin. They did not develop from cathedral schools, for the cathedral of Lincoln was about 120 miles distant from Oxford ; and the cathedral of Ely, though not far from Cambridge, seems to have had nothing to do with the origin of that university. There is no sufficient evidence that either university originated from monastic schools. Rather, like the university of Bologna, those of Oxford and Cambridge most probably originated from private schools. Oxford had become a commercial and political centre in the eleventh century. There were students in Oxford early in the twelfth century. Theobaldus Stampensis had sixty to one hundred clerks under his instruction there, prior to 1117. Robert Pulleyn taught theology there in 1133. Giraldus, the Welshman, tells how, in 1184-1185, he read his *Topography of Ireland* to students and doctors of the different faculties. Walter Map, archdeacon of Oxford, was then one of the masters. Richard of Devizes, the chronicler, writing in 1192, says that the city could scarcely feed her clerks, so great was their number.[1]

It is supposed that the organisation of the university was due to the recall of English scholars from Paris, and elsewhere on the continent, by Henry II., in 1167 or 1168.[2] The head of Oxford University was a rector, chosen by the masters of the schools, and himself a master. Later he became subordinate as chancellor to the bishop of Lincoln.

Cambridge University seems to have originated from a migration thither of students from Oxford, due to a conflict between town and gown, in 1209.

There were two nations at Oxford with their proctors,

---

[1] Richard of Devizes, *vide English Historical Society*, 1838, pp. 61 *seq*.
[2] *Vide* Rashdall, ii. pp. 330 *seq*.

the northern and the southern; but, in 1274, these were amalgamated. In 1254 a bull of Innocent IV. confirmed Oxford in its 'immunities and ancient customs.' The oldest colleges were: (1) *University*, founded by William of Durham (designed 1249, begun 1280); (2) *Merton*, founded by Walter de Merton, (designed *c.* 1263, begun in 1264-1265); (3) *Balliol*, founded by Sir John de Balliol (designed 1260, begun 1266).

As Rashdall says:

'The great work of the universities was the consecration of learning: and it is not easy to exaggerate the importance of that work upon the moral, intellectual and religious progress of Europe.' [1]

4. *Early in the thirteenth century a widespread revival of religion gave birth to the mendicant orders. The Franciscan order was founded at Assisi in 1210, the Dominican at Toulouse in 1215. These were followed by other lesser orders. All of these furnished scholars and teachers to the universities.*

Dominic († 1221), the founder of the Dominican order, was born in Castile, and trained in theology and philosophy at Palencia. Under the influence of his bishop, Diego de Azevedo, he undertook to lead a crusade against heresy by a body of preachers trained for the service, and spending their lives in imitation of the apostles. His first followers he sent to Toulouse for training in theology. The Dominicans were essentially preachers and teachers; and they established themselves in the great cities and seats of education: at Bologna and Paris, in 1217; and in Oxford, *c.* 1221, at the Church of St. Edward in the Jewry, where they opened the school in which Robert Bacon taught theology. The rule of the order required eight years of study in theology after the close of the novitiate. In the

[1] *Vide* Rashdall, ii. p. 693.

latter part of the century each province of the order had its own *studium generale* ; and Dominicans filled the chairs of theology at Bologna, Padua, Vienna, Cologne, Prague, Oxford, and Salamanca.[1]

Among the scholars trained by the Dominicans may be mentioned *Nicolaus de Gorran*, preacher and exegete (*c.* 1210-1295), whose work outlived his reputation. His commentaries cover a great part of the Bible, including the Gospels, Epistles, and Revelation. He also wrote *Distinctions*, a collection of ' sentences or thoughts from the Holy Books, arranged in alphabetical order,' of which a number of copies still exist. His sermons also have been printed in several editions. According to Feret, his commentaries on the Catholic Epistles appeared in Paris, in an edition of the year 1543, under the name of Thomas Aquinas.[2]

The Franciscans were less intellectual, and rather mystic ; but they also established themselves in the great centres at Oxford and Cambridge *c.* 1224, and at Paris in 1230. Their founder, *St. Francis of Assisi* († 1226), had also as his ideal the exact imitation of Christ in a life of apostolic service ; but he emphasised the practical side of that ministry, and its condition, voluntary poverty. ' When once these orders had been founded,' as Sandys says, ' all the great schoolmen were either Franciscans or Dominicans.'[3] The first Franciscan to open a school at Oxford was *Agnellus of Pisa*. He it was who introduced into the Franciscan school Robert Greathead, the first great teacher of Oxford. *Adam Marsh* († 1258), the friend of Greathead, was the first Franciscan to lecture there. Roger Bacon calls these scholars ' majores clerici de mundo.'[4]

[1] *Vide* Grützmacher, 'Dominic,' in *New Schaff-Herzog Encyclopedia.*
[2] Feret, *La Faculté de théologie de Paris*, ii. pp. 511 *seq.*
[3] Sandys, i. p. 573.
[4] Bacon, *Op. tert.* (Op. ined.), p. 75 ; cited by Rashdall, ii. p. 255, *n.* 3.

The Carmelites settled at Oxford in 1256, the Augustinians two years later, and lesser orders soon followed.

5. *Several other important universities were established in the thirteenth century, including those at Naples, Rome, Toulouse, Padua, Salamanca, and Lisbon.*

The university of Naples was founded in 1224, and was designed to be the centre of all departments of learning for the kingdom. But the *school of Salerno* had long been a *fons medicinæ*, and the attempt to establish a medical faculty at Naples failed. In 1231 the right of examination in the department of medicine was limited to the doctors of Salerno. In 1253 an effort was made to transfer all the faculties from Naples to Salerno, and to unite them with the old school of medicine in that place ; but this experiment also failed ; and in 1258 the three faculties returned to Naples, and the faculty of medicine remained alone at Salerno. Eight years later, however, Naples recovered its faculty of medicine. Innocent IV. established in *Rome* (1244-1245) a university for theology and law. In *Padua* a university was organised in 1222, and re-established in 1260 by a migration from Bologna, with all the faculties save theology, which was added in 1363. A number of colleges sprang up around it in the fourteenth century, and it eventually became the great university of Venice.

In France a university was founded at *Toulouse* by Pope Gregory IX., after the model of Paris (*c.* 1229). *In Spain* universities were established at *Salamanca* in 1230, and *Valladolid* in the middle of the century. *In Portugal* a university was recognised as already founded in *Lisbon* by papal bull, as early as 1290, but was transferred to *Coimbra* (*c.* 1308), and after several migrations between the towns, finally settled there in 1537.[1]

[1] *Vide* Rashdall, ii. pp. 101 *seq.*

A number of colleges grew up about the *university of Paris* in the thirteenth century. There were ten monastic colleges, founded between 1209 and 1269, including those of the Trinitarians, Dominicans, Franciscans, Bernardines, Augustinians, Carmelites, and those ' de Sainte Catherine, des Prémontrés, de Saint-Denys, de Cluny.' Six years of study were required for the regulars and seven for the seculars, before the Baccalauréat. Eight years of study in theology were prescribed for the doctor's degree. For three years students devoted themselves to the study of the Scriptures as *Biblici*, for one to the *Sentences* of the Lombard as *Sententiarii*, for four they prepared as candidates for licence. The candidate had to be present at the ' public acts ' of the faculty, to speak, discuss theses, sustain arguments and preach.[1] The theological course was extended in the following century, by the reform of 1366, over a period of sixteen years.[2] The *Baccalarius Formatus* was required to give lectures on the Bible. ' The Secular's lectures on the Bible were merely delivered " in course "—because they were required by the faculty as a condition of proceeding to the higher degrees. . . . The "ordinary" lectures on the Bible were delivered by " religious " Bachelors. Each of the mendicant orders in Paris . . . was required to supply a fresh lecturer (*Biblicus ordinarius*) every year.' [3] So there was no such neglect of Biblical study in favour of the scholastic theology as has been claimed. In fact, there has been a greater emphasis on systematic theology since the Reformation than before. The difference between theological study then and now is less in subject-matter than in method and emphasis. Then the emphasis was on the higher exegesis—the use of the Bible as a means of union and communion with God ; but there was a neglect of the historico-critical

[1] *Vide* Feret, ii. pp. 41 *seq.*   [2] *Vide* Rashdall, i. p. 463.
[3] *Ibid.*, i. pp. 465 *seq.*

in favour of the allegorical method. Now the neglect is of the spiritual in Biblical study. The difference as to the subject-matter of study, then and now, is chiefly in that gained by the inductive method, especially in the realm of natural science. Outside of this realm there is not much new material.

Of the secular colleges founded at Paris before the close of the thirteenth century, eight may be mentioned, *i.e.* those of Constantinople, St. Honoré, St. Nicolas du Louvre, St. Victor, Trésorier, Harcourt, Cholets, and above all the Collège de Sorbonne (1257-1258), founded by Robert de Sorbonne and richly endowed, with provision for all expenses. For admission the study of philosophy was required as well as the liberal arts. According to Rashdall, the Sorbonne

'was a college for men who had already taken the degree of Master of Arts and were desirous of entering upon the long and laborious career which led to the theological doctorate. . . . Originally . . . the "Sorbonne" was nothing more than a college of theologians. . . . In the sixteenth and seventeenth centuries, however, the title came to be popularly applied to the whole theological faculty of Paris. . . . Membership of the Sorbonne . . . became an honorary distinction which was usually sought by most of the theological doctors of the university. . . . The Hall or Schools of the Sorbonne became the scene of disputations and other public acts of the theological faculty, especially of its meetings to discuss and pronounce judgment upon heresies or theological novelties. . . . According to Richer, all doctors of theology in his time styled themselves Doctors of the Sorbonne.' [1]

The course of study embraced ten years, but by the close of the seventh the student must have shown some ability as teacher or preacher to be retained. [2]

6. *Robert Greathead, Alexander of Hales, and Vincent of Beauvais begin a series of great doctors of the Church.*

1. *Robert Greathead* (Grosseteste, *c.* 1175-1253), bishop

---

[1] Rashdall, i. pp. 488 *seq.*   [2] Feret, ii. pp. 11 *seq.*

of Lincoln, was a great teacher and author, an ethical
and practical theologian, who made much use of the
Scriptures. He was trained in Oxford and Paris ; and
his education is said to have been ' built on the foundation of the liberal arts and on an abundant knowledge
of literature.' [1]   Matthew of Paris calls him ' vir in
Latino et Græco peritissimus ' ; [2] Gower, ' the grete
clerc Grosseteste.' [3] He dominated English thought for
two centuries, and was ranked by Wyclif with Augustine
and above Aristotle.

Greathead wrote an encyclopædic work entitled
Compendium scientiarum, classifying all departments of
knowledge ; also *Dicta theologica,* and many other works.
He gave, in Stevenson's words, ' a powerful impulse to
almost every department of intellectual activity, revived
the study of neglected languages, and grasped the central
idea of the unity of knowledge.' [4] He wrote commentaries on Dionysius the Areopagite and John of Damascus,
Aristotle and Boëthius. He had studied Hebrew, and
in his work, *De cessatione legalium,* he sought to convert
the Jews. He was a great preacher, and a devoted
student of the Scriptures. In a letter to the regents of
Oxford he wrote :

' Let the foundation-stones be well laid ; on them the whole
building rests. The morning is the best time for study, and the
good old Paris custom should be observed of reserving those
early hours for the lectures on Scripture, giving the later part
of the day to other subjects.'

In 1235 Greathead was made bishop of Lincoln, and
began a work of reformation among the monks and the
clergy that brought him into conflict with both king and
pope. At his death the university of Oxford certified
Rome of his ' splendid learning and that he most admir-

---

[1] Giraldus Cambrensis, cited by Sandys, i. p. 575.
[2] *Hist. Angl.,* ii. 467.
[3] *Conf. Am.,* iv. 234 ; *vide* Sandys, i. p. 578.
[4] Stevenson, *Robert Grosseteste,* p. 337 ; *vide* Sandys, i. p. 578.

ably governed Oxford, in his degree of doctor of holy theology.' [1] Associated with Greathead was *Adam Marsh*.[2] These were the teachers of Roger Bacon and many other distinguished scholars.

2. *Alexander of Hales*, Gloucestershire († 1245), was ' the first of the Schoolmen who was familiar with the whole range of Aristotle's philosophy, and with his Arabic commentators, and who employed the same in the service of theology.' [3] He was called *doctor irrefragabilis* and *theologorum monarcha*. He went to Paris, to study and teach, and there became a Franciscan. His principal work is his *Summa universæ theologiæ*, completed by his pupils some years after his death.

The pupil and successor of Alexander at Paris was *John of Rochelle* (c. 1200-1253), whose chief work was *De anima*.

The establishment of the mendicant orders in Paris soon brought about a conflict of jurisdiction in the university. The friars were unwilling to take part in the great secession of the members of the university from Paris in 1229, but took advantage of the situation in their own interests, and started an independent theological school. *Roland of Cremona* and *John of St. Giles* taught in the Dominican convent, the latter changing from a secular into a regular. *Alexander of Hales* continued in the Franciscan convent the lectures he had begun as a secular. This increased the friction. Finally an appeal of the friars to Rome resulted in a papal bull (1255) authorising the chancellor to grant licences without the consent of the masters. This brought the conflict of jurisdiction to a crisis. It became clear that the friars wished to have all the privileges of the university without yielding to its authority. There was a long struggle, in which the pope continued to take the part of the friars, until the pontificate of Urban IV. (1261), a

---

[1] *Vide* Drane, *Christian Schools and Scholars*, pp. 484 *seq.*
[2] *Vide* p. 47.   [3] *Vide* Sandys, i. p. 574.

Parisian canonist, who thoroughly understood the whole situation and succeeded in restoring peace.

3. One of the earliest and most learned of the Dominicans was *Vincent of Beauvais* († 1264). He was tutor to the sons of Louis IX., and wrote *De institutione filiorum regiorum sive nobilium.* He was the author of the greatest encyclopædia of the Middle Ages, *Speculum mundi*, written in four parts : *Naturale, Doctrinale, Historiale* and *Morale*, the last completed long after his death (*c.* 1310-1320). His numerous works included *Tractatus de gratia Dei* and *De sancto Johanne evangelista.*

7. *The three great scholars of the thirteenth century were Albert the Great, Bonaventura and Thomas Aquinas, who gave shape to the Scholastic Theology which has dominated the Western Church until the present day.*

1. *Albert von Bollstädt, Albertus Magnus* (1193-1280), was born at Lauingen, not far from Augsburg, was educated at Padua, and became a Dominican. He taught in convent schools in Germany, and lectured in Paris (*c.* 1245) and Cologne (*c.* 1248). He was made provincial of the Dominicans at Cologne (1254) and bishop of Ratisbon six years later ; but in 1262 he resigned and returned to Cologne. He is known as the *Doctor universalis.* Albert's principal theological work is his *Summa theologiæ.* He followed the method of the Lombard's *Sentences*, and wrote a commentary on these in three volumes. He was the first scholastic to use the entire Aristotelian philosophy in systematic arrangement in the interest of the dogmatic system of the Church.[1] His work is rich in detail in the discussion of all kinds of subtle questions. He taught the Aristotelian Realism, and made the important distinction of the *universale ante rem* in the Divine Mind (Neo-Platonic and Augustinian), the *universale in re* in the Aristotelian

[1] *Vide* Ueberweg, *Geschichte der Philosophie* (ed. Heinze), ii. p. 287.

sense, and the *universale post rem* in the human mind.
This was a comprehension of Realism and Conceptualism.
Albert was also the author of commentaries on the
Psalms, Lamentations, Daniel, Baruch, the Minor
Prophets, the Four Gospels and the Apocalypse, sermons,
and a commentary on Dionysius the Areopagite.

As Schaff has said :

'He traversed the whole area of the physical sciences.   No one
for centuries had been such a student of nature. . . . His knowledge is often at fault, but sometimes his statements are prophetic
of modern discovery.'

His great *Study of Created Things* is ' an attempt, whose
boldness has never been exceeded, to explain the great
phenomena of the visible universe.' [1]

2. *Bonaventura*, the *Doctor seraphicus* (1221-1274), was
born in Tuscany, became a Franciscan (*c.* 1238), and
studied in Paris under Alexander of Hales and John of
Rochelle.   He succeeded John of Parma as teacher in
Paris in 1247, and as general of the Franciscan order ten
years later.   He was chosen cardinal-bishop of Albano
in 1273, and died at the Council of Lyons, where he spoke
in favour of union with the Greeks.   Bonaventura wrote
in defence of his order *De paupertate Christi* and *Deter-
minationes questionum circa regulam Francisci* ; and has
been called its second founder.   His principal works on
theology are his commentary on the *Sentences* of the
Lombard, and his *Breviloquium* and *Centiloquium*.   He
uses especially Augustine, Anselm, and Hugh and
Richard of St. Victor, in their combination of the mystic
and dialectic methods.   Bonaventura is more practical
and less speculative than Albert.   Like the other great
mystics he sought union and communion with God in
seraphic vision.   The difference between these mystics
and the great dogmatic theologians was chiefly one of
emphasis.   The mystic uses the religious imagination :

[1] Schaff, *History of the Christian Church*, v., i. pp. 655 *seq.*

the dogmatist, the reasoning powers. The one is absorbed in mystic, the other in logical contemplation. Mystic contemplation may attach itself to external things, but does not depend on such things. Gerson preferred Bonaventura to all the other doctors, 'because in his teaching he is solid and sure, pious and just'; because he abstains, so far as he can, from all curiosity, and knows how to avoid secular, dialectical, or physical matters hidden under theological forms; because in working to enlighten the spirit his aim is by means of that light 'to bring piety to birth in the heart.'[1] Bonaventura wrote commentaries on Luke, John, the Psalms, and Ecclesiastes. He uses the method called *Collationes*, or *Collativa expositio*, a selection of important passages of the Bible for exposition, and the use of a large number of others to illustrate and confirm these. He also wrote *Postilla seu expositio in Canticum canticorum*, and many mystical and practical works, including *Itinerarium mentis in Deum*, and Meditations on the Life of Jesus, also hymns still in use. According to Sixtus v. 'nothing more fruitful for the Church of God' had appeared than the theology of Bonaventura.[2]

3. *Thomas Aquinas*, the *Doctor angelicus* (c. 1225-1274), was of noble birth, and was educated at Monte Cassino and the university of Naples. He became a Dominican in 1243, and was sent to Cologne, where he studied under Albert the Great. He followed his master to Paris, and some years later back again to Cologne. 'This long association of Thomas with the great polyhistor' is called by Seeberg 'the most important influence in his development; it made him a comprehensive scholar and won him permanently for the Aristotelian method.'[3]

---

[1] Gerson, *Opera*, ed. Du Pin, i. 21; Feret, *La Faculté de théologie de Paris*, ii. p. 300.

[2] *Encyclical*, ed. Peltier, i. p. viii; cited by Schaff, v., i. p. 680, *n.* 4.

[3] Seeberg, 'Thomas Aquinas,' in *New Schaff-Herzog Encyclopedia*.

Albert is reported as saying of Thomas : ' He will give
forth in teaching such a roar as will resound through the
whole world.' [1] Thomas taught himself at Cologne,
Paris, Bologna, Rome, Naples, and elsewhere. He is
the greatest and most comprehensive of the scholastics,
and the standard theologian of the Roman Catholic
Church. The papal encyclical of 1879 praises him as
' inter scholasticos doctores omnium princeps et magister
. . . veritatis, unice amator, divina humanaque scientia
prædives.' [2] Aquinas sought the reunion of the Greek
and Latin Churches, and died on his way to the Council
of Lyons. He is the author of many dogmatic works,
including : a Commentary on the *Sentences* of the
Lombard, *Quæstiones disputatæ*, *Quæstiones quodlibetales XII.*, *Compendium theologiæ*, *Summa theologiæ*,
and an Exposition of the Creed. While he builds on the
Lombard and Albert, he is independent in judgment, and
more comprehensive and able in his scholarship. It is
said that in his *Summa* he considers over three thousand
articles and fifteen thousand arguments or difficulties.[3]
Among his apologetic works the most important are :
Summa de veritate catholicæ fidei contra Gentiles, *Contra
errores Græcorum*, and *De unitate intellectus contra
Averrhoistas*. Thomas is also the author of many commentaries on Job, the Psalms, Song of Songs, Isaiah,
Jeremiah, Matthew, John, the Pauline Epistles, and also
of *Catenæ* on the Gospels. He uses for these commentaries various terms : *Continua expositio*, *Continua glossa*,
Aurea glossa, and *Catena*. He is said to cite more than
eighty Greek and Latin Fathers. He also wrote many
works on philosophy, including thirteen commentaries on
Aristotle. He is called by Sandys ' on the question of
" universals " . . . a Realist in the moderate Aristotelian
sense.' [4] He conceives of theology and philosophy as

[1] *Vide* Schaff, v., i. p. 663, *n.* 1.   [2] *Vide* Schaff, v., i. p. 662, *n.* 1.
[3] *Vide* Flügge, *Theol. Wiss.*, iii. p. 521.   [4] Sandys, i. p. 583.

searching for the truth by different methods. ' Non eodem ordine utraque doctrina procedit.' [1] ' In his consideration of ethics,' according to Schaff, ' he rises far above the other mediæval writers, and marks an epoch in the treatment of the subject. He devotes to it . . . one third of his entire system of theology.' [2]   Three of his hymns are in the Roman Breviary.

Among the other celebrated doctors of this century three more call for special mention.

4. *Roger Bacon, Doctor mirabilis* (1214-1294), was a Franciscan, who studied at Oxford and Paris, and taught in both universities. His teachers at Oxford, Robert Greathead, Adam Marsh and Thomas Wallensis, were all said to have been pupils of *Edmund Rich* of Canterbury († 1240), of whom it was said, ' (studebat) discere, quasi semper victurus ; vivere, quasi cras moriturus.' [3] Bacon was a student of the same temper. He became famous, especially for his studies in natural science ; but produced important works in philosophy and theology also. His principal work on theology, written shortly before his death, was a *Compendium studii theologici* in five books (1292). He found fault with the scholastic method of instruction, and, in his *Compendium studii philosophiæ*, he criticised at the same time Aristotle and the great scholastics, Alexander of Hales, Albert the Great, and Thomas Aquinas. His *Opus majus* treats of the relations of theology with science and philosophy, and the study of the natural sciences. It has been recognised as ' at once the Encyclopædia and the Organon of the thirteenth century.' His *Opus minus* abbreviates the former work. His *Opus tertium* reproduces both works in the aphoristic form. Bacon writes :

' Ignorance of the truths set forth by the ancients is due to the little care that is spent on the study of the ancient languages.

---

[1] *Vide* Schaff, v., i. p. 667, *n.* 5.   [2] *Vide* Schaff, *ibid.*, p. 672.
[3] *Vide* Sandys, i. p. 589.

It is vain to object that some of the Fathers neglected that study and misunderstood its advantages. Worthy as they are of respect in many ways, they cannot serve as our models in everything. . . . It is impossible to obtain a perfect knowledge of the Scriptures without knowing Hebrew and Greek, or of philosophy without knowing Arabic as well. . . . There are not five men in Latin Christendom who are acquainted with the Hebrew, Greek and Arabic grammar. . . . There are many among the Latins who can *speak* Greek, Arabic, and Hebrew; very few who understand the *grammar* of these languages, or know how to teach them. . . . The scientific works of Aristotle, Avicenna, Seneca, Cicero, and other ancients cannot be had except at a great cost; their principal works have not been translated into Latin. . . . Slowly has any portion of the philosophy of Aristotle come into use among the Latins.' [1]

' In urging the study of Greek as well as Hebrew, he adds :

" We are the heirs of the scholars of the past, and (even in our own interests) are bound to maintain the traditions of learning, on pain of being charged with infinite folly." ' [2]

Bacon himself wrote Hebrew and Greek grammars.[3] His *Epistola de laude Scripturæ sacræ* emphasises the study of the Sacred Writings in the original languages. Bacon was suspected of magical arts and heresy, and was imprisoned in a monastery for ten years, but was temporarily released by Clement IV., to whom he sent his three encyclopædic works. He was imprisoned again in the time of Nicolaus III. (*c.* 1278), and was not finally liberated until Nicolaus IV., his former accuser, had become pope, when influential friends interposed on his behalf.[4]

5. *Richard Middleton, Doctor solidus* († *c.* 1300), was also a Franciscan. He lectured both at Paris and at

---

[1] Bacon, *Opus majus*, 18, 44; *Opus tertium*, 33, 55; *Compendium studii theologiæ*, lv.; cited by Sandys, i. pp. 590 *seq.*

[2] Bacon, *Compendium studii philosophiæ*, 434 *seq.*; *vide* Sandys, i. p. 594.

[3] *Vide* edition of Nolan and Hirsch, London, 1902.

[4] *Vide* preface to *Opus majus*, ed. Bridges, Oxford, 1897.

Oxford. His principal works are *Quæstiones super IV. libros Sententiarum,* and *Quodlibeta.* He was one of the best commentators of the Lombard, and follows him strictly. He was also a skilful interpreter of Scripture and was versed in canon law. His writings include commentaries on the Pauline Epistles and the Gospels, *De distinctione decreti,* and other lesser works. He was held in great esteem, and was described as *fundatissimus* and *copiosus.* A scholar of the fifteenth century calls him ' doctor profundus et magnæ autoritatis in scolis.' Martigné classes him with Alexander of Hales, Bonaventura, and Duns Scotus as one of the four great teachers of the Franciscan order, and cites the Life of a Franciscan, a bishop of Toulouse, whose great-nephew was taught by Richard, in which he is described as ' doctor of the university of Paris, and one of the most learned theologians of the century.' [1]

6. *Ægidius de Columna, Doctor fundatissimus* († 1316), a Roman, was a pupil of Thomas Aquinas, and an Augustinian monk. He studied and taught at Paris for many years, was made general of his order, 1292-1295, and archbishop of Bourges, 1296. He spent years in the papal court at Rome and Avignon, and is supposed to have written the bull *Unam sanctam.* His works include commentaries on the *Sentences,* on Romans and the Song of Songs ; also a treatise, *De potestate ecclesiastica.*

8. *In this period the Syrian Church produced a scholar of lasting importance, Gregory, Bar-Hebræus, physician, theologian and philosopher.*

Bar-Hebræus (1226-1286) is described by Wright as ' one of the most learned and versatile men that Syria ever produced.' [2] He ' cultivated nearly every branch of

---

[1] *Vide* Feret, *La Faculté de théologie de Paris,* ii. pp. 379 *seq.*
[2] Wright, *Syriac Literature,* pp. 265 *seq.*

science that was in vogue in his time,' and wrote com-
pendiums on many of them.   His *Sapientia sapien-
tiarum* is an encyclopædia, comprising ' the whole
Aristotelian discipline.'   He wrote commentaries on
Hippocrates and Galen, grammatical works that are
' now well known and appreciated by Orientalists,' and
verse that is still admired.   His most important contribution to theology is *The Storehouse of Secrets*, ' a
critical and doctrinal commentary on the text of the
Scriptures of the Old and New Testaments, based on the
Peshitta, but taking note of the various readings of the
Hebrew text, the Septuagint, and other Greek versions,
the later Syriac translations, and even the Armenian
and Coptic, besides noting differences of reading between
the Nestorians and Jacobites.'   His lesser works on
theology include an anaphora, a confession of faith, and
a *Nomocanon* of great authority in the Jacobite Church.
His historical works are now of special importance.   The
Universal History, extending to 1286, has been brought
by other writers down to the year 1496.

CHAPTER IV

THE DECLINE OF SCHOLASTICISM IN THE FOUR-TEENTH AND FIFTEENTH CENTURIES

AT the beginning of the century there were several great scholastics ; but they divided Scholasticism into different schools, and really gave the impulse to the decay that followed, by their criticism of the great scholastics of the previous century.

1. *Duns Scotus introduced the Scotist school of Scholasticism, characterised by criticism of traditional theories, and emphasis upon the will, divine and human.*

John Duns Scotus, Doctor subtilis (c. 1267-1308), was a native of England. He became a Franciscan, studied in Merton College, Oxford, and took his degrees of bachelor and doctor in Paris. He taught successfully in Oxford and Paris, and finally in Cologne, where he died at the age of about forty. His great work is *Opus Oxoniense*, a commentary on the *Sentences* of the Lombard, abridged in *Reportata Parisiensia*. He also wrote commentaries on Aristotle's *De anima*, and *Refutations*, and his treatises on physics, metaphysics, and meteorologics. His writings include also : *Grammatica speculativa* ; *Disputationes subtilissimæ* ; *Conclusiones metaphysicæ* ; *Quæstiones quodlibetales*, and other works.[1] He is the most hair-splitting of ecclesiastics, and raised a multitude of new questions ; and in his discussion of

[1] *Opera*, 12 vols., Lyons, 1639 ; 26 vols., Paris, 1891-1895.

the older ones questioned not a few of the traditional answers. As Seeberg says :

> ' Characterising God as Will, and finding the essence of man's nature also in his Will, he naturally emphasises the individual and his freedom in his view of humanity. Thus by his sharp criticism of traditional theories and by his bold creation of new terms and combinations, he set forces at work in the domain of theology which did much to prepare the way for the still more thoroughgoing criticism of the Reformers.' [1]

2. *William of Occam began as a Scotist, but subsequently made a new departure by the revival of Nominalism, which continued to influence theological education until after the Reformation.*

William of Occam (c. 1280-1349) was born at Occam, in Surrey, England. He studied at Oxford and Paris, and became a Franciscan in early life. He taught at Paris for some years, and was made a provincial of his order (1322). A rigid advocate of poverty, the original principle of St. Francis, he was imprisoned and finally excommunicated for supporting Michael of Cesena in his attempts to reform the order. Occam began as a pupil of Duns Scotus, but subsequently made a new departure by his revival of Nominalism in a better form, which continued to influence theology until after the Reformation, and some schools even till the present day. Occam was known as the *Doctor singularis et invincibilis.* His writings include : (1) important philosophical works, the chief of which are an *Expositio aurea*, which gives ' in the form of commentaries on Aristotle and Porphyry, Occam's logic, epistemology and metaphysic,' [2] and *Summa logices* ; (2) theological works : *Quæstiones et decisiones in IV libros sententiarum, Centiloquium theologicum, Quodlibeta VII, De corpore Christi, De sacramento altaris, De prædestinatione et futuris con-*

---

[1] Seeberg, 'Duns Scotus,' in *New Schaff-Herzog Encyclopedia.*
[2] Seeberg, ' Occam,' in *New Schaff-Herzog Encyclopedia.*

tingentibus ; (3) many practical works : in advocacy of poverty, the chief of which was *Opus nonaginta dierum* ; and in defence of the German emperor, Louis of Bavaria, against the intrusion of the pope, John XXII., into the domain of civil affairs. Seeberg says of Occam :

'His historical importance rests on three achievements in particular : he carried the banner of nominalism to victory in the philosophy of his age ; he encouraged the critical spirit in regard to traditional dogma, and taught men how to use it as a counterpoise to ecclesiastical positivism ; and he struck out a new line of thought as to the relations of temporal and spiritual authority of Church and State.'

He is said to have been 'the pioneer of modern epistemology.'[1] Luther called him 'my dear master,' and declared : 'I am of the Occamist faction.' Sandys follows Mullinger in the opinion :

'His chief service to philosophy is that "he brought again to light . . . the true value of the inductive method, as auxiliary to the deductive."'[2]

Several other nominalists of the period may be mentioned : 1. *Durand of Saint Pourçain* (Porciano), *Doctor resolutissimus* († 1334), studied in the Dominican convent at Clermont, and then at Paris, where he became a teacher, and a doctor (*c.* 1312). He was made Master of the Sacred Palace at Avignon, and in 1326 bishop of Meaux. His principal work is a *Commentarius in IV libros sententiarum Lombardi*. Durand is usually classed as a nominalist ; but he was rather a critic, and independent in his judgment, mediating between Thomas Aquinas and Occam. He stated many opinions, which, if not heretical, tended that way ; but as they were tentative and subject to the authority of the Church, he escaped condemnation. He taught a kind of impanation or consubstantiation, in his doctrine of the Eucharist.

[1] Seeberg, 'Occam,' in *New Schaff-Herzog Encyclopedia.*
[2] Sandys, i. p. 601.

2. *Franciscus de Mayronis, Doctor illuminatus* († *c.* 1325-1327), one of the principal pupils of Duns Scotus, taught theology in Paris early in the fourteenth century. His works include : *Commentaria in IV libros sententiarum*, printed at Venice [1] in the sixteenth century in many editions (1504 +) ; *Expositio in VIII libros Physicorum Aristotelis* (Venice, 1490, 1517) ; *Passus super universalia et prœdicamenta Aristotelis* (Venice 1517, Boulogne 1479) ; commentaries on Anselm, Dionysius the Areopagite, and *Genesis* ; *De divinorum nominum explanatione*, works on ethics, sermons, and many other writings.

3. *Petrus Aureolus*, a Franciscan and *Doctor fœcundus* († 1322), taught at Paris, became provincial of Aquitaine, and finally archbishop of Aix. He also began as a follower of Duns Scotus. His works include : *Commentarius in IV libros sententiarum* (Rome, 1596-1605), *Tractatus de conceptione Mariœ Virginis, Tractatus de paupertate, Breviarium Bibliorum, Quodlibeta, Postilla super Job, Isaiam prophetam*, and numerous other writings. Feret remarks : ' To judge by the printing of many of his works, and above all by the large number of editions of the *Breviarium Bibliorum*, the thinker in Pierre Auriol was esteemed no less by the following generations than by his cotemporaries.' [2]

4. *John Buridan* († after 1350), rector of the university of Paris, was a pupil of Occam, and ' one of the best known of the supporters of (his) revived nominalism.' [3] He wrote a text-book on logic, and commentaries on various works of Aristotle, including his *Ethics*. Buridan is chiefly important in theology for his researches on the freedom of the will.

5. *Robert Holcot* († 1349), an English Dominican, taught theology at Oxford. He also is classed among

---

1 Also *Conflatus*, Basle, 1489, Lyons, 1579.
2 Feret, iii. p. 355.   3 Sandys, i. p. 603.

the nominalists, but he was rather an intermediate man. He wrote commentaries on the Minor Prophets and Proverbs, and also on the *Sentences*.

6. The last great nominalist was *Gabriel Biel* († 1495). He was born at Speyer, studied at Heidelberg, became a preacher at Mainz, and professor of theology and philosophy at the new university of Tübingen (founded in 1477). He too was a follower of Occam, and his chief work is *Epitome et collectorium ex Occamo super IV libros sententiarum*, 1495. He also wrote very influential practical works : *Lectura super canonem missæ*, 1488 ; *Expositio canonis missæ*, 1499 ; and *Sermones*, 1499. Late in life he joined the Brethren of the Common Life.

3. *Raymond Lully was a Franciscan of another type, whose special service was the revival of the study of the Oriental languages and of comparative religion, connected with missionary effort.*

Raymond Lully (c. 1232-1315) was born on the island of Majorca ; and his life-work was from the Balearic Isles as a centre, although he taught in Paris, Montpellier, and elsewhere, and journeyed to Rome and other parts in the interest of his missions to the Moslems and the study of the languages of the East. He became a Franciscan in early life, and devoted himself to the study of physics, natural philosophy, and the Oriental languages. He wrote against Averroès' philosophy. His most important work is entitled *Ars magna*. This won him the title of *Doctor illuminatus*, and ' seemed to offer an easy road to the co-ordination of all sciences in one master science.' [1] Raymond greatly promoted the study of the languages of the East ; and through his influence missionary colleges and professorships of Oriental languages were established at Avignon, Paris, Bologna, Oxford, and Salamanca. He was one of the earliest writers on

[1] Zöckler, 'Lully,' in *New Schaff-Herzog Encyclopedia*.

Comparative Theology. He wrote : *Liber de quinque sapientibus*, a dialogue of disputation between a Roman, a Greek, a Nestorian, a Jacobite, and a Saracen ; also *Liber de gentili et tribus sapientibus*, a discussion between a Pagan philosopher, a Jew, a Christian, and a Saracen. The former may be regarded as Comparative Theology, the latter as Comparative Religion. Raymond also wrote a number of practical and devotional works,[1] and still has a reputation among his countrymen as a poet.

4. *The most influential Thomists of the period were Hervæus Natalis and Thomas Bradwardine.*

The Dominican order continued to perpetuate the teachings of Thomas Aquinas. 1. *Hervæus Natalis* († 1323) studied at Paris, and taught there as doctor of theology. He was one of the most noted scholars of his time. He became a provincial of the Dominicans in 1309, and general of the order nine years later. He wrote : *In IV Petri Lombardi sententiarum volumina* (Venice 1505, Paris 1647), *Quodlibeta* (Venice 1486, 1513), *De intentionibus* (Paris, 1489, 1544), and many other works. Seeberg calls him ' a moderate Thomist, (who) distinguished himself by his opposition to the views of Duns Scotus.' [2]

2. *Thomas Bradwardine* (1290-1349) was both student and teacher at Oxford, and became archbishop of Canterbury, 1348. He was a Thomist, and especially an Augustinian ; and was called *Doctor profundus*. His great work was *De causa Dei contra Pelagium* (ed. Savile, 1618).

Two other Dominicans deserve special mention :

3. *Johannes Capreolus* (1380-1444) became a doctor of theology in Paris, where he explained the *Sentences*. He

---

[1] *Works*, Mainz, 1721-1748, in ten volumes, ed. Salzinger (vol. vii. and viii. not published) ; earlier edition, 1617, incomplete.
[2] Seeberg, ' Hervæus Brito,' in *New Schaff-Herzog Encyclopedia*.

was called to Toulouse to preside over the *studium generale* of the Dominicans there. He wrote a commentary on the four books of *Sentences*, and *Defensiones theologiæ divi Thomæ* (Venice 1483-1484, 1514 +), which gained him the surname of ' the Prince of Thomists.'

4. *Juan de Torquemada* (Turrecremata) was born at Valladolid and died at Rome (1388-1468). He became a Dominican at sixteen, studied in the monastery of St. Jacques at Paris, and was licensed in theology, 1424. Returning to Spain, he was made prior in the convents first of Valladolid and then of Toledo. He became Master of the Sacred Palace of Eugene IV., in 1431, and an ardent defender of the papacy at the Council of Basle. Torquemada wrote many treatises upon the Church and the papacy after the teaching of Thomas Aquinas, and also upon the sacraments against the Hussites. He was made cardinal in 1439, and was active at the Council of Florence, having a hand in the composition of the decree of reunion. His writings cover a wide range, including works on the Scriptures, dogma, canon law, the sacraments, and practical Christianity. He was called ' the honour of his nation and of his order,' ' a luminary and a pillar ' for ' the Church universal.' [1]

5. *There was a great revival of mysticism in the fourteenth century in Eckhart, Tauler, Suso, and Ruysbrœck.*

1. *Meister Eckhart* (c. 1260-1329) was a Dominican mystic. He studied at Erfurt and Cologne, and became prior at Erfurt and provincial of Thuringia. He went to Paris to study and lecture, and there took his degrees (1300-1303). He was made provincial of Saxony, and then vicar-general for Bohemia. In 1311 he was appointed to teach in Paris, and some years later he appears as teacher at Cologne. The mysticism of Eckhart was

---

[1] *Scriptores ordinis Prædicatorum*, i. p. 837 ; cited by Feret, *La Faculté de théologie de Paris*, iv. p. 336.

extreme and tended towards pantheism. He said and
wrote many things that led to his condemnation by the
archbishop of Cologne and finally by the pope, to whom
he appealed. Twenty-six propositions were condemned
as *Errores Ekardi*.[1] He is said to have submitted before
his death. He was willing to admit the eternity of the
world. The Christian may be converted into God just
as the bread of the Eucharist is converted into the body
of Christ. Whatever God gives to His only-begotten Son
in human nature, all that He may give to the Christian.
Whatever is proper to the divine nature, that is also
proper to the just man. External acts do not make us
good, but only interior acts. ' *Si homo commisisset mille
peccata mortalia, si talis homo esset recte dispositus, non
deberet velle se ea non commisisse.*' [2]

There are in such statements as these pantheism and
antinomianism, the forerunners of similar tendencies
in modern times. Eckhart combined scholasticism with
a mysticism run wild. The earlier mystics had been
Franciscans. They were comparatively sober, and
attached the mystic element to the scholastic theology.
The later Dominican mystics tended towards heresy.
Protestants ignore the heretical tendencies of these men,
and regard them as ' preparing the way for the Reformation.' Eckhart was called by Hegel ' the father of
German philosophy ' ; by Cruel, ' the boldest and most
profound thinker the German pulpit has ever had.'
According to Pfleiderer his spirit is ' the spirit of the
Reformation, the spirit of Luther.' [3]

2. *John Tauler* (c. 1300-1361) was a Dominican of
Strasburg. He is known to have come under the influence of the mystics Johann Sterngasser and Nicholas
of Strasburg, possibly also of Eckhart and Suso. Little

[1] Denzinger, *Enchiridion Symbolorum*, pp. 141 *seq.*
[2] *Ibid.*, pp. 501 *seq.*
[3] *Vide* Schaff, v., ii. pp. 243, 248, 256.

is known about his life, and of the works ascribed to him only the Sermons, and a part of these, are certainly genuine. These have passed through many editions, the first being that of Leipzig, 1498. Tauler was more practical than Eckhart, but no less pantheistic and antinomian in his tendency. Yet his sermons have been great favourites with Christians of the mystic type. Beza called him a visionary ; but Luther and Melanchthon praised him.[1]

3. *Henry Suso* (1300-1366), ' the Swiss mystic,' was born on Lake Constance, became a Dominican at thirteen years, and studied at Strasburg and at Cologne. The greater part of his life was spent in the monasteries of his order at Constance and Ulm. In his twenty-eighth year he came under the influence of Eckhart. Suso and his writings were condemned as heretical also by a council of unknown date, but what he taught is not clear. *The Book of Truth* is a defence of Eckhart ; *The Book of Eternal Wisdom* ' became one of the favourite books of meditation of the Middle Ages.' [2] Schaff quotes Denifle as calling it ' the consummate fruit of German mysticism.' [3] Suso was beatified by Pope Gregory XVI.

4. *John Ruysbrœck* († 1381) was prior of the regular canons at Gröndal, near Brussels. He was called *Doctor ecstaticus*. His works were written in Dutch, but translated into Latin by his pupils Jordæns and Groote. They include mystical, ethical, and monastic treatises, and a short exposition of the Athanasian Creed. Ruysbrœck shows the influence of Eckhart, and was visited by Tauler. His pupil Groote founded the Brethren of the Common Life.

The greatest works produced by the mystics of this age are of uncertain authorship. 5. *The Imitation of*

---

[1] *Vide* Schaff, v., ii. p. 261.
[2] Cohrs, 'Suso,' in *New Schaff-Herzog Encyclopedia.*
[3] Schaff, v., ii. p. 266.

Christ has been attributed to Gerson, but is now generally supposed to be the work of *Thomas à Kempis* († 1471), to whom are ascribed other popular works, including meditations on the life of the Saviour and on the incarnation.   Thomas was educated at the famous school at Deventer conducted by the Brethren of the Common Life, and is called a follower of Groote.   Whatever may be thought of its authorship, *De imitatione Christi* takes rank with the *Confessions of St. Augustine* as a devotional book of the universal Church.[1]

6. The unknown author of the *Theologia Germanica* has been called 'one of the Reformers before the Reformation.'   Luther published this work in two editions (1516, 1518), the title of the second being : *Ein Deutsch Theologia.*   He called it a 'noble little book,' in which he had found his God 'in the German tongue' as he had not 'found Him in the Latin and Hebrew tongues.'[2]   It contains, however, pantheistic elements.

6. *The Eastern Church had also its great mystics at this period, chief among whom were Nicolas Cabasilas and Simeon of Thessalonica.*

1. *Nicolas Cabasilas,* archbishop of Thessalonica († *c.* 1371), was a cotemporary of Tauler ; and as Adeney says, the two 'agree in their vital principles.'[3]   The great work of Cabasilas is *Concerning the Life of Christ,* in seven books.   His writings include 'a mystical exposition of the Liturgy' and a philosophical work against scepticism.

2. *Simeon* († *c.* 1428), also archbishop of Thessalonica, was an influential writer and 'one of the chief mystagogic theologians of the later Greek Church.'[4]   His most important works were : *The Faith, the Rites, and the*

[1] *Vide* Schaff, 'Kempis,' in *New Schaff-Herzog Encyclopedia.*
[2] Schaff, *History of the Christian Church,* v., ii. pp. 242, 293 *seq.*
[3] Adeney, *The Greek and Eastern Churches,* p. 282.
[4] Meyer, 'Simeon,' in *New Schaff-Herzog Encyclopedia.*

Mysteries of the Church, described by Adeney as ' a store-house of ecclesiastical archæology ' ; [1] and a dialogue *Against All Heresies*. He also wrote expositions of the Nicene Creed, and other treatises.

7. *The chief reforming movement in the fourteenth century was that of Wyclif.*

John Wyclif (*c.* 1325-1384) was born in Yorkshire and educated at Oxford, where he became a scholar of Balliol, and then master (*c.* 1360). He was interested in mathematics and natural science, as well as in philosophy and theology. He became a doctor of theology not later than 1372, and then gave lectures on theology. About two years later he was made rector of Lutterworth, Leicestershire, a living which he held until his death. Wyclif revived the study of the Scriptures, and sought a reformation of the Church, especially on the religious and ecclesiastical side. He was sustained and protected by John of Lancaster. His principal writing was his *Summa theologiæ*, which is strongly polemic in character. Like Bradwardine he was an Augustinian. He was, indeed, a realistic philosopher ; but based himself chiefly on the Scriptures, and so received the title of *Doctor evangelicus*. With the help of his associates he translated the Latin Bible into English, assigning to himself the New Testament, and to his friend, Nicholas of Hereford, the Old Testament. The whole was revised in 1388 by John Purvey. Wyclif wrote :

' Christen men and women, olde and young, shulden study fast in the New Testament, and no simple man of wit shulde be aferde unmeasurably to study in the text of holy Writ. Pride and covetise of clerks is cause of their blyndness and heresie and priveth them fro verie understonding of holy Writ. The New Testament is of ful autorite and open to understonding of simple men, as to the pynts that ben most needful to salvation.' [2]

---

1 Adeney, *The Greek and Eastern Churches*, p. 282.
2 Cited by Schaff, v., ii. pp. 341 *seq.*

Wyclif opposed the abuse of the allegorical method of exegesis, and exalted the authority of the Scriptures above the authority of the Church. He made an all-important statement, which became the Puritan watchword in later times: 'The Holy Spirit teaches us the sense of Scripture as Christ opened the Scriptures to His apostles.' [1]

Wyclif established an order of poor preaching priests, who went about like the earlier Dominicans preaching to the people. These and their followers were called Lollards, and were speedily declared heretical. The reforming energies of Wyclif were at first directed against abuses of an ecclesiastical and economic kind; but his activities, like his writings, covered a wide range. The latter included: *De civili dominio, De officio regis, De incarcerandis fidelibus*, as well as sermons, polemic treatises, and the famous *Trialogus, Dialogus*, and *Opus evangelicum*. According to his disciple Thorpe, 'from him one could learn in truth what the Church of Christ is, and how it should be ruled and led.' [2]

8. *The reforming spirit was transferred from England to Bohemia through John Huss, who adopted essentially the teaching of Wyclif.*

John Huss (1369-1415) was a native of Bohemia, and studied at the university of Prague, where he took his degrees. He was ordained priest in 1400, became dean of the philosophical faculty a year later, and rector of the university in 1402. A contest over the rival popes brought about a secession of the German professors and students in 1409. They removed to Leipzig, where a new university was established. Huss adopted the views of Wyclif, and his teaching spread with great rapidity all over Bohemia until the mass of the

---

[1] *Vide* Briggs, *Study of Holy Scripture*, p. 455.
[2] Cited by Loserth, 'Wyclif,' in *New Schaff-Herzog Encyclopedia.*

Bohemians had become Hussites. The archbishop appealed to the pope, and Huss and his adherents were put under the ban. A civil war ensued, which lasted for a long time, even after the condemnation of Huss. He was summoned to the Council of Constance, and burned at the stake as a heretic ; but he died protesting his innocence, saying : ' In the truth of the Gospel which I have written, taught, and preached, will I die to-day with gladness.' His writings are for the most part polemic. In his sermons he often reproduces Wyclif. In pastoral activity he was ' unsurpassed.' [1]

The friend and follower of Huss, Jerome of Prague, was not long in sharing his fate. *Jerome* († 1416) studied in Prague, Oxford, Paris, Cologne, and Heidelberg. At Oxford he came under the influence of Wyclif, and carried back with him to Bohemia two of Wyclif's writings, the *Trialogus* and the *Dialogus*. He supported Huss in his attempts at reformation and in spreading the teachings of Wyclif, and remained true to both these masters until after the death of Huss. Then for a time his courage gave way ; but at the close of a winter's imprisonment he defended both them and himself with great spirit before the Council. Bracciolini describes his bearing with great admiration, crying : ' He stood there fearless and unterrified, not alone despising death, but seeking it, so that you would have said he was another Cato. . . . I praise not that which he advanced, if anything contrary to the institutions of the Church ; but I admire his learning, his eloquence, his persuasiveness of speech, his adroitness in reply. . . . Not Mutius himself suffered his arm to burn with such high courage as did this man his whole body. Nor did Socrates drink the poison so willingly as he accepted the flames.' [2]

He suffered on the very spot where Huss was burned.

---

[1] *Vide* Loserth, ' Huss,' in *New Schaff-Herzog Encyclopedia.*
[2] Cited by Schaff, v., ii. pp. 390 *seq.*

9. *The study of the Scriptures was greatly promoted by Nicolaus de Lyra, Ludolph of Saxony and others.*

1. *Nicolaus de Lyra* (c. 1270-1340) was born at Lyre, France, and died at Paris. He was a Franciscan, and in 1325 was made a provincial of his order. He studied the Oriental languages as well as theology, and taught at the Sorbonne for many years. He spent his life in the study and exposition of the Scriptures, and thirty-eight years in writing his commentaries. He also wrote a commentary on the Lombard's *Sentences, Quodlibeta*, and three books against the Jews. His *Postillæ* are written in fifty books of running commentary on the whole Bible, including the Apocrypha; also thirty-five books of *moralia*. There are three prologues: (1) a eulogy of Scripture; (2) a study of method; (3) of the mystical meaning. Lyra mentions the four senses of Scripture, and then says:

'All of them presuppose the literal sense as the foundation. As a building, declining from the foundation, is likely to fall; so the mystic exposition, which deviates from the literal sense, must be reckoned unbecoming and unsuitable.'

And yet he adds:

'I protest, I intend to say nothing either in the way of assertion or determination, except in relation to such things as have been clearly settled by Holy Scripture on the authority of the Church. All besides must be taken as spoken scholastically and by way of exercise; for which reason, I submit all I have said, and aim to say, to the correction of our holy mother the Church.' [1]

It is astonishing that Lyra accomplished so much while working within such limits. However, it is only in the field of the spiritual and practical interpretation of Scripture that the Church has ever claimed infallibility. It is certain that piety and communion with God are absolutely essential to an understanding of His Word.

[1] Nicolaus de Lyra, *Postillæ perpetuæ*, prol. ii.; *vide* Briggs, *Study of Holy Scripture*, p. 454.

To know the Bible it is necessary to know God and His Christ. The supreme interpreter of the Scriptures is the Holy Spirit. Lyra regarded the Church as more completely under the influence of the Spirit than any of its individual members. He therefore submitted all questions of faith and morals to the decision of the Church ; and, in so doing, was not disloyal to that fundamental principle, upon which the greatest leaders of the Church in all ages have acted, however defective their apprehension of it may have been.[1] He exerted a healthful, reviving influence on Biblical study, and is certainly the chief exegete of the Middle Ages. There is truth in the saying : ' If Lyra had not piped, Luther would not have danced.' [2] By Lyra and Wyclif the seeds of a new exegesis were planted, which burst forth into fruitful life at the Reformation.[3]

2. Next to Lyra may be mentioned the Carthusian, *Ludolph of Saxony*, who flourished *c.* 1330, and wrote a life of Jesus Christ, which became influential and so remained until after the Reformation. It was not an historical study, but was useful for ethical purposes. Ludolph also wrote *scholia* on the Psalms.

Among the other exegetes of the time may be mentioned : 3. *Peter Berchorius* († 1362), a French Dominican, who wrote *Opus reductorii moralis super tota biblia*, in thirty-four books. He urged tropology, or moral exposition.

4. *Peter Herentalius* († 1436), a native of Flanders, wrote *Catenæ* on the Psalms and the Gospels, taking as his model the *Glossa continua* of Thomas Aquinas on the Gospels.

5. *Alphonsus Tostatus* († 1455), lecturer at Salamanca, bishop of Avila, and lord high chancellor of Castile, was

---

[1] *Vide* Briggs, *Study of Holy Scripture*, pp. 484 *seq.*, 660 *seq.*
[2] *Si Lyra non lyrasset, Lutherus non saltasset.*
[3] *Vide* Briggs, *Study of Holy Scripture*, p. 455.

F

one of the most learned men of his time. He wrote a
commentary on the greater part of the Bible, published
at Venice 1728, in twenty-seven volumes folio, which
is diffuse and dry, but learned. His Introduction to
the Biblical writings, prefixed to the commentary on
Matthew, is of little value.

Laurentius Valla († 1457) returned to the grammatico-
historical method of exegesis. As a humanist he belongs
rather to the Modern Age.[1]

6. *Bernardine of Siena* († 1444), a Franciscan, and the
first Vicar-general of the Observantists, was noted for
his preaching, and was called by Pius II. a second Paul.
In addition to sermons he wrote a commentary on the
Apocalypse.

7. *Augustine of Rome* wrote commentaries on the
Epistles of Paul, the Catholic Epistles, and the
Apocalypse.

8. *Paulus Burgensis*, bishop of Burges († 1435), is
described by Flügge [2] as a converted Jew who showed
many traces of Jewish learning. He wrote *Additiones
ad Nicolai Lyræ postillas in sacram Scripturam.*

9. *John Lattebur*, a Franciscan of England, wrote
Moralia super Threnos Jeremiæ, and commentaries on
Jeremiah, the Psalms, and the Acts.

10. *Many universities were founded in the latter part
of the fourteenth, the fifteenth, and the early sixteenth
centuries, the most important of which were in Germany
and after the model of Paris.*

In Germany were founded the universities of *Prague*
(1348), *Vienna* (1365), *Heidelberg* (1386), *Cologne* (1388),
Erfurt (1379-1392), *Würzburg* (1402-1582), *Leipzig* (1409),
Rostock (1419), *Trèves* (1454-1473), *Greifswald* (1456),

[1] *Vide* pp. 87 f.
[2] Flügge, *Versuch einer Geschichte der theologischen Wissenschaften*, iii.
p. 272.

Freiburg (1457), *Ingolstadt* (1459-1472), *Mainz* (1477), *Tübingen* (1477), *Wittenberg* (1502), and *Frankfurt* (1506).

In Italy were opened the universities of *Perugia* (1308) ; *Pisa* (1343), subsequently the university of the Florentine government ; *Pavia* (1361), which served for the Milanese ; *Ferrara* (1391), and *Turin* (1405).

France established those of *Avignon* (1303), *Cahors* (1332), *Grenoble* (1339), and *Orange* (1365), in the fourteenth century, and eight others in the fifteenth century.

In the Low Countries the university of *Louvain* was established in 1425.

In Switzerland was opened the university of *Basel*, 1459.

In Poland and Hungary were founded those of *Cracow* (1364-1397), *Fünfkirchen* (1367), and *Ofen Pest* (Budapest, 1476-1477).

In Spain a large number were founded, including those at *Lerida* (*c.* 1300), *Perpignan* (1349), *Huesca* (1359), *Barcelona* (1450), *Saragossa* (1474), *Palma* (1483), *Sigüenza* (*c.* 1489), *Alcalá* (1499), and *Valencia* (1500).

In Sweden a university was opened at *Upsala* (1477).

In Denmark one was established at *Copenhagen* (1478).

In Scotland three were founded : one at *St. Andrews* (1411-1413) ; one at *Glasgow* (1450) ; and one at *Aberdeen* (1494).

The greater universities had for the most part the four faculties : those of *arts*, in which instruction was based on Aristotle ; *medicine*, in which the chief text-books were the works of Hippocrates, Galen, and Avicenna ; *law*, the study of which was based on civil and ecclesiastical canons, collected in the *Corpus juris canonici* ; and *theology*, based on the Lombard's *Sentences*.

According to Rashdall,

'There were . . . in every university town, as in other important places, grammar schools proper. . . . In many cases . . . the university acquired jurisdiction over these schools. This

was the case in most German universities. In others they remained under the ecclesiastical inspection to which they had
been subject before the rise of the university corporations. . . .
The old ecclesiastical schools, in connection with cathedrals or
other important churches, were not destroyed by the growth
of the universities, and other schools of the same kind were founded
from time to time. . . . In districts remote from universities
there were ecclesiastical schools of a higher type. . . . In some
countries the bulk of the inferior clergy must have received their
education in such schools.' [1]

Rogers says :

' I am convinced that [grammar schools] were attached to
every monastery, and that the extraordinary number of foundation schools established just after the Reformation of 1547 was
not a new zeal for a new learning, but a fresh and very inadequate
supply of that which had been so suddenly and disastrously
extinguished.' [2]

11. *The conflicts between the rival popes involved all
Europe in political and ecclesiastical confusion. The
University of Paris, under the lead of the great mystics,
D'Ailly and Gerson, led in an attempt at reform through
œcumenical councils ; but they simply succeeded in
strengthening the papacy, after the schism was healed.*

The great schism in the papacy, which began in 1378
between Urban VI. and Clement VII., the former at Rome,
the latter at Avignon, France, involved the whole of
Europe in civil and ecclesiastical war, to the serious
injury of religious and theological education. Various
attempts to heal the schism were made from time to
time ; until at last the chief civil governments, under
the lead of the university of Paris, determined to bring
it to an end. Three successive reforming Councils were
held : those of Pisa (1409), Constance (1414-1418), and
Basel (1431-1443). These reforming Councils were ably
and conservatively conducted ; but they could not

---

[1] Rashdall, ii. pp. 597, 601.
[2] Rogers, *Six Centuries of Work and Wages*, i. p. 165 ; *vide* Rashdall,
ii. p. 600, *n.* 2.

succeed, because of the unwillingness of the papacy to be reformed, or to submit to the Councils, and because of the rivalry of the civil governments. The *Council of Pisa* deposed both of the rival popes, and elected a third ; but as neither of the rivals would yield, the result of this action was that three popes were in the field. The *Council of Constance* succeeded better in this regard. John XXIII. was deposed ; Gregory XII. resigned voluntarily ; and Benedict XIII. could be disregarded, as he was recognised only in Peniscola, a small town of Valencia, Spain. A new pope was elected (1417), under the name of Martin V. ; and apparently the schism was healed. This Council, however, disgraced itself by violating the safe-conduct of John Huss, and burning him at the stake. The new pope failed to carry out the reforms proposed by the Council ; and so, after his death, the *Council of Basel* was summoned to deal with his successor, Eugene IV. The Council suspended him in 1438, deposed him in 1439, and elected as pope Amadeus of Savoy under the name of Felix V. As Eugene would not submit, two rival popes were in the field. After his death the cardinals elected Nicolas V. (1447-1455), an exceedingly able, wise, and irenic pope, who soon persuaded Felix to resign, the Council to dissolve, and all Europe to unite under his jurisdiction. This reunion was celebrated by a Jubilee at Rome in 1450, which closes the period of the Middle Ages, leaving the papacy at the height of its supremacy over the world.

The most influential men in connection with the Council of Pisa were Petrus de Alliaco, bishop of Cambrai, and his pupil John Gerson, chancellor of the University of Paris.

1. *Petrus de Alliaco* (Pierre D'Ailly, 1350-1420) was a student of theology at the university of Paris (1372), and lectured on the *Sentences* of the Lombard from 1375 onward. In 1380 he was made doctor of theology and

professor, four years later Director of the College of
Navarre, and in 1389 chancellor of the university.
Among his pupils were Gerson and Nicolaus Clémanges.
He became bishop of Puy in 1395, of Cambrai in 1397,
and cardinal in 1411.   He wrote on many subjects, including : commentaries on the Song of Songs, and the
Penitential Psalms ; *Quæstiones super IV libros sententiarum*, which were nominalistic ; *De reformatione ecclesiæ*,
and *De potestate ecclesiæ*.   He was especially prominent
at the Council of Constance, where he maintained the
supreme authority of œcumenical councils.   He also
urged the cause of union in the papacy and the reformation of the Church.   Yet he took an active part against
heresy in the condemnation of John Huss.   D'Ailly distinguished between the Bible and tradition, between
pope and council ; and as a nominalist was critical of
Scholasticism, and especially of the exaggeration and
abuse of dialectic, which had degenerated into mere
sophistry.   At the Council of Constance he ' urged the
appointment of "institutores Rhetoricæ et linguarum
Græcæ et Latinæ." ' [1]

2. *John Gerson* (1363-1429) studied at Paris with
Pierre D'Ailly for seven years, and succeeded him as
professor of theology and chancellor of the university.
He was called *Doctor christianissimus*.   He sought to
enrich scholasticism with mysticism, and wrote mystical
and practical works, and commentaries on the Song of
Songs, the Penitential Psalms, and the Lord's Prayer,
with mystical, allegorical, and moral interpretations.
He also wrote *Monotessaron*, a harmony of the Gospels,
and *Propositiones de sensu literali sacræ Scripturæ et
de causis errantium*, in which he states the principles of
catholic hermeneutics over against the literalism of
heretics.   He wrote against the vain curiosity of the
degenerate Scholasticism in matters of faith, and made

[1] Rashdall, i. p. 541, *n*. 1 ; citing Von der Hardt, I. iv. c. 427.

the profound statement that 'those who prefer the
new works, conduct themselves after the manner of
boys who eat the new and bitter fruits rather than the
mature, digestible and healthful.' [1] In his tract *De modis
uniendi ac reformandi Ecclesiam in concilio universali*
he takes a general view of the Church as consisting of all
those who believe in Christ, ' be they Greeks or Latins or
Barbarians.' [2] This larger Church he distinguishes from
the particular Roman Catholic Church. Other works of
importance were *De reformatione theologiæ, De unitate
ecclesiastica, De auferibilitate papæ ab ecclesia.* Trithemius at the close of the century called Gerson ' theologorum sui temporis longe princeps.' [3]

[1] Gerson, *Opera*, i. col. 119 *seq.*   [2] Gerson, *Opera*, ii. col. 161 *seq.*
[3] Cited by Schaff, v., ii. p. 218.

PART II

THE MODERN AGE

CHAPTER I

THE REVIVAL OF LEARNING

1. *There was a preliminary revival of classical scholarship in the late fourteenth and early fifteenth centuries, which tended to the corruption of life and manners in the direction of heathenism, and to the undermining of Christian life and education.*

We have seen that the university of Paris grew out of the cathedral school, and that the other early universities of Northern Europe for the most part grew out of the migration of students and masters from Paris and Bologna, or the daughters of these universities. The inevitable result of the growth of the universities was the decline of the older cathedral schools; for the best teachers and the most energetic scholars resorted to the universities by preference.

The establishment of the mendicant orders, the location of their chief seats at the universities, and their active, energetic life, replacing the older contemplative life of the Benedictines, drew the most vigorous of the young men to the new orders. The Benedictines declined in influence as the Franciscans, Dominicans, Augustinians and other friars increased in reputation. And so the monastic schools lost their importance, as the mendicant orders established their schools in connection with the universities. Accordingly the universities became the great seats of theological as well as of philosophical and grammatical education ; and the cathedral and monastic schools were either discontinued, or reduced to small importance as mere grammar schools, or schools of piety, from which the best students went to the universities. The study of theology was practically given over to the mendicant orders, and especially to the Dominicans and the Franciscans, whose contests agitated the universities and the Church until the Reformation.

The study of theology at the universities was chiefly a study of the *Sentences* of the Lombard, elaborated by the great scholastics, Thomas, Bonaventura, Duns Scotus and Occam, with their numerous disciples. The dogmas of Christianity were elaborated by the Aristotelian logic, and in accordance with the Aristotelian categories, into the most refined and hair-splitting definitions and speculations. The dogmas of Christianity became abstract dogmas, of little practical interest or importance, mere intellectual balloons, or castles in the air. The inevitable result was a barren and dead orthodoxy. The study of the Bible had been thrust into the background. It had become a preliminary study, leading up to the dogmatic system. The allegorical sense gave the dogmatic theologian whatever he wanted for his purpose.

The great teachers of Paris, especially Gerson and Clémanges, recognised and strove to overcome these evils. The latter says :

‘ I am astonished that the theologians of our time read so carelessly the pages of the divine Testaments, enfeebling their spirits by the research for sterile subtilties, and, to use the term of the Apostle, “ doting about questionings and disputes of words,” [1] that which is proper for sophists, but not for theologians. The Apostle indicates here the procedure of those men who leave the

---

[1] 1 Tim. vi. 4.

vigorous and fertile tree of the Holy Scriptures, and seek their nourishment in doctrine in desert and sterile places. It is there that they anguish, in other terms, that they suffer of fasting, die of hunger, because they find no fruit; or if they encounter it, that fruit is like the apples of Sodom, which are beautiful and bright in appearance, but which at the touch resolve themselves into dust and smoke. Yes, at first sophisms appear beautiful, ingenious, penetrating, keen; but, if you tear away the envelope of words to get at the fruit, it is nothing but smoke, because all is empty within.' [1]

The most practical study of theology at the universities was that of canon law; for this study involved the practice of law in the law-courts, and gave those skilled in it the highest places in Church and State.

Paris was the great school of Theology, Bologna the great school of Law, so recognised by the pope and the bishops for centuries. The Scholastic Theology and the Canon Law played into the hands of the pope and the curia.

There gradually arose, as we have seen, various movements for reform, chiefly on the practical side of the religious life or of religious institution, and through the revival of mystic theology; but all of these movements failed for the time, though not without some good results. So far as theological education is concerned, they accomplished nothing of importance. The reforming movements did not go deep enough; and they did not propose any thorough-going principle of reform, or find for it a sufficiently authoritative basis.

In the meanwhile divine Providence was preparing the way for the great Reformation in an extraordinary way and an unexpected manner, such as is usual with God, by the revival of classical scholarship and a return to Greek and Roman antiquity. This was brought about

[1] Clémanges, *De studio theologico; vide* D'Achery, *Spicilegium,* i. 476; Feret, *La Faculté de théologie de Paris,* iv. 19,

in several ways, all of which conspired to the common end.

It is generally recognised at present that the revival of classical scholarship was led by two great literary men : *Petrarch* (1304-1374) and *Boccaccio* (1313-1375). These were especially interested in the literature of Rome and Greece. *Petrarch* has been called the ' first modern man.' [1] ' In a new age he was the first to recognise the supreme importance of the old classical literature ' ; he ' prepared the soil of Italy for the reception of Greek culture,' but he regarded ' the study of the classics as the handmaid of Christianity.' [2] *Boccaccio* was ' the first of modern men to study [classical] Greek in Italy, and indeed in Europe.' [3] He learned his Greek from the pupils of the Calabrian monk Barlaam. Florence became the centre of a classical scholarship, which did not at first connect itself with the universities, but organised itself in associations or academies entirely apart from universities or organised schools. The new learning was at first acquired by private study, from private teachers, as in ancient times. The students of classical antiquity were known as *Humanists*. This classical revival at the beginning had nothing to do with theology ; its tendency was rather away from theology. Indeed for a long time it was demoralising to Christian theology, and really a revival of heathenism.

In the latter part of the fifteenth century there arose at Florence a reformer who ' represents a religious reaction against the pagan tendencies of some of the Humanists,' and who wrote a tract ' describing all learning as dangerous unless limited to a chosen few.' [4] *Savonarola* (1452-1498) was a mystic of a different type from those of Paris. He was a preacher of repentance, and exposed from the pulpit the abuses existing among clergy and laity. He says of himself : ' I preach the regeneration of the Church, taking the Scriptures as my sole guide.' He complains :

---

[1] Renan, *Averroès*, p. 328 (ed. 1882).
[2] Sandys, ii. pp. 4 *seq.*   [3] *Ibid.*, p. 15.   [4] *Ibid.*, p. 88.

'In the mansions of the great prelates there is no concern save for poetry and the oratorical art.' 'The theologians of our time . . . do not know a shred of the Bible; yea, they do not even know the names of its books.'[1] Savonarola claimed the gift of prophecy, and predicted ruin for the impenitent. Even his enemies saw in him a resemblance to John the Baptist. In his denunciations he spared neither Rome nor the papacy. When his own city, which had protected him, was threatened with the interdict, he prepared an appeal from the pope to an œcumenical council. His enemies, by challenging him to an ordeal of fire, succeeded in destroying his influence with the people; and they tortured him into a retraction. But like Jerome of Prague, he overcame his physical weakness and faced death with unflinching courage. At his deposition, when the officiating prelate declared: 'Separo te ab ecclesia militante et triumphante,' Savonarola cried: 'Militante, non triumphante: hoc enim tuum non est.' The Meditations, which he wrote in the intervals of torture, were translated and circulated in Germany, Spain, France, and England, as well as Italy. Luther published them with warm commendation.

2. *The Council of Florence* (1439), *in the interest of the reunion of the Eastern Churches with the Western, brought a large number of Orientals to Italy, and resulted in a revived interest in the study of Theology, especially of Comparative or Irenic Theology.*

The Council held at Ferrara in 1438, and removed to Florence in 1439, brought a large number of Greeks and Orientals to Italy in the interest of the reunion of the East and the West. Among them came a considerable number of learned men, who established themselves permanently in Italy. These scholars brought with them the Greek language and Greek literature. Students of theology learned to know the Greek Bible and the Greek Fathers; students of philosophy read Plato and Aristotle in the original. The Latin Church became once more acquainted with the Greek and Oriental Churches.[2]

[1] *Vide* Schaff, vol. v. part ii. pp. 688 *seq.*
[2] *Vide* Briggs, *Theological Symbolics*, pp. 142, 154.

Of these Eastern scholars the chief were:

(1) *Bessarion* (*c.* 1395-1472), archbishop of Nicæa, who for his services in behalf of reunion was made cardinal, and so spent his last years in Italy. He surrounded himself with numbers of Greek scholars, and became a great patron of classical learning.

(2) Another of these learned Greeks was *Theodore of Gaza* (1400-1475), the first professor of Greek at Ferrara, who also taught philosophy in Rome. He wrote a Greek grammar, which was used as a text-book in Paris, Cambridge and Germany. Among his pupils was the great German Humanist, Rudolphus Agricola.

(3) *Argyropulos* of Constantinople (1416-1486) taught first at Padua, then at Florence, and finally in Rome, where he became the instructor of the famous German, Reuchlin, concerning whom he exclaimed: 'Lo! Greece through our exile has flown across the Alps.' [1] He became noted for his translations of Aristotle.

(4) *Gemistos Plethon* of Constantinople (*c.* 1356-1450) was one of the champions of the Greek Church at the Council of Florence. He taught the Platonic philosophy in Florence, and renewed the struggle between Plato and Aristotle.

The Greeks in Italy were divided between these two philosophers, and a great controversy arose as to their relative merits. The result was an increasing attention to Plato among the Humanists, and an increasing desire to get rid of the dominant Aristotelian Scholasticism.

The study of the classics carried with it the study of Christian antiquity and the rise of historic investigation.

The most important scholar in this regard was *Laurentius Valla* (1407-1457).

Valla became the father of historical criticism. He was trained in Humanistic studies, and, while professor of rhetoric at the university of Pavia, wrote *Quæstiones dialecticæ* and *De elegantiis latini sermonis*, works characterised by Wagenmann as 'Humanism's open declaration of war' against the logic and the Latin of the Schools.[2] The treatise on Latin passed through fifty-nine editions in the years 1471-1536. 'In his treatise on Dialectic he denounces the mediæval Aristotelians, Avicenna

---

[1] *Vide* Sandys, ii. p. 64.
[2] Wagenmann, 'Laurentius Valla,' in Herzog's *Real-Encyklopädie für protestantische Theologie und Kirche.*

and Averroès, and attacks the philosophers of his time for their belief in the infallibility of Aristotle.'[1] The philosophers, theologians and jurists all rose up in arms, and Valla left Pavia. Some years later he entered the service of the Humanist, Alfonzo, king of Aragon and Sicily (c. 1435). During this period of his life he investigated the sources of Canon Law, and proved that the so-called *Donation of Constantine* was a pseudonymous work of much later date. He also produced a *Collatio Novi Testamenti*, first published by Erasmus (1505), who praises the 'remarkable sagacity' with which Valla has 'examined the whole New Testament,' and considers him 'unrivalled both in the sharpness of his intelligence and the tenacity of his memory.'[2] About the year 1445 Valla opened a school of Greek and Latin literature in Naples, and attracted a multitude of students. Two or three years later Pope Nicholas v. made him *scriptor apostolicus*. In 1450 he became also professor of rhetoric in Rome, and under Calixtus III. (1455) papal secretary. In addition to numerous translations from the Greek, his works include the famous *Elegantiæ* and *Declamatio*, and several influential treatises on Ethics. Luther declares that 'the like of (Valla) neither Italy nor the whole Church produced in many centuries.'[3] 'Laurencius Valla ist der best wahl, den ich mein lebtag gesehn oder erfaren hab. De libero arbitrio bene disputat.'[4] Erasmus wrote: 'Where is the man whose heart is so narrowed by jealousy as not to have the highest praise for Valla, a man who with so much energy, zeal and labour refuted the stupidities of the Barbarians, saved half-buried letters from extinction, restored Italy to her ancient splendour of eloquence, and forced even the learned to express themselves henceforth with more circumspection?' To strike at Valla is to wound 'all men of letters.' He is 'eloquent above all others,' and 'has been rightly called "The Marrow of Persuasion."'[5]

3. *The capture of Constantinople by the Turks in* 1453 *drove large numbers of learned Greeks into exile in Italy, and other parts of the West, where they greatly increased the knowledge of Greek literature, both classical and theological.*

Students of classical antiquity resorted to Italy from

---

[1] Sandys, ii. p. 67.
[2] Erasmus, *Epp.* 21, 182.
[3] Benrath, 'Valla,' in *New Schaff-Herzog Encyclopedia.*
[4] Preger, *Tischreden Luthers*, 237.
[5] Erasmus, *Epp.* 26, 27.

all over Europe to acquire the new learning, and they carried it back with them to their native lands. Thus Humanism spread rapidly as a new intellectual force throughout the West.

Erasmus expressed the conviction of many when he said :

'Latin erudition, however ample, is crippled and imperfect without Greek. We have in Latin at best some small streams and turbid pools, while they have the clearest springs and rivers flowing with gold. I see it is the merest madness to touch with the little finger that principal part of theology which treats of the divine mysteries, without being furnished with the apparatus of Greek.' 'They have neither sense nor shame who presume to write upon the Sacred Books, or indeed upon any of the books of the ancients, without being tolerably furnished in both literatures.' [1]

Among the exiles from Constantinople came also learned men from among the Jews and the Oriental Churches, who introduced the study of Oriental languages, especially Hebrew. The Hebrew Bible, the Talmud and the Jewish commentators began to be studied by Christian scholars.

4. *The spread of the new learning was greatly aided by the invention of printing at Mainz in* 1440.

Printing was introduced into Italy by two of the workmen of Fust the inventor, who set up a press at Subiaco in 1465, and then at Rome in 1467. The great printing press of Italy, however, was the *Aldine* at Venice, established in 1494, and sustained by the 'New Academy' of Hellenists which was founded in 1500 by Aldus Manutius. This society proposed to print each month an edition of at least 1000 copies of some good author.

'By the year 1500 about 5000 books had been produced in Italy, of which about 300 belong to Florence and Bologna, more than 600 to Milan, more than 900 to Rome, and 2835 to Venice.' [2]

---

[1] Erasmus, *Epp.* 143, 182.   [2] Sandys, ii. p. 97.

Erasmus testifies to the liberality of the Italians, and especially of Aldus, in matters of literature ; saying :

> ' When I, a Hollander, was publishing in Italy my work on Proverbs, all the learned who were within reach, came forward to supply me with the authors, not yet printed, that they thought likely to be of use to me. Aldus had nothing in his treasures which he did not place at my service. . . . I was assisted by some whom I knew neither personally nor by name.' [1]

5. *Humanism found an early entrance into the Netherlands by attaching itself to the mystic tendency of the Brethren of the Common Life.*

Gerhard Groote (1340-1384) and *Florentius Radewyns* (1350-1400) founded the Brotherhood of the Common Life, which established schools for moral and religious education in the Netherlands and in Northern Germany. The instruction given was based upon the study of the Latin language. This led to a revival of the study of the Latin classics in these schools.

Nicolaus Cusanus and *John Wessel* were trained in them, and both added Greek and Hebrew to their Latin, and gathered ancient manuscripts.

Nicolaus of Cusa (1401-1464) was trained in Law, Mathematics and Astronomy, as well as Theology and Philosophy. He belonged to the Mystics who sought the reformation of the Church, and wrote *De concordantia catholica*. Like Gerson he subordinated the pope to the œcumenical council. In his work, *De docta ignorantia*, he criticised the scholastic method.

John Wessel (1420-1489) was noted for breadth of interest and a spirit of inquiry, that won for him the name *magister contradictionum*. Rudolphus Agricola and John Reuchlin studied with him before going to Italy to enlarge their knowledge of Greek.

6. *Erasmus summed up in himself all that was best in Humanism, and by his editions of the Greek Testament and of the Fathers gave a basis of authority, Biblical and Patristic, for the reformation of the Church.*

---

[1] Erasmus, *Adagia ; vide* Nichols, *Epistles of Erasmus*, i. pp. 437 *seq.*

The most distinguished of the pupils of the Brethren of the Common Life was *Erasmus of Rotterdam* (1466-1536). He received his primary education among the Brethren at Deventer and Bois-le-Duc, and in 1487 entered the Augustinian monastery near Gouda, where he remained a close student for ten years. The bishop of Cambrai then sent him to Paris, where he studied and taught in the university. He devoted special attention to Greek, and wrote :

' My Greek studies are almost too much for my courage ; while I have not the means of purchasing books, or the help of a teacher.' Again he says : ' I have been applying my whole mind to the study of Greek ; and as soon as I receive any money, I shall first buy Greek authors, and afterwards some clothes.' He complains of ' a great penury of books ; leisure none ; health infirm ; ' yet declares : ' My whole soul is bent on acquiring the most perfect learning, and hence I have a supreme disregard for learning of a trivial kind.'

' I am determined that it is better to learn late than to be without the knowledge which it is of the utmost importance to possess.' ' I began to look at Hebrew, but frightened by the strangeness of the idiom, and in consideration of my age and of the insufficiency of the human mind to master a multitude of subjects, I gave it up.'

In his enthusiasm he declares :

' If there is any fresh Greek to be bought, I had rather pawn my coat than not get it ; especially if it is something Christian, as the Psalms in Greek or the Gospels.' [1]

Erasmus travelled about from university to university in France, England, Italy, the Netherlands and Switzerland, in the interests of higher scholarship ; and became the greatest scholar of his age. He paid several visits to England, and the English Humanists, Colet and Sir Thomas More, became his devoted friends. Both the great universities ' sought to have ' him, and he ' spent several months at Cambridge teaching Greek and

---

[1] Erasmus, *Epp.* 112, 113, 139, 143, 156, 180.

Divinity.' [1]   The latter part of his life was passed chiefly in Basel, and most of his works appeared from the famous press of Froben.   Erasmus sought and obtained release from his monastic vows, and came into conflict with the monks in the interests of learning.   He ardently espoused the cause of classic scholarship and of the study of the Fathers, as over against mediæval scholarship and the ignorance of the religious orders of his time.   His editions of the Greek Testament, and of many of the Fathers, laid a basis for sound scholarship.   He says himself :

'Many are induced to study the Sacred Writings, who would otherwise never have read them, as they themselves admit ; and a great many have begun to study Greek ; indeed, that is going on everywhere.' [2]

He regarded himself as called to do 'the humblest part of the work' to be done for theology, and says :

'I wanted to construct a road for other persons of higher aims, so that they might be less impeded by pools and stumbling blocks in carrying home those fair and glorious treasures.' [3]

The works of Erasmus include editions or translations of many of the greatest authors of the Christian and classical world.   Of his original works the best known are his famous satire *Moriæ encomium*, the *Colloquies*, letters, treatises on education, and on the Greek and Latin languages, the *Enchiridion militis christiani* and its companion *Institutio principis christiani*, and *Ecclesiastes*, which emphasises the prophetic function of the Christian ministry.

There are countless testimonies from his cotemporaries to the unique place held by Erasmus.   Reuchlin writes from Germany : 'You alone bring us back some image of the ancient eloquence ; the rest of us are a mob.'   More writes from England concerning his *Utopia* : 'I want to know whether Tunstall approves, and Busleiden, and your Chancellor . . . but your vote alone will

[1] Erasmus, *Ep.* 290.   [2] *Ibid.*, 400.   [3] *Ibid.*, 522.

be abundantly sufficient for my judgment. We two are to my
mind a multitude, as I think I could live happily with you in any
solitude.' Henry of Glarus cries: 'It was a great thing to have
learned morality from Socrates . . . but I have received much
more from you. Besides innumerable other benefits, the chief
is this: that you have taught me to know Christ, and not to
know Him only, but to imitate, to reverence and to love Him.' [1]
Watson writes: 'You are celebrated everywhere in Italy,
especially among the learned of the highest note. . . . Your
fame is spread throughout all the Christian world. . . . Wherever
you are, you so live as to seem present everywhere in Christendom,
and will continue to live by the immortality of your fame and the
noble monuments you will leave behind you. By your correction of the New Testament accompanied by your notes, you have
thrown a marvellous light on Christ, and deserved well of all His
zealous followers.' [2] But Erasmus says: 'For myself I think
nothing settled, unless I have the approval of Christ, on whose
single vote all our felicity depends.' [3] 'Huc discuntur disciplinæ,
huc philosophia, huc eloquentia, ut Christum intelligamus, ut
Christi gloriam celebremus. Hic est totius eruditionis et elo-
quentiæ scopus.' [4]

Erasmus worked for a reform of the Church, especially
on the side of learning and morals ; and he, like most of
the Humanists, finally opposed Luther and the other
Reformers, in the interests of learning and the unity of
the Church. His dread of a conflict in the Church may
be gathered from the fervour of his appeal against
national strife for those ' who glory in the name of
Christ, of a Master who taught and exhibited nothing but
gentleness, who are members of one body, and are one
flesh, quickened by the same Spirit, fed by the same
sacraments, attached to the same Head, called to the
same immortality, hoping for that highest communion,
that as Christ and the Father are one, so we may be one
with Him.' [5]

[1] *Vide* Nichols, *Epistles of Erasmus*, ii. pp. 276, 386, 426 *seq.*
[2] *Vide* Nichols, *ibid.*, ii. pp. 334 *seq.*   [3] Erasmus, *Ep.* 184.
[4] Erasmus, *Ciceronianus* ; *vide* Woodward, *Desiderius Erasmus concerning the Aim and Method of Education*, p. 59.
[5] Erasmus, *Ep.* 281.

7. *The Humanists of France were more of the Italian type. Their chief theologian Clémanges combined mystic with humanistic studies.*

The earliest French Humanist was *Jean de Montreuil* (1354-1418), who had, however, no position as a teacher. *Nicolas de Clémanges* (*c.* 1367-1437), his friend, was the first great Humanist of France. He was educated in the university of Paris, at the college of Navarre, by Pierre D'Ailly and Gerson ; and taught rhetoric there. In 1393 he became rector of the university, and, four years later, papal secretary under Benedict XIII. But in 1408 he retired to a Cistercian cloister, and gave himself to Biblical study, which he felt had been neglected. In his work *De studio theologico* he exalts the parish priest above the student, yet recommends the study of theology and especially of the Scriptures. He felt the influence of the Italian Humanists. In 1425 he returned to Paris to teach rhetoric and theology in the college of Navarre. Clémanges was influential in the calling of the Council of Constance, but disappointed and displeased with its final action as to the papacy. Like his masters, D'Ailly and Gerson, he was opposed to the sophistry of the time. These three great mystics were sound in their mysticism, and emphasised direct communion with God and the Christian life. Like Erasmus they worked for reform as middle men, and accomplished more than is recognised. All three have been neglected by both Protestants and Catholics—by the latter because, in the three reforming councils which they dominated, they exalted the authority of the œcumenical council above that of the pope. Among the writings of Clémanges may be mentioned the tracts, *De ruina ecclesiæ, De corrupto ecclesiæ statu, De fructu rerum adversarum*, and his letters to D'Ailly, Gerson and others.

The first scholar officially appointed to teach classical Greek in Paris was *Gregorio Tifernas* († 1466). He was followed in 1476 by *Hermonymus*, the 'somewhat incompetent' instructor of Reuchlin, Erasmus and Budæus. *Aleander* was introduced there by Erasmus (1508), and became rector of the university in 1512, librarian of the Vatican in 1517, and finally a cardinal.

The greatest French Humanist was *Budæus* (1467-1540), who won from Italy the supremacy in classical scholarship. Calvin calls him : 'primum rei literariæ decus et columen.' His influence secured the establishment of the Corporation of the Royal Readers (1530), which developed into the *Collège de France*. Sandys regards this foundation as 'perhaps his most important, certainly his most permanent, service to the cause of scholarship.'[1]

Faber Stapulensis, Jacques Lefèvre d'Étaples (†1536), Humanist, philosopher, and theologian, was influential as a teacher in Paris. He is praised by Sir Thomas More ' as the restorer of true Dialectic and true Philosophy, especially that founded upon Aristotle,' and by Erasmus for his work on the New Testament.[2] He published *Psalterium quintuplex* (1509), French versions of the New Testament (1523), and the Psalter (1525), and finally one of the entire Bible (1530), which served as a basis for the better known version of Olevitan (1535). Stapulensis also produced commentaries on the Scriptures and on Aristotle, and Latin translations of the Fathers and the Mystics. In the preface to his commentary on St. Paul's Epistles, he maintained the authority of the Scriptures and urged a reform of the Church.

8. *Humanism made its way into Germany and German universities. The earliest representatives were Æneas Sylvius and Regiomontanus. The chief German Humanist, however, was Reuchlin, who laid the foundation for the study of the Old Testament in Hebrew.*

1. *Æneas Sylvius de Piccolomini* (1405-1464) ' represented Italian Humanism in Vienna (1442-1455),' and won 'the gratitude of Germany for the teaching and the example which had led that land to admire the studies of Humanism.'[3] As Pope Pius II. (1458) he collected many valuable manuscripts and encouraged all the arts.

2. *Regiomontanus* (1436-1476), archbishop of Ratisbon,

---

1 Sandys, ii. pp. 172 *seq.*
2 *Vide* Nichols, *Epistles of Erasmus*, ii. pp. 224 327.
3 *Vide* Sandys, ii. p. 251.

was a friend of Bessarion, and taught and translated both Greek and Latin works.

We may quote the summary statement of Sandys as to the different classes of Humanists in Germany :

'The Humanists of Germany may be divided into three successive schools distinguished from one another in their relation to the Church. (1) The *Earlier* or *Scholastic* Humanists, who were loyal supporters of the Church, while they were eager for a revival of classical learning, and a new system of education. They are represented by the three great teachers of North Germany, Rudolfus Agricola, Rudolf von Langen, and Alexander Hegius ; also by Wimpfeling, the restorer of education in South Germany ; by Trithemius, one of the founders of the Rhenish Society of Literature ; and by Eck, the famous opponent of Luther. They worked for the Revival of Learning in all branches of knowledge, while they hoped that the new learning would remain subservient to the old theology. (2) The *Intermediate* or *Rational* Humanists, who took a rational view of Christianity and its creed, while they protested against the old scholasticism, and against the external abuses of the Church. "They either did not support Luther, or soon deserted him, being conscious that his movement would lead to the destruction of all true culture." Their leaders were Reuchlin and Erasmus, and Conrad Muth, the Canon of Gotha. "Their party and its true work of culture were shipwrecked by the tempest of the Reformation." (3) The *Later* or *Protestant* Humanists, who were ready to " protest " against everything—young men of great talent, but of less learning, whose love of liberty sometimes lapsed into licence. Their leading spirit was Ulrich von Hutten. In course of time, some of them became Rational Humanists ; others, supporters of Luther. "While Erasmus, Reuchlin and Muth viewed Luther's propaganda with distrust," these younger Humanists "flocked to the new standard of protest and revolt, and so doing brought culture into disgrace and shipwrecked the Revival of Learning in Germany." "The revolt of Luther caused the Church to reject Humanism, and was the deathblow of the Erasmian Reformation." '[1]

This last statement, however, is rather extreme and unfair to the Reformers, who counted on their side one

---

[1] Sandys, ii. pp. 258 *seq.*, citing Pearson, *The Ethic of Free Thought*, pp. 166 *seq.*

of the greatest of the Humanists, Melanchthon, the
'Preceptor of Germany,' Camerarius, John Sturm, and
many others.

3. *Rudolphus Agricola* (1444-1485) was trained at
Deventer, Erfurt, Louvain, Cologne, Pavia, and Ferrara ;
and taught at Heidelberg. He learned Greek of Theo-
dorus Gaza, and in his last years studied Hebrew. He
is said to have been to Germany what Petrarch was to
Italy, and was called by his cotemporaries ' a second
Virgil.' [1]

4. *Hegius* (1433-1498) 'made the school of Deventer
the great educational centre of North Germany.' [2]
In his time ' the number of scholars rivalled those of a
university, amounting, it is said, at one time to 2200.' [3]
Erasmus writes of Agricola as ' the preceptor of my
schoolmaster, Alexander Hegius, himself no degenerate
disciple of such a master.' [4]

5. *Jacob Wimpheling* (1450-1528) studied at Schlettstadt, Freiburg, Erfurt, and finally at Heidelberg, where
he afterwards (1498) became a professor and lectured on
Jerome. At Strasburg and other cities he founded
societies of literature. Through these as well as through
his text-books and treatises on education he became
widely influential in promoting liberal learning and
improved methods of instruction. His numerous writings
include works on theology, and he laboured for the
Church as well as for the school. Erasmus calls him
' the chief man of letters in his country, and the high
priest of every Humanity.' [5]

6. *Johannes Trithemius* (1462-1516), abbot of Spon-
heim, transformed his monastery into a centre of learning
and gathered a great library there. He was a student of
Hebrew and Greek, and of the natural sciences ; but

---

[1] *Vide* Pearson, *The Ethic of Free Thought*, p. 173.
[2] Sandys, ii. p. 255.   [3] Nichols, *Epist. Erasm.*, i. p. 17.
[4] Erasmus, *Ep.* 22.   [5] *Ibid.*, 298.

exalted theology above them all, and urged theologians to study the Scriptures.

7. *Reuchlin* (1455-1522) was trained in law, philosophy, and 'the three languages,' and studied at Schlettstadt, Freiburg, Paris, Basel, Orléans, Poitiers, Florence, and Rome. Greek he learned of native Greeks; Hebrew of John Wessel and Jewish Rabbis. He published a Greek grammar, and a Latin lexicon that passed through many editions. He laid the foundation for Hebrew scholarship among Christians by publishing the first Hebrew grammar and lexicon, combined in the work *De rudimentis hebraicis* (1506).[1] Twelve years later he brought out a treatise *De accentibus et orthographia linguæ hebraicæ.* He also studied Rabbinical literature, and wrote on the cabala. There was a stiff battle in Germany between the Humanists and the Obscurantists about Reuchlin and the study of the Hebrew language and the Jewish Talmud. Erasmus wrote to Raphael, the cardinal of St. George:

'I do most earnestly beseech and adjure you for the sake of good letters . . . that that distinguished man, Doctor John Reuchlin, may enjoy your protection and goodwill. . . . He is one to whom all Germany is indebted, having been the first to arouse in that country a love of Greek and Hebrew literature.'[2]

To Reuchlin Erasmus wrote:

'When I read your apology, composed with so much spirit and eloquence, and such an exuberance of learning, I seemed to myself to be listening not to a culprit making his defence, but to a conqueror celebrating his triumph.'[3]

Fisher, bishop of Rochester, says of Reuchlin:

'He appears to me to hold the palm over all living authors, whose works I have read, in the treatment of abstruse questions of Theology and of Philosophy.'[4]

---

[1] *Vide* Briggs, *Study of Holy Scripture,* pp. 140 *seq.*
[2] Erasmus, *Ep.* 319.   [3] *Ibid.,* 294.
[4] *Vide* Nichols, *Epistles of Erasmus,* ii. p. 292.

8. *Mutianus*, Conrad Muth of Erfurt (*c.* 1471-1526), a schoolmate of Erasmus at Deventer, was the chief of the group of Humanists which produced the *Epistolæ obscurorum virorum*, a series of satires which threw their opponents into confusion and contempt. The first volume was mainly composed by Johann Jäger (*Crotus Rubeanus*), the second by *Ulrich von Hutten* (1488-1523), ' the stormy petrel ' of the German Reformation.[1] Cologne was the chief seat of the opponents of Humanism, Erfurt of its friends.

9. *Johann von Staupitz* († 1524), the first dean of the theological faculty at Wittenberg, became vicar-general of the German Augustinians, and the teacher of Luther and his counsellor in the early stages of his reform. He was a man without stain and above reproach, a saint in the estimation of Protestant and Catholic alike, an apostle of love and good works. He ranks with Erasmus and Sir Thomas More among those irenic spirits that sought a reform of the Church from within.[2] Luther was strongly influenced by his practical mysticism and calls him his ' reverend father in Christ,' ' per quem primum cœpit Evangelii lux de tenebris splendescere in cordibus nostris.' [3] His chief mystic works are *Von der Nachfolgung des willigen Sterbens Christi*, *Von der Liebe Gottes*, and *Von dem heiligen rechten christlichen Glauben*.

9. *Humanism in England was represented chiefly by Linacre, Sir Thomas More, and Colet.*

Sandys says that ' Modern English scholarship begins with Linacre and his two friends, William Grocyn and William Latimer.' [4] These introduced the humanistic classic study into the British universities.

1 Lindsay, *History of the Reformation in Germany*, p. 75.
2 *Vide* Briggs, *Church Unity*, p. 420.
3 *Vide* Schaff, vol. vi. p. 119, *n.* 1.
4 Sandys, ii. p. 228.

1. *Thomas Linacre* (*c.* 1460-1524) was a nephew and pupil of William Selling, the first English Humanist to study Greek. Linacre studied at Oxford, and became Fellow of All Souls (1484). A year or two later he went to Italy, studied with Humanists in Rome, Florence, and Venice, and graduated in medicine at Padua (1492). Returning to England he gave lectures on. Aristotle's *Meteorologica*, which were attended by Sir Thomas More, either at Oxford or London. In 1509 he was appointed physician to King Henry VIII., and nine years later he founded the College of Physicians. In addition to his scientific treatises and translations he wrote *De emendata structura latini sermonis*, which was reprinted on the continent with a letter of recommendation by Melanchthon.

2. *John Colet* (*c.* 1467-1519) studied at Oxford, and then for three years in Italy, where he learned the rudiments of Greek. Returning to Oxford he introduced there the study of Plato, and gave lectures on the New Testament 'like one inspired.'[1] Among his hearers were all the doctors of Oxford.[2] At this time Erasmus visited Oxford, and became his intimate friend. In 1504 Colet was made dean of St. Paul's, London, where he introduced expository preaching, and founded a great school. According to Erasmus, Colet united 'the highest learning with admirable piety,' and 'exerted a great and general influence.' England had not 'another more pious, or one who more truly knew Christ.' When he died, Erasmus exclaimed : 'What a man England has lost, and I—what a friend !'[3] Colet's tract, *A Right Fruitful Admonition concerning the Order of a Good Christian Man's Life*, was first published in 1534, and afterwards incorporated in a book of *Daily Devotions*.

[1] *Vide* Plummer, *English Church History, 1509-1575*, p. 29.
[2] *Vide* Erasmus, *Epp.* 108, 290.
[3] *Vide* Schaff, v., part ii. p. 652.

3. *Thomas More* (1478-1535) studied at Oxford, and then went to London for the study and practice of law. He became the most able and learned jurist of his time ; but was also interested in theology, and lectured in London on Augustine's *City of God*. In 1529 More succeeded Wolsey as Lord Chancellor. Five years later he was sent to the Tower, and in 1535 was beheaded. Erasmus writes of yielding to the influence of

' Thomas More, whose eloquence is such that he could persuade even an enemy to do whatever he pleased, while my own affection for the man is so great, that if he bade me dance a hornpipe, I should do at once just as he bade me. . . . I do not think, unless the vehemence of my love leads me astray, that Nature ever formed a mind more present, ready, sharp-sighted, and subtle, or, in a word, more absolutely furnished with every kind of faculty than his. Add to this a power of expression equal to his intellect, a singular cheerfulness of character and an abundance of wit, but only of the candid sort ; and you miss nothing that should be found in a perfect advocate.' [1]

More maintained the rights of the crown of England over against papal encroachment, and the rights of the pope as the supreme head of the Church over against the royal ecclesiastical supremacy. He died a martyr to the great cause of the separation of the jurisdictions of Church and State. More's great work is his *Utopia*, in which he embodies his ideas of reform. Among his writings are controversial tracts against Luther and Tyndale.

4. *John Fisher*, bishop of Rochester († 1535), was trained at the university of Cambridge, and served there as master, vice-chancellor, professor of divinity and chancellor. He took part in the establishment of Christ's College and St. John's, and was president of Queens' College for a time. Erasmus calls him ' that great chieftain of literature and piety.' [2] Fisher admired Reuchlin and Erasmus, but wrote against Luther and

[1] Erasmus, *Ep.* 191.   [2] *Vide* Erasmus, *Ep.* 446.

Œcolampadius. As an opponent of the royal supremacy he shared the fate of More.

The English Humanists, like the Continental, desired a peaceable reform by education, not a revolution. They were in general accord with Erasmus, who wrote of them :

'I have found in England . . . so much learning and culture, and that of no common kind, but recondite, exact and ancient, Latin and Greek, that I now hardly want to go to Italy, except to see it. When I listen to my friend Colet, I can fancy I am listening to Plato himself. Who can fail to admire Grocyn, with all his encyclopædic erudition ? Can anything be more acute, more profound, more refined, than the judgment of Linacre ? Has nature ever moulded anything gentler, pleasanter or happier, than the mind of Thomas More ? '[1]

These men wished a reform through a study of the original Scriptures and the Fathers.

Among the Humanists of England who sought to promote theological education were also :

5. *Cardinal Wolsey* († 1530), founder of Christ Church (College), Oxford ; 6. *Warham*, archbishop of Canterbury († 1532), whom Erasmus praised as ' the patron of all the learned ' ;[2] and 7. *Richard Fox*, of Winchester († 1528), founder of Corpus Christi College, Oxford, and of the first Greek lectureship in an English university.[3] Sir Thomas More saw no reason to prefer the universities of Paris and Louvain to those of Oxford and Cambridge.[4] Erasmus wrote in 1516 : ' About thirty years ago nothing was taught at Cambridge but Alexander, the *Parva Logicalia*, as they are called, those old " dictates " of Aristotle, and questions from Scotus. In process of time Good Letters were introduced ; the study of Mathematics was added, and a new or at least a renovated Aristotle. Then came some acquaintance with Greek, and with many authors, whose very names were unknown to the best scholars of a former time. Now I ask, what has been the result to the University ? It has become so flourishing, that it may vie with the first schools of the age, and possesses men, compared with whom those old teachers appear mere shadows of theologians.'[5]

---

[1] *Vide* Sandys, ii. p. 229.   [2] Erasmus, *Ep.* 242.
[3] *Vide* Briggs, *Theological Symbolics*, pp. 159 *seq.*
[4] *Vide* Nichols, *Epistles of Erasmus*, ii. p. 224.
[5] Erasmus, *Ep.* 441.

10. *The Humanists gradually succeeded in transforming the greater part of the universities and schools of Europe early in the sixteenth century. The study of the Greek and Latin classics, of the Hebrew and Greek Scriptures, and of the Greek and Latin Fathers, was gradually introduced, and the Scholastic Theology was pushed into the background.*

This transformation took place in Italy and Spain, no less than in Germany and England ; and was permanent in its results. The Humanist reformation was interrupted, and the Humanists were divided into hostile camps, by the outbreak of the revolutionary Reformation, led by Luther and Zwingli. This was a reformation of religion, which pushed the reformation of scholarship into the background. Its immediate effects were disastrous to scholarship, especially in Northern Europe. Insurrections and civil wars spread rapidly over Europe, and continued to work mischief for more than a century. But there was a permanent gain to theological scholarship in spite of all. The Holy Scriptures were studied in the original languages by all the great scholars of the time, and Biblical texts were published by Protestants, Catholics and Jews.

In Spain the *Complutensian Polyglot* was published by Cardinal Ximenes (1514-1517). In Italy the *Octaplum Psalterium* was issued at Genoa by Bishop Justinianus in 1516, the Aldine text of the Septuagint at Venice in 1518. Erasmus published his Greek Testament at Basel in five editions (1516-1535). From the second edition (1519) Luther made his translation. Stephens published three editions in Paris (1546-1550), and one in Geneva (1551). The Hebrew Bible was printed at Soncino, Lombardy, in 1488, and at Naples in 1491-1493. Another edition was printed at Brescia in 1494, which Luther used in making his version. The same text appeared in Bomberg's Rabbinical Bible (1516-1517), edited by Felix Pratensis. A second Rabbinical Bible was published by Bomberg in 1524-1525, carefully revised after the Massora by Jacob ben Chayim.[1] The Mishna

---

[1] *Vide* Briggs, *Study of Holy Scripture*, pp. 186 *seq.*, 206 *seq.*

was published at Naples in 1492, the Babylonian Talmud at Venice by Bomberg (in twelve volumes folio, 1520), the Jerusalem Talmud at Venice by Bomberg (1522-1523). The Christian Fathers were also published in original editions, as well as the heathen classics in Greek and Latin, by the great presses at Venice, Basel, Paris, Geneva and elsewhere.

The whole world, Jew and Christian, Catholic and Protestant, had Hebrew and Christian antiquity opened to them as never before.

CHAPTER II

THE REFORMATION

THE New Learning made its way gradually into the midst of the universities and schools of Europe, not without severe conflicts with the Old Learning. The Humanists, early in the sixteenth century, divided on the deeper question of religious reform. The most of the Humanists remained Catholics, with Erasmus and Reuchlin, Sir Thomas More and Fisher, John Eck, and the Italian and Spanish Humanists in a body. Few of them followed Melanchthon and Calvin into the Protestant camp. The Humanists wished a reform by scholarship, and especially by a return to Christian antiquity, the study of the Scriptures and the Fathers in the original languages. The Protestants, under the lead of Luther and Zwingli, were more concerned to bring about a religious reform and do away with the abuses of religion. The Humanists in the main were unwilling to sacrifice Christian scholarship in the confusion and storms of a religious revolution.

1. *The revival of the study of Theology was due in the main in the Protestant world to Melanchthon and John Calvin, and among Catholics to John Eck and Ignatius Loyola.*

The original hostility of the New Learning to the Old had to be overcome, and a more comprehensive plan devised for the healthful and harmonious combination of the two. This was in a measure accomplished by

Melanchthon, Calvin, and their associates among Protestants, and among Catholics especially by John Eck, Ignatius and the Jesuit Order. Calvin and Ignatius had the same teachers in the university of Paris, and both alike saw the defects of the university education. Both alike organised colleges for the better training of the Christian ministry.

2. *Luther introduced new life and spirit into theological education in Northern Germany. Melanchthon gave it form and organisation.*

1. *Martin Luther* (1483-1546) was trained in law at the university of Erfurt, entered the Augustinian Order in 1505, and two years later became a priest. In 1508 he was appointed professor of philosophy at the newly established university of Wittenberg, where he continued his studies in theology, and took his bachelor's and doctor's degrees. About the year 1513 he turned to lecturing on the Bible. He became intensely hostile to the Aristotelian philosophy and to Scholasticism, and built his theology on the Scriptures and on St. Augustine. He gave to Wittenberg a Biblical rather than a humanistic character, and a mystic rather than a dogmatic spirit. The master of the German Reformation was a professor of theology, and began his work by training students in the exegesis of the Psalter and the Pauline Epistles. These writings, expounded in the lecture-room at Wittenberg, became the pillars of the Reformation.

'Hæc scripta sic illustravit, ut post longam et obscuram noctem nova doctrinæ lux oriri videretur.'[1]

Luther entirely reformed theological instruction by introducing new principles and new methods. The concrete was substituted for the abstract, the intuitive method for the analytical. Luther taught the Bible in

[1] Melanchthon, *Vita Lutheri*, p. 12 ; *vide* Gieseler, iv. p. 18, *n*. 6.

place of the Lombard and Thomas Aquinas. He followed the Apostles and Prophets in preference to the
Fathers and the Schoolmen.[1] Above all ' he recalled the
minds of men to the Son of God.' [2] He said :

' All right holy books agree in this, that they altogether preach
and urge Christ. This also is the true touchstone to test all
books, . . . since every scripture shows Christ.' [3]

Luther insisted that the Scripture should be its own interpreter, and urged the one literal sense against the
fourfold sense, yet claimed that faith was absolutely
essential to the exegete.

' Every word should be allowed to stand in its natural meaning,
and that should not be abandoned unless faith forces us to it.'
' It is the attribute of Holy Scripture that it interprets itself by
passages and places which belong together, and can only be
understood by the rule of faith.' [4]

Zwingli said :

' Luther . . . has searched out the meaning of Scripture with
greater earnestness than any one on earth has done for a thousand
years. . . . What I have read of his writings (so far as concerns
dogma, doctrine, opinions, and the sense of Scripture, for I have
nothing to do with his quarrels) is generally so well fortified and
grounded in the Word of God, that it is not possible for any
creature to refute them.' [5]

Ambrose Blaurer declared in 1523 :

' Luther, . . . above all other men, has so restricted his understanding, according to the exhortation of Paul, and forced it
into subjection to the word of Christ, that he seldom decides by
his own opinion, but by comparing and explaining Scripture
with Scripture, which is the highest art in commenting.' [6]

---

[1] Vide Briggs, in A Symposiac on Martin Luther by the Professors of
the Union Theological Seminary in New York, 1883, pp. 9 seq.
[2] Melanchthon, Vita Lutheri, p. 12.
[3] Walch, xiv. 149 ; vide Briggs, Study of Holy Scripture, pp. 652 seq.
[4] Walch, iii. 2042 ; xix. 1601 ; Briggs, Study of Holy Scripture, p. 456.
[5] Zwingli, Uslegung des XVIII. Art., 1523 ; vide Gieseler, iv. p. 83,
n. 39.
[6] Blaurer, in Füssli's Beyträge zur Reformationsgeschichte, iv. 195 ;
vide Gieseler, iv. pp. 73 seq., n. 119.

Melanchthon testifies to his extraordinary power as a teacher :

'One man is an interpreter ; another a logician ; and still another an orator, affluent and beautiful in speech ; but Luther is all in all. . . . Whatever he writes, whatever he utters, pierces to the soul, fixes itself like arrows in the heart.' [1]

But the chief merit of Luther as a teacher was his un-flinching fidelity to truth. The truth of God swayed him with irresistible power. At the Diet of Worms (1521) he cried : ' My conscience is bound in the Word of God : I cannot and will not recant anything. . . . Here I stand. I cannot do otherwise. God help me.' [2]

He wrote to Melanchthon in 1530 :

'To your great anxiety, by which you are made weak, I am a cordial foe ; for the cause is not ours. . . . So far as the public cause is concerned, I am well content and satisfied ; for I know that it is right and true, and, what is more, it is the cause of Christ and God Himself. For that reason, I am merely a spec-tator. If we fall, Christ will likewise fall ; and if He fall, I would rather fall with Christ than stand with the emperor.' [3]

Luther first appeared as a reformer in the publication of ninety-five Theses against the sale of indulgences (1517). He claimed that he was upholding the Scriptures and the teaching of the Church ; but in the heat of controversy he came into conflict with the common teaching and practice of the Church as expressed in the writings of great theologians and in papal decrees. He challenged the Scholastic Theology and the authority of the pope, holding that only a general council could finally deter-mine articles of faith. But in a controversy with Eck at Leipzig (1519) he was forced by inevitable logic to justify Huss in some matters, and so to deny the infallible authority of councils as well as of popes.[4] In the follow-

---

[1] *Vide* Painter, *Luther on Education*, p. 108.
[2] *Vide* Kidd, *Documents Illustrative of the Continental Reformation,* p. 85 ; Briggs, *Theological Symbolics*, pp. 262 *seq.*, 271 *seq.*
[3] *Vide* Kirn, ' Melanchthon,' in *New Schaff-Herzog Encyclopedia.*
[4] *Vide* Briggs, *Theological Symbolics*, pp. 162 *seq.*, 165 *seq.*

ing year he published his tracts : *To the Christian
Nobility of the German Nation, The Babylonian Captivity
of the Church*, and *The Liberty of a Christian Man*. In
these he appealed to the Scriptures over against pope
and council. Two years later he began to print in parts
translations of the Bible in German.[1] This work was
completed in 1534, but he continued to revise it for the
rest of his life. He secured the help of Melanchthon,
Cruciger, Bugenhagen, Justus Jonas, and Aurogallus.[2]

The translation was based upon the original Hebrew
and Greek texts, compared with the Vulgate and the older
German versions. Luther's Bible has been the Bible
of the German people from that day to this. Widely
scattered in cheap editions, it greatly helped the progress
of the Reformation. Luther also produced numerous
commentaries, *postillœ* and expository sermons, which
were of great influence. The *Kirchenpostille* Luther
calls ' the very best book that I ever made.' [3] The
commentaries on Genesis, the Psalms, and Galatians
were of special value. In addition to his dogmatic and
polemic writings and his numerous letters, Luther
published works of fundamental importance for symbolics
and liturgics. His catechisms were given symbolical
authority by the Formula of Concord, as ' the Bible of the
laity.' [4] The smaller catechism is an abridgment of the
larger, and is based on the Decalogue, the Apostles'
Creed, the Lord's Prayer and the Sacraments. In the
preface to the Larger Catechism Luther writes :

' I read and recite word by word, in the morning and when I
have leisure, the Ten Commandments, the Articles of the Creed,
the Lord's Prayer, the Psalms, etc. . . . and I must remain and
do cheerfully remain a child and pupil of the catechism.'

---

[1] *Vide* Briggs, *Theological Symbolics*, p. 168 ; *Study of Holy Scripture*,
pp. 216 *seq.*
[2] *Vide* Schaff, *History of Christian Church*, vi. pp. 346 *seq.*
[3] Walch, xx. 1112 ; *vide* Gieseler, iv. pp. 554 *seq.*, *n.* 12.
[4] *Vide* Briggs, *Theological Symbolics*, pp. 11 *seq.*

Löhe remarks of the smaller work : ' No other catechism in the world can be made a prayer of but this.' Leopold von Ranke cried :

' Happy he whose soul was nourished by it, he who clings to it ! He possesses . . . under a thin shell the kernel of the Truth, which is sufficient for the wisest of the wise.' [1]

Luther's hymns are also household treasures among the German people. Luther came into conflict with Erasmus on the freedom of the will, and with Zwingli on the Eucharist. He alienated the greater number of the Humanists, and destroyed the unity of the Reformation by insisting that it should go in his way and in no other. He lacked the faculty of nice discrimination, and did injury to some of the cherished institutions and well-established doctrines of Christianity. But the Church was in bondage to a vast system of legalism, and it was Luther who spoke the master word that set men free. He had passed through an experience almost identical with that of St. Paul, and so was enabled to understand him better than any one since Augustine. It was the merit of Luther that he set forth the teaching of the Apostle Paul as the great transforming power of the age.[2] Like the Baptist, ' monstravit agnum Dei, qui tulit peccata nostra.' [3]

2. *Philip Melanchthon* (1497-1560) was educated in humanistic studies at the Latin school of Pforzheim and at the universities of Heidelberg and Tübingen. He was strongly influenced by Reuchlin, his great-uncle, and later by Erasmus, and so became a thorough Humanist. Œcolampadius recommended him to the latter as ' a person plainly worthy of Erasmus' love, who may himself become a second Erasmus.' [4] Melan-

[1] Von Ranke, *Deutsche Geschichte im Zeitalter der Reformation* (1852³), ii. p. 357 ; *vide* Schaff, *Creeds of Christendom*, i. pp. 250 *seq.*
[2] *Vide* Briggs, *Theological Symbolics*, pp. 156 *seq.*, 167 *seq.*, 170 *seq.*
[3] Melanchthon, *Vita Lutheri*, p. 12 ; *vide* Gieseler, iv. p. 18, *n.* 6.
[4] *Vide* Nichols, ii. p. 536.

chthon began his career by teaching the classics at Tübingen, and then went to Wittenberg as professor of Greek. At Wittenberg he represented the humanistic culture, which he combined with the more Biblical methods of Luther. His inaugural address, *De corrigendis adolescentiœ studiis*, excited extraordinary interest, and his lecture-room was thronged with students. In 1533 he reformed and reorganised the methods of the university, and this reform furnished the model for most of the Protestant universities of Germany. There were three professors of theology, the first of whom lectured on the New Testament, and the second on the Old Testament, while the third gave a more practical exposition of the Bible. Hebrew, Greek, and ethics were taught in the philosophical faculty. The *Sentences* of the Lombard and the old compendium of dogmatic were done away with. Melanchthon devoted himself for a time chiefly to the philosophical faculty, in strictly humanistic studies; but such interest was aroused by his lectures on the Greek Testament, that he was transferred to the theological faculty.

Matthesius relates that he came to Wittenberg at the age of twenty-five (in 1529), and there heard *Melanchthon* lecture on the Epistle to the Romans, and on Rhetoric, Dialectic and Ethics; also *Luther* on Isaiah; *Jonas* on the Psalms; *Bugenhagen* on Corinthians; *Aurogallus* on Hebrew grammar; *Frank* of Weimar on Greek, etc.[1]

Melanchthon became the great theologian of the Lutheran type of the Reformation. He rejected the Scholastic Theology; and, following the method of the Positive Theology, based his teaching on the Scriptures, especially on the Epistle to the Romans. He was more comprehensive in his scholarship than Luther, and more irenic in his disposition.[2] Luther contrasts himself with

---

[1] *Vide* Paulsen, *Geschichte des gelehrten Unterrichts*, i. p. 221.
[2] *Vide* Briggs, *Theological Symbolics*, pp. 168 *seq.*, 203 *seq.*

his friend in the preface which he wrote to Melanchthon's
Commentary on Colossians, saying :

'I am rough, boisterous, stormy, and altogether warlike. I
am born to fight against innumerable monsters and devils. I
must remove stumps and stones, cut away thistles and thorns,
and clear the wild forests ; but Master Philippus comes along
softly and gently, sowing and watering with joy, according to
the gifts which God has abundantly bestowed upon him.' [1]

After the death of Luther, Melanchthon developed
still more in the irenic and humanistic direction toward
which he was naturally inclined, but he became involved
in the Interimistic and Adiaphoristic Controversies, and
was charged with yielding too much in the interests of
peace. The *Augsburg Confession*, the *Apology* for that
Confession, and the so-called *Variata* were all the work
of Melanchthon. He also prepared other symbols in
whole or in part.[2] His *Loci communes rerum theologicarum*, published in many editions (1521-1559), grew out
of a course of lectures on the *Romans*. Luther called
it, ' *liber invictus, non solum immortalitate, sed et canone
ecclesiastico dignus.*' [3] It became the standard system of
theology of the Lutheran Reformation. Dorner classes
it with Luther's three great tracts of the year 1520,
saying : ' To the reformation proclaimed in these writings
and to no other did the German people subscribe.' [4]
Melanchthon's commentaries were also of great value,
especially those on the Romans and Colossians. His
numerous writings include important works on the
sacraments, worship, and government of the Church,
on ethics, homiletics, catechetics, and pedagogics, as
well as on dogma, philosophy, and philology. He
perpetuated the influence of Reuchlin, Wimpheling and

[1] *Vide* Schaff, vi. p. 193.
[2] *Vide* Briggs, *Theological Symbolics*, pp. 176 *seq.*, 184, 189 *seq.*, 193
354 *seq.*
[3] *Vide* Herrlinger, ' Melanchthon,' in Herzog's *Real-Encyklopädie*,
1881².
[4] Dorner, *Geschichte der protestantischen Theologie*, p. 93.

Agricola ; and he was the first Protestant to write on the proper method of studying theology, and the first to 'attempt a history of dogma.' 'It may safely be said that by his influence every department of theology was advanced.' [1]

The most of the German universities became Protestant : *Wittenberg, Erfurt, Leipzig, Frankfort, Greifswald, Rostock,* in the north ; and *Tübingen* and *Heidelberg,* in the south ; also *Copenhagen* in Denmark, and *Upsala* in Sweden. Upon all of these the influence of Melanchthon was strong. New universities were organised under the same influence at *Marburg* (1527), *Königsberg* (1544), *Jena* (1556-1558), *Helmstädt* (1576). The most of the universities, however, declined after the Reformation, with the exception of Wittenberg and Marburg in the north, and Tübingen and Heidelberg in the south.

Among the scholars of *Wittenberg* were : 3. *Justus Jonas* († 1555), who called Erasmus his 'father in Christ,' and was entrusted by Luther and Melanchthon with the translation of their works from German into Latin, or the reverse ; 4. *Johann Bugenhagen* († 1558), who was influenced by Erasmus to study the Scriptures, helped Luther in his Biblical translation, published notable commentaries, and, as superintendent of the reform in Denmark, reorganised the University of Copenhagen ; 5. *Matthias Flacius Illyricus* († 1575), leader in the Interimistic, Adiaphoristic and Synergistic controversies, author of works of great value to Church historians and Biblical exegetes, among them the famous *Magdeburg Centuries,* which originated with him ; 6. *Martin Chemnitz* († 1586), a leader in the preparation of several of the minor Protestant symbols and in the Adiaphoristic and Eucharistic controversies, and noted for his polemic against Rome, especially his *Examen Concilii Tridentini.*

The University of *Marburg* had among its first professors of theology : 7. *François Lambert* († 1530), a Franciscan of Avignon who came under the influence of both Zwingli and Luther, took a leading part in the Reformation in Hesse, especially in the Homberg Synod, and published practical commentaries and dogmatic and polemic treatises ; 8. *Andreas Hyperius* († 1564),

---

[1] Kirn, 'Melanchthon,' in *New Schaff-Herzog Encyclopedia.*

' the spiritual head of the Hessian Church ' and ' the father of Practical Theology,' [1] who wrote works of great importance, *De ratione studii theologici, De methodo in conscribenda historia ecclesiastica consilium, De formandis concionibus sacris*, and valuable commentaries.

The University of *Königsberg* numbered among its professors: 9. *Andreas Osiander* († 1552), Hebrew scholar, controversialist, and leader of the Reformation in Nüremberg, whose works include a Latin version of the Bible, a Harmony of the Gospels, and various polemic treatises. He is to be distinguished from his son *Lucas* († 1604), also preacher, teacher, controversialist, and the author of important Biblical, historical and doctrinal works.

Among the theologians of *Heidelberg* were: 10. *John Brenz* († 1570), the leading reformer of the Duchy of Würtemberg, active in many of the religious controversies of the time and in the reform of the University of Tübingen (1537), author of the *Confessio Wirtembergica*, the Church Order of 1553-1559, and of several catechisms of great usefulness ; also an exegete of whom Luther said : ' No one of the theologians of our time so explains and discourses of the Holy Scriptures as does Brentius ; in such a way that I often wonder at his mind, and doubt my own capacity. I believe that no one of us could do what he has done in explanation of the Gospel of John.' [2] 11. *Zacharias Ursinus* († 1583), an associate of Melanchthon at Wittenberg, and teacher in the *Collegium Sapientiæ* at Heidelberg, who helped to prepare the *Heidelberg Catechism*, and wrote on the *Augsburg Confession* and the *Formula of Concord* ; 12. *Caspar Olevianus* († 1587), trained in theology at Geneva, whose chief work was done at Heidelberg, in the preparation of the *Heidelberg Catechism*, in teaching, preaching and church organisation.

At the University of *Leipzig* valuable work was done in preparation for a sounder exegesis of the Greek Testament by the Greek scholar : 13. *Camerarius* († 1574), a disciple of Melanchthon.

The leading spirit in the University of *Rostock* in his day was : 14. *Chytræus* († 1600), another pupil of Melanchthon and ' the last of the fathers of the Lutheran Church.' He was a mediating theologian, and an encyclopædic scholar, and produced *Regulæ studiorum, De studio theologiæ recte inchoando* (1562, 1572), and other works of great influence in the fields of dogmatics, catechetics, Church history and Biblical exegesis.

---

[1] Achelis, ' Hyperius,' in *New Schaff-Herzog Encyclopedia*.
[2] Walch, xxii. 2290 ; *vide* Gieseler, iv. p. 555, *n.* 14.

The University of *Tübingen* trained such scholars as: 15. *Jacob Andreæ* († 1590), who helped to prepare the Swabian-Saxon *Concordia*, the Torgau Book, and the Formula of Concord, and wrote *De instauratione studii theologici, De studio sacrarum literarum*, and numerous other works; 16. *Piscator* († 1625), author of a German version of the Bible, Latin commentaries on both Testaments, and an *Anhang des herbonischen biblischen Wercks*, 'noted for its wealth of archæological, historical, and theological material.' [1]

In the University of *Copenhagen* the Danish theologian: 17. *Niels Hemmingsen* († 1600), a devoted pupil of Melanchthon, taught for thirty-seven years (1542-1579). He published valuable works in Exegetical, Doctrinal and Practical Theology, including the *Way of Life* (1570, English, 1575), in which the material is arranged on the principle of the Law and the Gospel.[2]

3. *The University of Basel perpetuated the influence of Erasmus, but went over to the Zwinglian type of the Reformation under the chief reformer Œcolampadius.*

1. *Œcolampadius* (Johann Heussgen, 1482-1531) was trained at Heilbronn, then studied law at Bologna, and at last philosophy and theology at Heidelberg, where he was greatly influenced by Thomas Aquinas and the Scholastic Mystics, especially Richard of St. Victor and Gerson. He spent some years in tutoring and preaching, and then went to Tübingen, where he met Melanchthon. In 1514 he returned to Heidelberg, and the following year was called to preach at Basel. There he entered into fellowship with Erasmus, and helped him in the publishing of his Greek Testament. In 1516 he began to lecture on the New Testament in the university, and two years later he assisted Erasmus in his second edition of the Greek text. The group of scholars to which both belonged is thus described by Erasmus:

'I seem to be living in some charming sanctuary of the Muses, where a multitude of learned persons, and learned in no common fashion, appears a thing of course. No one is ignorant of Latin;

---

[1] E. F. Karl Müller, 'Piscator,' in *New Schaff-Herzog Encyclopedia.*
[2] *Vide* Briggs, *Theological Symbolics*, pp. 8 *seq.*

none of Greek ; most of them know Hebrew. This one excels in the study of History, that one is deeply versed in Theology ; one is skilled in Mathematics, another is a student of Antiquity, and another is learned in the Law. Certainly up to this time it has never been my good fortune to live in such an accomplished society. But not to dwell upon that, what a sincere friendship prevails among them all, what cheerfulness, what concord ! You would swear they had only one mind among them.' [1]

In 1520 the mystic tendencies of Œcolampadius led him to retire to a monastery ; but after two years he left, and became the chaplain of *Franz von Sickingen*. A few months later he accepted a call to Basel, where he spent the remainder of his life. He became a leader of the Reformation in Basel, though not its originator. After a long conflict the reforming party triumphed (1529), and *Simon Grynœus* († 1541) and *Sebastian Münster* were added to the faculty of the university. The lectures of Œcolampadius in the university were chiefly upon the Scriptures, and his commentaries are among the most valuable of the time. His writings include sermons, exegetical and polemical treatises, letters and translations from the Fathers. He stood in close relations with Zwingli, and aided Bucer in his efforts for peace. At the conference of Marburg (1529) he showed a conciliatory spirit, and in the following years he continued to work for union. In 1534 he drew up with the help of *Myconius* the first Confession of Basel, which is simple and moderate in statement.[2]

The successor of *Œcolampadius* at Basel was: 2. *Oswald Myconius* († 1552), an associate of Zwingli, who helped to prepare both the First Confession of Basel and the First Helvetic Confession.

Among the theologians trained at Basel may be mentioned : 3. *Urbanus Rhegius* († 1541), a follower of Eck, who came under the influence of Erasmus and Zwingli, and took his doctor's degree at Basel. He became a leader of the Reformation in

---

[1] Erasmus, *Ep.* 366.
[2] *Vide* Briggs, *Theological Symbolics*, p. 185.

Lüneburg and Hannover, and published numerous doctrinal and polemical works, many of which were translated into English ; 4. *Johannes a Lasco* († 1560), author of the *Emden Catechism* and the *Confessio Londinensis,* a friend of Erasmus and other leading Humanists, who was charged with the superintendence of all the churches in East Friesland (*c.* 1542), of all the congregations of foreign Protestants in London (1550), and of all the Reformed churches in Little Poland (*c.* 1557).

4. *Zwingli began a revival of the study of Theology in Zürich ; and his influence was carried on by Bullinger, who organised both common and theological education, and laid the basis for the subsequent university.*

1. *Huldreich Zwingli* (1484-1531) was educated at Bern and Vienna, and finally at Basel, where *Thomas Wyttenbach* († 1526), professor of theology, taught him ' to seek remission of sins in the death of Christ alone.' [1] He began his work as pastor at Glarus in 1506 ; and some years later, under the influence of Erasmus, he undertook the study of the Greek Testament, that he might ' draw the doctrine of Christ from the original.' [2]   In 1516 he removed to Einsiedeln, where he began to proclaim the mediatorial work of Christ and the authority of the Scriptures.   Three years later he was called to the Great Minster at Zürich, where he remained until his death.   In Zürich he studied Hebrew with a pupil of Reuchlin, and began a series of expository sermons by which he covered the entire New Testament, save for the Apocalypse, in four years.   These sermons produced a profound impression.   In 1523 he published sixty-seven Theses, exalting Christ as the only Saviour, and Holy Scripture as the only infallible authority.   These articles are more comprehensive and dogmatic than those of Luther.   They may be regarded as the basis of the Swiss Reformation.   Zwingli defended them in a series of disputations.   He began his work of reform independently

[1] *Vide* Schaff, vii. pp. 23 *seq.*   [2] *Vide* Gieseler, iv. p. 78, *n.* 17.

of Luther, and from a different point of view. He was
stirred against idolatry rather than against the abuse of
indulgences. But, like Luther, he appealed to the
Scriptures.[1] In 1525 Zwingli introduced in Zürich the
study of the Bible in Hebrew, Greek and Latin, forming
a kind of theological school. It seems to have been to
some extent a revival of the ancient cathedral school.
Under the name of the *Carolinum* it developed into a
famous institution. Myconius declared that, if Zwingli
had lived to bring his plan to complete fulfilment, this
school would have had no equal.[2] Bullinger, Myconius,
Pellican, Bibliander and other noted scholars took part
in the building up of the institution. Zwingli sent a confession of faith to the Diet of Augsburg (1530), and an
Exposition of the Christian Faith to Francis I. (1531). He
wrote a *Commentarius de vera et falsa religione*, which is
said to be ' the first systematic exposition of the Reformed faith ' ; [3] also treatises on Divine Providence and
Christian education, polemical, exegetical, liturgical, and
political works, sermons and letters.

2. *Henry Bullinger* (1504-1575) was educated at
Emmerich by the Brethren of the Common Life, and
then at the university of Cologne. Influenced by a study
of the Fathers and the Scriptures, as well as by the
writings of Luther and Melanchthon, he became a
Protestant in 1522. The following year he began to
teach at the Cistercian monastery in Kappel, near
Zürich, and there remained for six years, teaching the
classics and the Bible. He became a close friend and
supporter of Zwingli, and after his death the leader of
the German Swiss Protestants. Bullinger raised the
schools of Zürich to a high standard of excellence, and
did much to promote theological scholarship. Peter

[1] *Vide* Briggs, *Theological Symbolics*, pp. 169 *seq.*
[2] *Vide* Christoffel, *Huldreich Zwingli*, in *Leben und ausgewählte
Schriften der Väter und Begründer der reformirten Kirche*, i. p. 97.
[3] *Vide* Schaff, vii. p. 63.

Martyr, Pellican and Bibliander were called to teach in
the *Carolinum*. Protestant refugees from France, Italy,
England, and Germany came to Bullinger for refuge.
Like Bucer he worked on behalf of Church Unity, and
Beza called him ' the common shepherd of all Christian
Churches.' [1] He was one of the authors of the First
Helvetic Confession (1536), and joined with Calvin in the
production of the *Consensus Tigurinus* (1549), which
united the French and German Swiss on a common platform. The Second Helvetic Confession (1566) he wrote
as his own confession of faith, in expectation of death
(1562) : it became the bond of unity of all the Reformed
Churches.[2] His writings consist of Latin commentaries
on the whole New Testament save the Apocalypse ;
sermons on several of the Prophets and on the Apocalypse ; treatises *De providentia, De gratia Dei justificante,
De Scripturæ sanctæ auctoritate et certitudine,* and other
dogmatic works ; *Sermonum decades quinque,* on the
Decalogue, the Apostles' Creed and the sacraments,
highly valued in England and Holland ; historical works,
and letters of great importance for the history of the
Reformation ; and a book of Church Order, prepared
with the help of Leo Judæ, which remained in use for
three centuries.

Among the scholars that assisted Zwingli and Bullinger the
most important was : 3. *Leo Judæ* (1482-1542). He was trained
at Schlettstadt, and was a fellow-student of Zwingli at Basel.
He began as a student of medicine ; but, influenced by Wyttenbach's lectures on *Romans,* he joined Zwingli in the study of
theology. He succeeded his friend at Einsiedeln, and afterwards
became his colleague and helper at Zürich (1523). He prepared
several catechisms, and became famous for his work as a translator, especially for his Latin version of the Old Testament. He
taught Hebrew in the *Carolinum,* and was the chief of the group
of scholars which produced the Zürich Bible (1525-1529). What

---

[1] *Vide* Schaff, vii. p. 207.
[2] *Vide* Briggs, *Theological Symbolics,* pp. 185, 193, 196 *seq.*

Melanchthon was to Luther, that Leo was to Zwingli; and he helped Bullinger to carry on the great Reformer's work.

Prominent among the reformers of Zürich were the Biblical scholars: 4. *Pellican* († 1556), a disciple of Reuchlin, and former associate of Œcolampadius at Basel, who taught Hebrew and Greek at Zürich for over thirty years, and published *Commentaria Bibliorum*; 5. *Bibliander* († 1564), 'homo grammaticus,' a pupil of Pellican, Capito, Œcolampadius and Myconius, and Zwingli's successor as professor of theology, regarded by Hottinger as the father of Exegetical Theology in Switzerland.[1]

Zürich became the refuge of several disciples of the Spanish mystic, *Juán de Valdés* († 1541), who produced a profound impression by his tract, *Del Beneficio di Christo*, and in his *Alfabeto christiano* summed up Christian perfection in holy love. One of the most noted of his many followers was: 6. *Pietro Martire Vermigli* (1500-1562), prior of the Augustinians at Lucca, who sought to reform theological study in his monastery, and published a tract on the Twelve Articles of the Christian Faith. Called to account by his Order, he retired to Strasburg, and there became professor of Hebrew (1543-1547). Cranmer invited him to England, and he was made professor of Divinity at Oxford (1549). Forced to leave England by Mary's accession, he finally settled at Zürich (1555), where he taught Hebrew in the *Carolinum*. His principal writings are commentaries, *Loci communes*, and doctrinal tracts. Among his disciples at Lucca was *Zanchi* († 1590), who taught Hebrew at Strasburg (1553) and theology at Heidelberg (1568), and wrote on the nature of God, His works and His law.

7. *Bernardino Occhino* (1487-1564), a native of Siena and member of the new order of Capuchins, became the most popular preacher of Italy after Savonarola. He was strongly influenced by Juan de Valdés and Peter Martyr, and was suspected of heresy. Taking refuge in Geneva (1542), he published many volumes of sermons and a commentary on Romans. Calvin praised him for 'eminent learning and exemplary life.'[2] In 1547 he was called to England by Cranmer, and for some years worked in London as an evangelist (1547-1554). On the accession of Mary he removed to Zürich, where he came under the influence of *Lælius Socinus*. In 1561-1563 he published works which excited doubts of his orthodoxy, and led to his expulsion. Driven from place to place, he died in Moravia the following year.

---

[1] *Vide* Egli, 'Bibliander,' in *New Schaff-Herzog Encyclopedia*.
[2] *Vide* Schaff, vii. p. 646.

Mention may also be made of : 8. *Hospinian* (1547-1626), who was head of the *Carolinum* for nearly twenty years, and produced numerous polemical and historical works, especially in the field of Christian Institutions.

5. *John Sturm organised the gymnasium of Strasburg in 1538, and Martin Bucer organised the theological seminary there in 1544.*

John Sturm and Martin Bucer were jointly responsible for the organisation of education at Strasburg.

1. *Sturm* (1507-1589) studied in the famous school of Liége and the university of Louvain, and began his teaching at Paris. Through the influence of Bucer's writings he became a Protestant. He is chiefly responsible for the organisation of the gymnasium of Strasburg (1538), which he conducted for over forty years as the public school of the city. According to his plan the study was carried on for ten years in as many classes. It was in preparation for the higher studies of the learned professions, law, medicine, and theology, and was humanistic throughout. Sturm's aims found expression in the phrase : *Sapiens atque eloquens pietas* ; his ideas and methods in the treatise : *De literarum ludis recte aperiendis.* His school had at one time more than a thousand pupils assembled from all parts. Among the teachers of theology were Bucer, Calvin, Capito, Hedio, Peter Martyr, and Fagius. Sturm was called upon to organise other schools on the model of that at Strasburg. His writings were numerous, including polemical tracts and letters of value, as well as works on pedagogy, rhetoric, etc.

Among the pupils of Sturm at Paris was the celebrated Humanist and philosopher, *Petrus Ramus* († 1572), noted for his criticism of the Aristotelian philosophy and logic, who published *Commentariorum de religione Christiana libri IV.*

2. *Martin Bucer* (1491-1551) was trained at Schlettstadt, joined the Dominican Order, and continued his

education among the Humanists at Heidelberg. He
left the monastery in 1520, and served as pastor at
Landstuhl, Wissenburg, and finally at Strasburg (1523),
where he united with Zell, Capito, and Hedio in the
reformation of the city. He organised evangelical
worship, Church government, and the teaching of
theology. Between the years 1524 and 1544 he published
no less than three catechisms, and in 1530 prepared the
Tetrapolitan Confession for the Diet of Augsburg. He
also helped Sturm in his school, and subsequently, in
1544, organised a seminary for training in theology.
Bucer was the chief mediating theologian on the Reformed side. He was influenced by both Luther and
Zwingli ; but took an independent position, and in his
turn influenced both Calvin and Melanchthon. It was
Bucer who, with the help of Melanchthon, composed the
Consultation of Hermann of Cologne, which Cranmer
used in the preparation of the Book of Common Prayer.[1]
Bucer was called by Cranmer to England, and settled
at Cambridge in 1550, only to die the following year.
His remarkable literary activity bore fruit in the fields
of Biblical Exegesis, Dogmatics, Symbolics, Apologetics,
Polemics, Irenics, Liturgics, Church Order, Pastoral
Theology, and the History of Councils and Conferences.
As an exegete he deserves special mention. Grynæus
wrote to him in 1533 : ' Palmam tibi in sacris literis
inter Germanos concedo.' [2]

3. *Capito* (Wolfgang Koepfel, 1478-1541) was educated at
Pforzheim and Ingolstadt, and finally at Freiburg, where he
studied medicine, law and theology. He became professor and
preacher at Basel (1515), and there, under the influence of Erasmus and other Humanists, took up the study of the Scriptures.
Erasmus describes him as ' a man who, besides other accomplish-
ments, is pre-eminently skilled in three tongues, Greek, Latin,
and Hebrew, and finally is a person of so much integrity and piety,

---

[1] *Vide* Briggs, *Theological Symbolics*, pp. 174 *seq.*, 180 *seq.*, 184 *seq.*, 191.
[2] *Vide* Gieseler, iv. p. 556, *n.* 15.

that I have never seen anything more stainless.' [1]   Capito published a *Psalterium hebraicum* (1516), and a Hebrew grammar in
several editions (1516, 1518, 1525), translations of Hosea and of
Chrysostom, two catechisms (1527, 1529), *Von der Kirchen-
lieblicher vereinigung* (1533), and above all the *Berliner Synodus*
(1532).   He became with Bucer a leader of the reform in Strasburg, and assisted him in preparing the Tetrapolitan Confession
(1530).

4. *Caspar Hedio* (1494-1552) was trained at Pforzheim,
Freiburg and Basel, and became one of the leading reformers
at Strasburg (1523).   He was also active in building up the
schools there, and taught theology in the higher school.   He
has been called the first Protestant Church historian, and his
works include translations of Eusebius, Rufinus, Sozomen, etc.,
and a chronicle extending from the beginning of the world to
the year 1543.

The successor of Capito at Strasburg was: 5. *Paulus Fagius*
(† 1549), one of his students, and a pupil of *Elias Levita*, the great
Jewish scholar, who, together with *Jacob ben Chayim*, exerted
a strong influence upon the Protestant reformers in their study
of the Old Testament.[2]   Fagius was called to England and
appointed professor of Hebrew at Cambridge (1549), but died
soon afterwards.   His writings are on the Hebrew language and
Old Testament exegesis.

Among the students of Hebrew at Strasburg in the time of
Capito and Bucer was: 6. *Musculus* (Muesslin, † 1563), a mediating theologian and worthy to stand with Bullinger, Œcolampadius and Melanchthon by the side of Luther, Zwingli and
Calvin, as one of the great exegetes of the Reformation.[3]   In
addition to his valuable commentaries Musculus published translations of the Greek Fathers, *Loci communes*, a catechism, and
doctrinal tracts.   He preached for some years at Augsburg, but
was driven from there by the *Interim* (1548), and became professor of theology at Bern.

6. *John Eck at the University of Ingolstadt reformed
the study of Theology by a combination of Positive Theology
with Humanistic studies and the traditional Catholic
Theology.*

John Eck (1486-1543) was educated at Heidelberg,

[1] Nichols, *Epistles of Erasmus*, ii. p. 328.
[2] *Vide* Briggs, *Study of Holy Scripture*, pp. 140 *seq.*, 219 *seq.*
[3] *Vide* Briggs, *ibid.*, pp. 224, 457.

Tübingen, Cologne, and Freiburg, at which last
university he became a successful teacher. He was
called to a theological chair at Ingolstadt in 1510 ; and
by his influence there, which continued until his death,
he made it the great Catholic university of Germany.
He was no less a Humanist than Melanchthon, and no
less a Biblical scholar than Luther, having been trained
in Greek and Hebrew as well. He differed from them
in maintaining the traditional Roman Catholic Faith
and Institutions, which he defended with such great
ability that he was regarded as the chief champion of
Rome on all occasions. His *Enchiridion* went through
forty-six editions between 1525 and 1576, and is as
truly Positive Theology, based on the Bible, as any of
the writings of Luther or Melanchthon. He also issued
(1537) a German translation of the Bible over against
that of Luther.[1]

Among the peacemakers on the side of Rome at the time of
the Reformation may be mentioned : 1. *John Gropper* († 1559),
a follower of Erasmus and supporter of Hermann of Cologne
in his first efforts at reform. Gropper took part in several conferences on behalf of Church Unity, and drew up the canons of the
reforming council held at Cologne in 1536.[2] But he differed from
the Protestants irreconcilably on matters concerning the Church,
and became the opponent of Hermann after the appearance of
his *Reforming Constitution*. Gropper's chief works are his
Enchiridion (1538), and *Institutio catholica* (1565), in which he
makes use of the Positive Theology. 2. *George Cassander*
(† 1566), the greatest of all the Catholic peacemakers, in his *De
officio pii ac publicæ tranquillitatis, etc.* (1561), and his *Consultatio*
(1564), considers the differences between Catholics and Protestants in an irenic spirit and makes useful proposals for recon-
ciliation.[3] 3. *George Witzel* († 1573), a pupil of Erasmus, in
his *Methodus concordiæ ecclesiasticæ* (1537) urged reforms in
doctrinal statements and ecclesiastical usages, and in his *Via*

---

[1] *Vide* Greving, *Eck als junger Gelehrter*, 1906.
[2] *Canones provincialis concilii Coloniensis*, 1538 ; *vide* Briggs, *Theological Symbolics*, p. 184.
[3] *Vide* Briggs, *Church Unity*, p. 421.

regia (1564) proposed the laying aside of scholastic dogmatism and a return to the simplicity of doctrine and usage of the early Church.[1]

7. *The Universities of Louvain and of Alcalá combined Humanistic studies with a reformed Scholasticism.*

The University of Alcalá, Spain, was established *c*. 1500 by *Cardinal Ximenes*, who organised several colleges for humanistic studies, Latin, Greek and Hebrew, and for the study of theology. The theological degrees were given the precedence of all the others. There were six professorships of theology proper, six of Church Law, and four of Greek and Hebrew. Biblical studies were emphasised by those who gave the first great Polyglot, the *Complutensian*, called after the ancient *Complutum*, where the first college was established. Some of the greatest scholars of Spain took part in this work, among them *Alphonso de Zamora*, also *Demetrius Ducas* of Crete.

The University of Louvain was founded in Brabant *c*. 1425 with all the faculties save that of theology, which was added in 1431. Louvain was given in charge of the Dominicans and became the great seat of the Thomist Theology. Humanistic studies were introduced *c*. 1517 by the establishment of the *Collegium Trilingue* after the model of that of Alcalá, for the study of Latin, Greek, and Hebrew. These two reformed universities, combining Humanism with the Scholasticism of Thomas Aquinas, were chiefly responsible for the newer Scholasticism of the sixteenth century, which put aside the corrupt and hair-splitting Scholasticism of the fifteenth century and reverted to the pure Scholasticism of Thomas. The study of theology throughout the Roman Catholic world was greatly influenced by this.

1. *Ximenes* († 1517) rose to the highest positions in the Church, as archbishop of Toledo, primate of Spain, cardinal, and in-

---

1 *Vide* Briggs, *Theological Symbolics*, pp. 20 *seq.*

quisitor-general. He reformed the clergy, regular and secular, reorganised and strengthened the universities, issued the *Complutensian Polyglot*, and revived the study of the Scholastic Theology of Thomas Aquinas.

2. *Francisco Vittoria* († 1546) was influenced by Ximenes, and became the father of the newer Scholasticism. His pupils, *Melchior Cano* and *Dominico Soto,* exerted immense influence in the reformation of theology, especially in the Council of Trent.

3. *Melchior Cano* († 1560), of the Universities of Alcalá and Salamanca, a Dominican, and a bitter opponent of the Jesuits, maintained in his *Loci theologici* the fundamental importance of the Positive over against the Scholastic Theology.[1]

4. *Dominico Soto* († 1560) was noted both as a Biblical exegete and as dogmatic theologian.

5. *Thomas de Vio Cajetanus* († 1534), Italian Dominican and cardinal, who conferred with Luther as papal delegate (1518), was one of the foremost scholastic theologians of the age, and the author of a notable commentary on Thomas Aquinas. But he also realised the importance of Biblical study, and prepared a literal translation of the Bible, and commentaries on most of its books.

Among the Biblical scholars of the time were the Dominicans : 6. *Santes Pagninus* of Lucca († 1541), whose studies in the Hebrew language bore fruit in several important works, including a Latin version of the Hebrew Bible and *Isagogæ ad sacras litteras liber I.* ; 7. *Sixtus of Siena* († 1560), whose *Bibliotheca sancta* contains valuable material for Biblical criticism and the history of exegesis ; [2] 8. the cardinal, *Sadoleto* († 1547), a member of the Oratory of Divine Love, and one of the ablest men in Rome ; [3] and 9. *Masius* († 1573), councillor of the Duke of Cleves, and collaborator with *Arias Montanus* and others in the preparation of the Antwerp Polyglot.[4]

8. *John Calvin in his organisation of the Academy of Geneva made it the centre and norm of theological education for all the Churches of the Reformed type.*

The Academy of *Geneva* was based on those of Strasburg and Lausanne. The Academy at *Lausanne* was organised by *Mathurin Cordier* in 1545. It was preceded

[1] *Vide* Heinrici, *Theologische Encyklopädie*, pp. 271, 349.
[2] *Vide* Heinrici, *ibid.*, p. 80.
[3] *Vide* Briggs, *Theological Symbolics*, p. 161.
[4] *Vide* Briggs, *Study of Holy Scripture*, pp. 222, 250.

by a school of religion, founded by the citizens of Bern
in 1537, in which *Viret* taught the Greek Testament.
The Academy of Lausanne was the first academy of the
Reformed Church using the French language, and to it
large numbers of Frenchmen resorted. In 1558 there
were as many as seven hundred students. Hebrew was
taught there by *Merlin*, theology by *Rebit*, the Hellenist,
Greek (after 1549) by *Beza*. But the institution was
soon eclipsed by the Academy of *Geneva*, founded by
Calvin in 1559.

1. *Mathurin Cordier* (1479-1564) was one of the chief Humanist teachers of France. *Ubicunque docebit Maturinus Corderius,
florebunt bonæ litteræ.* He had been the instructor of Calvin
at Paris, and was always esteemed by him as a great teacher and
his own adviser in all matters of education. Calvin dedicated
his *Commentary on Thessalonians* to Cordier, saying : ' Your
principles have been to me of such help that I regard myself as
indebted to you for my subsequent progress. And I have
wished to bear witness to posterity ; so that, if they should
attach any value to my writings, they may recognise that these
proceed in part from you.'

In 1557 Cordier resigned from the headship of the academy
in Lausanne on account of his age, but two years later was called
to Geneva to assist in the founding of the Geneva Academy.
There he finished his famous *Colloquies*, which were published in
the year of his death.

2. *William Farel* († 1565), a pupil of *Stapulensis* at Paris,
and an associate of Œcolampadius at Basel, became a leader of
the Reformation, at first in Geneva (1532), and then in Neuchâtel. It was Farel who secured for Geneva the services of
Calvin.

3. *Pierre Viret* († 1571), the reformer of Lausanne, having
worked in Geneva as Farel's assistant and afterwards at Neuchâtel, settled as pastor and teacher in Lausanne for twenty-two
years. In 1559 he went to Geneva as preacher, and spent his
last years in service as an evangelist at Nîmes, Lyons and elsewhere, and as teacher of theology in the Academies of Nîmes
(1561) and Orthez (1566). He wrote many useful works on the
Scriptures and Christian Doctrine and Institutions, the most
important being an *Instruction chrestienne en la doctrine de la
oy et de l'évangile.*

4. *John Calvin* (1509-1564) was born at Noyon, in Picardy, and went to Paris to study for the priesthood (1523). He was trained in the classics under Cordier at the Collège de la Marche, and then was transferred to the Collège de Montaigu, which Loyola entered before Calvin left. In 1528 he turned his attention to legal studies, and went to Orléans, and in the following year to Bourges. In 1531 he returned to Paris to study theology. There the Humanist became a Protestant. In 1534 he was compelled to flee from Paris, and, after some months of wandering, retired to Basel, where he remained for over a year. At Basel he studied Hebrew with *Grynæus*, and completed and published his *Institutes of the Christian Religion* (1536), the most important product of the Positive Theology of the sixteenth century. Like the other reformers, Calvin discarded the Scholastic Theology, and turned to the Scriptures as alone possessed of divine authority, and to the Creeds of the ancient Church as valid summaries of the doctrines of Scripture. He sought his material in the Bible, and his structural principle, not in the Aristotelian philosophy, but in the Apostles' Creed, whose order he followed strictly, only making a fourfold instead of the traditional twelvefold division. That same year Calvin went to Geneva, and there took part in the work of reform ; but in 1538 he was forced to retire. He then went to Strasburg, where for three years he preached to the French refugees and taught in the academy. In 1541 he was recalled to Geneva, and at once became the chief reformer, not only of Geneva, but also of Switzerland, and of the Reformed branch of Protestantism in all other countries. Calvin was distinguished especially as a teacher, and by his practical executive ability. His chief merit as a reformer was in the field, not of doctrine, but of institution : in his organisation of the Church on a presbyterial basis, in his pre-

paration of a normal liturgy for the Reformed Churches, and in his establishment of a thorough theological education.[1] He greatly valued religious education, but was obliged to devote himself at first to more essential things, while the educational part of the reform was carried on at Lausanne. But in 1559 the Geneva Academy was founded, and *Beza* was called from Lausanne to aid in the work.

There were two departments: the *Schola privata*, consisting of seven classes, a preparatory school in the Classics, Dialectic and Rhetoric; and the *Schola publica*, in which theologians taught. Courses were given in *Theology, Hebrew, Greek,* and *Biblical Exegesis,* as well as in *Physics, Mathematics, Dialectic* and *Rhetoric.* Theology was taught by Calvin, or by Beza. A sermon was given every day, special prayers once a week: a conference was held weekly, so also a discussion on theological questions, making the total number of hours thirty a week, five each day. At the time of Calvin's death (1564) the number of students in his academy had reached 1500.

The school of Calvin educated the ministry for French Switzerland and Protestant France, and many of the fathers of Scottish and English Presbyterianism were trained there. Among Calvin's own students were John Knox, François du Jon, Lambert Daneau, and many other notable theologians.

Calvin was influential also as a practical and an irenic theologian. By friendly correspondence with Bullinger and other Zwinglians he brought the German and French Swiss into harmony and unified the Reformed Churches throughout Europe. He kept in touch with the leaders of the Church of England on the one hand, and with the Waldensians and Bohemian Brethren on the other. He always retained the respect of Luther and the friendship of Melanchthon.

In his Augustinianism Calvin was more moderate and cautious than Luther, and he is not responsible for the

[1] *Vide* Briggs, *Theological Symbolics,* pp. 183 *seq.*

higher and more polemic Augustinianism of his scholastic
successors. Beza, rather than Calvin, is the real father
of scholastic Calvinism.[1] In the Eucharistic controversy Calvin as well as Bucer took an intermediate
position, which was adopted by all the Reformed
Churches and the Church of England.[2] He was associated
with Bullinger in the preparation of the *Zürich Consensus* (1549), and composed the *Gallican Confession*
(1559) with the help of his pupil Chandieu. He also
drew up the *Consensus Genevensis*, and published three
catechisms (1537, 1542, 1545). His works on the worship
and government of the Church were of fundamental
importance. He also produced many polemic and
apologetic treatises, and an extraordinary number of
letters and sermons. He was the greatest exegete of
the Reformation, and remarkable for his insistence upon
the activity of the Holy Spirit in connection with the
Scriptures. He declared :

' As God alone is a sufficient witness of Himself in His own
Word, so also the Word will never gain credit in the hearts of
men till it be confirmed by the internal testimony of the Spirit.
It is necessary, therefore, that the same Spirit, who spake by
the mouths of the prophets, should penetrate into our hearts
to convince us that they faithfully delivered the oracles which
were divinely entrusted to them.' [3]

Arminius († 1609) wrote of Calvin : ' Next to the study of the
Scriptures, which I earnestly inculcate, I exhort my pupils to
peruse Calvin's *Commentaries*. . . . I affirm that he excels
beyond comparison in the interpretation of Scripture, and that
his commentaries ought to be more highly valued than all that is
handed down to us by the library of the Fathers ; so that I
acknowledge him to have possessed above most others, or rather
above all other men, what may be called an eminent spirit of
prophecy.' Hooker († 1600) declared that Calvin held among
the preachers of the Reformed Churches the same place that the
Master of Sentences held in the Church of Rome ; and Bishop

---

[1] *Vide* Briggs, *Theological Symbolics*, pp. 183 *seq.*, 209, 282 *seq.*
[2] *Vide* Briggs, *Church Unity*, p. 269.
[3] Calvin, *Institutes*, i. 7 ; *vide* Briggs, *Study of Holy Scripture*, p. 142.

Hall reckoned him 'among the best interpreters of Scripture
since the Apostles left the earth.'

Many since his time have cried with Scaliger († 1609) : *Solus
inter theologos Calvinus.*[1]

5. *Theodore Beza* (1519-1605) succeeded Calvin at
Geneva, and was in some respects a more dominating
personality. He also was a Frenchman, son of the royal
governor of Vézelay, Burgundy. He was educated in
the classics at Paris, Orléans, and Bourges ; and then
returned to Orléans for the study of law (1535-1539).
He practised law in Paris for a short time, but was
more interested in humanistic studies. In 1548 he
went to Geneva, where he was warmly received by Calvin.
The following year he became professor of Greek at the
Academy of Lausanne, where he remained till 1558,
when he became professor of Greek at Geneva. After
the death of Calvin in 1564 he became his successor
and the great leader of the Reformation in the French
Cantons, and indeed in France and all over the Reformed
world. As Choisy says : ' The Protestant youth for
nearly forty years thronged his lecture-room to hear his
theological lectures, in which he expounded the purest
Calvinistic orthodoxy.'[2] Beza's influence upon the
Churches of Great Britain and Holland was very great.
His editions of the Greek Testament (1565-1604), enriched by a study of two early texts, the *Codex Bezœ*
and the *Codex Claromontanus*, took the place of those of
Erasmus and Stephens. His numerous writings include
important Biblical, doctrinal, and historical works, and a
treatise *De theologo sive de ratione studii theologici* (1556).

9. *Theological study was promoted in Great Britain by
Tyndale, Cranmer, Knox, and their fellow-reformers.*

Among the scholars of Cambridge to welcome Erasmus'
Greek Testament was : 1. *William Tyndale*, a pupil of

---

1 For these and many other tributes, *vide* Schaff, vii. pp. 272 *seq.*
2 Choisy, ' Beza,' in *New Schaff-Herzog Encyclopedia.*

Colet (1484-1536). He devoted himself to the study of the Scriptures in their original tongues, and to their translation into the vernacular. Prevented from publishing his work in England, he laboured for over ten years on the Continent, and produced English versions of the New Testament (1524-1526), and of the Pentateuch (1530), Jonah (1531), Joshua, Judges, Ruth, and the Books of Samuel, Kings and 1 Chronicles. These translations were all made on the basis of the original Greek and Hebrew texts. *John Rogers* († 1555), a friend of Tyndale, incorporated these versions in the Bible which he published in 1537 under the name of *Matthew's Bible*, using for the remaining books the version of *Miles Coverdale* († 1568), ' out of Douche and Latyn ' (1535). Tyndale wrote commentaries on 1 John and Matthew v.-vii., a celebrated Prologue to Jonah, one to the New Testament, afterwards printed as *A Pathway into the Holy Scripture*, and tracts, including the *Practyse of Prelates* and the *Obedience of a Christian Man*. Tyndale carried on the movement begun by Wyclif, which emphasised the most far-reaching of the principles of the Reformation, *the Word of God as a means of grace*. The British Reformation from the beginning laid stress upon this principle, and in the British churches it received its fullest statement and development.[1] Tyndale died a martyr, praying, ' Lord, open the King of England's eyes.' That very year (1536) a *Proclamation for Uniformity in Religion* informed ' the loving subjects ' of Henry VIII. that he was pleased that they should have the Scriptures in English, and ' read the same in convenient places and times.' *Injunctions* further directed that ' a Bible of the largest volume in English ' be placed in every church.[2]

---

[1] *Vide* Briggs, *American Presbyterianism*, pp. 28 *seq.* ; *Study of Holy Scripture*, p. 653.
[2] *Vide* Proctor and Frere, *The Book of Common Prayer*, pp. 29 *seq.*

2. *Thomas Cranmer* (1489-1556) was trained at Cambridge, and undertook a systematic study of the Bible. As archbishop of Canterbury (1533) he conducted various projects of reform, including the publication of the Scriptures in several English versions, that of catechisms and articles of faith, and a revision of the worship, order and government of the Church.[1] The Reformation was advanced by Cranmer in the English universities. On Edward's accession (1547) he sent to the continent and secured the help of such teachers as *Bucer*, *Fagius*, *Vermigli*, *Occhino*, and *John a Lasco*. Bucer and Fagius were made professors at Cambridge, Vermigli at Oxford; Occhino and a Lasco became influential in London. In 1549 a reform of the universities was undertaken by royal commission. Cranmer conducted the reform of the Church in a gradual and conservative way, yet he followed *Rogers*, *Ridley*, and *Latimer* to the stake, atoning by a bearing of singular heroism for the retractions which his enemies had impelled him to make.

Among the theological scholars of England may also be mentioned : 3. *Matthew Parker* († 1575), the father of the episcopate of the Anglican Church, who took a leading part in the revision of the *Articles of Religion* and the preparation of the *Bishops' Bible*, and enriched the University of Cambridge with a priceless collection of ancient manuscripts ; 4. *John Foxe* († 1587), the friend of Tyndale and Latimer, and author of the celebrated *Book of Martyrs* (Latin, 1559 ; English, 1563) ; 5. *Richard Hooker* († 1600), whose *Laws of Ecclesiastical Polity* made him the chief Anglican authority on the Church.

6. *Patrick Hamilton* (c. 1503-1528), the 'first apostle' of the Reformation in Scotland, studied at the universities of Paris, Louvain, St. Andrews and Marburg, and was influenced by both Erasmus and Tyndale. Returning to Scotland in 1527, he began his short career as a preacher of reform, ' on fire with zeal to confess the name of Christ.' [2]   The substance of his teaching

---

[1] *Vide* Briggs, *Theological Symbolics*, p. 191.
[2] *Exegeseos Francisci Lamberti in Joannis Apocalypsim lib.* vii. ; *vide* Lorimer, *Precursors of Knox*, pp. 157, 240.

is preserved in *Patrick's Places*, which extol faith, and contrast the Law and the Gospel: 'The Law showeth us our sin; the Gospel showeth us remedy for it.'[1] Hamilton had 'a great following,' and was called to give account of his teaching in a conference at St. Andrews. For some weeks he held in his own defence 'public disputations and private interviews,' and so became 'the teacher of many of the present and future teachers of the country,'[2] including the faculty and students of the university, as well as many of the clergy, ecclesiastical lawyers, and members of religious orders. His martyrdom in 1528 roused much excitement. In the words of John Knox: 'Then within St. Andrews, yea, almost within the whole realm, there was none found who began not to inquire, Wherefore was Master Patrick Hamilton burnt? And when his articles were rehearsed, question was holden if such articles were necessary to be believed under the pain of damnation. And so within short space many began to call in doubt that which before they held for a certain verity.'[3]

7. *John Knox* (c. 1514-1572) was educated at Haddington and the University of Glasgow. He became a priest, but engaged for a time in private teaching. His conversion to Protestantism he owed chiefly to *George Wishart*, a pupil of Calvin, whose martyrdom (1546) he would gladly have shared. But Wishart refused his consent, saying: 'Nay, return to your bairns. One is sufficient for a sacrifice.' The following year Knox was taken prisoner, and forced to serve in the French galleys. On his release in 1549 he began to preach in England; but the death of Edward VI. drove him to the Continent. Taking refuge in Geneva, he studied with Calvin, and after a short pastorate in Frankfort, settled in Geneva as pastor of the English congregation. In 1559 he returned to Scotland, and became the triumphant leader of the Reformation in that country. He was the chief of the six divines who drew up the *Scottish Confession* and the first *Book of Discipline*. His

---

[1] Lorimer, *Precursors of Knox*, pp. 110, 112.
[2] Lorimer, *ibid.*, pp. 134 *seq.*
[3] Knox, *History of the Reformation*, i. p. 36; *vide* Lorimer, *Precursors of Knox*, p. 156.

writings include a *History of the Reformation*. At his
death he was mourned as ' the lycht of Scotland, the
comfort of the Kirke within the same, the mirrour of
Godliness and patrone and exemple to all trew ministeris';
and as one who ' never feared the face of man.' [1]

10. *Ignatius and his associates organised the Jesuit
system of education, which has predominated in the
Roman Catholic Church until the present time.*

1. *Ignatius of Loyola* (c. 1491-1556), a Spanish officer,
wounded in an engagement at Pampeluna in 1521, was
called to a religious life. He undertook severe religious
discipline, and in 1524 began a long course of study at
Barcelona, Alcalá, Salamanca, and finally at Paris
(1528-1535). He won as his associates, Faber, Xavier,
Lainez, and others ; and founded the Order of the Fathers
of Jesus, organised by mutual vows in 1534, and by
papal bull in 1540. The chief aim of the order was
missions to the heathen and to heretics. The methods
were : pastoral care, preaching, and religious education.
To give training in these was their main purpose. The
colleges which they established, wherever they could
get a foothold, became the chief seats of theological
education for two centuries.

2. *Peter Faber* († 1546) began his work in Western Germany at
Speyer, Mainz and elsewhere, removed subsequently to Cologne
(1543-1544), and with the help of his companions won the lower
Rhine and Westphalia back to the Roman Church.

3. *Peter Canisius* († 1597) entered the Jesuit order under the
influence of Faber. He laboured at Cologne, Ingolstadt, Vienna,
Dillingen, Prague, and other towns, teaching, preaching and
building up *Collegia*. He and his associates won Bavaria,
Austria and Bohemia back from Protestantism. His Catechisms
were widely influential. The *Summa doctrinæ christianæ per
quæstiones tradita* (1556) ' remained for about two centuries the
principal catechism of the Roman Catholic Church.' [2]

---

[1] *Vide* Lee, ' Knox,' in *New Schaff-Herzog Encyclopedia*.
[2] Cohrs, ' Catechisms,' in *New Schaff-Herzog Encyclopedia*.

The Jesuits established in Rome the *Collegium Romanum* (*c.* 1550) and the *Collegium Germanicum* (1552), which became the great theological institutions of the Roman Church, and so remained for centuries.

The founders of the Jesuit Order in their *Ratio Studiorum* combined the old learning with the new in more harmonious proportions and in better adjustments than did Melanchthon, Calvin, Ximenes or Eck, from whom, however, they learned much. The Scholastic Theology was reformed by falling back from the later corrupt, hair-splitting Scholasticism to the Scholastic Theology of Thomas Aquinas; and on him was built a newer and, for a time, a sounder Scholastic Theology than the Church had known for centuries. At the same time there was a great revival of Biblical and Patristic studies, and, indeed, in the original languages. While the Jesuit theologians carried this reformation through to success, it must be said that they built upon the reformed Scholasticism and Biblical study that had already begun in Alcalá under Ximenes' influence, at Louvain and at Ingolstadt.[1]

The Jesuits also united the theoretical and the practical in theology as these had never been united before; and while, for two centuries, they trained the best scholars of Europe, they also trained the best preachers, pastors, teachers and missionaries. They built on the ancient method of three gradations of study. The original constitution of the Jesuit Order distinguishes the three grades: the *grammatico-rhetorical*, the *philosophical*, and the *theological*; and sums up the whole as: ' *Litteræ Humaniores diversarum linguarum, Logica, naturalis ac moralis Philosophia, Metaphysica et Theologia, tam quæ Scholastica quam quæ Positiva dicitur, et sacra Scriptura.*' [2]

The training prescribed in the German college at Rome, as reorganised in 1573, was a course of ten years in philosophy and theology. The grammatical and rhetorical schooling was presupposed. Students were not received, unless properly qualified and specially recommended for real ability, and who were at least twenty years of age. They were placed for six months on probation, and then were required to take the vow for the ministerial life, or else retire from the college. The course of study extended over ten years, three for philosophy and the higher

---

[1] *Vide* pp. 125 f.
[2] Cap. **v.** ; *vide* Paulsen, *Geschichte des gelehrten Unterrichts*, **i.** p. 381.

sciences, four for Scholastic Theology, and three for Moral Theology. Almost all the great Catholic scholars of Germany were trained here for many generations. The training given for those who were to advance in the Jesuit Order was much more severe and prolonged. A novice, who entered the order at the age of sixteen or eighteen, must spend two years in quiet religious life before the first vow was taken and the *Scholasticus* began his career as a scholar. If he had had the required training in grammar and rhetoric, he might enter at once upon a three years' course of logic, physics and metaphysics ; if not, he was obliged to take the preparatory studies first. He was then required to serve for some years as a tutor in the studies already acquired. He might be required to remain in this position all his life. If he was deemed qualified to go on into the study of theology, he entered upon a four years' course, after the completion of which he must be a tutor in theology for two years more, or else take special training as preacher and pastor. The Jesuits in all their instruction, from the rhetorical schools upward, laid great stress upon practical discipline in writing and in speaking, both by declamation and by debate. Their students were made, therefore, ready, graceful speakers, easy and powerful writers, and also adroit and attractive members of society. They were disciplined by frequent confessions, in which not only mortal sins, but the most secret and delicate sins and motions to sin, and all the circumstances of the inner life, were exposed to the confessor ; so that they had practical as well as theoretical training in the whole range of moral theology and casuistry. It is not surprising that such discipline in scholarship and in its practical use made them the most adroit and able scholars of Europe in the late sixteenth and the seventeenth centuries.

The entire reforming influence of the Roman Church gathered about the Jesuits. Ignatius had as his advisers and strong helpers not only all the popes of his generation, but also the most able of the cardinals and the most capable scholars.

Among the theologians in the Jesuit Order may be mentioned : 4. *Maldonatus* of the University of Salamanca († 1583), who taught at Paris, Bourges and Rome with extraordinary success, and wrote commentaries on the Prophets and the Gospels ; 5. *Toletus* († 1596), the first cardinal of the order, eminent as an exegete, and one of the foremost in a long series of celebrated casuists ; and 6. *Vasquez* (†1604), one of the chief Roman Catholic divines of the sixteenth century,[1] the author of notable works in Moral and Polemic Theology.

11. *The Council of Trent advised the organisation of diocesan seminaries for the religious training of students, especially for the priesthood.   Under the influence of Borromeo, Pole and others, these were established with great success, and were called Tridentine Seminaries.*

Two cardinals may be mentioned especially in connection with this work, namely : *Reginald Pole* (1500-1558) of England, and *Carlo Borromeo* (1538-1584) of Milan.   These were in hearty sympathy with the educational reforms of Ignatius and his associates ; between them the plan of the theological seminary was devised, and was ordered by the Council of Trent in 1563.

The popes and the bishops now vied with one another in the establishment of diocesan seminaries for the training of the clergy.   These were given into the hands of the Jesuits chiefly ; but the other orders, old as well as new, rallied about the plan.   The older monastic schools revived ; and the friars and newer orders also, on their part, shared in a measure in this educational reform.   The result was the forcing back of Protestantism all along the line.   It was not so much religious persecution and the force of arms that stayed the progress of Protestantism in the latter half of the sixteenth century, and reconquered for Rome in that period, and still more in the seventeenth century, so large a part of the original strongholds of Protestantism.   Persecution does not usually succeed ; and, in fact, the Protestants were as zealous persecutors as the Roman Catholics, and even more prompt than the Catholics for religious warfare.   It was a superior religious education, not only of scholars, but of priests, secular as well as regular, that

---

[1] *Vide* Briggs, *Church Unity*, p. 280.

gave the Roman Catholics a succession of victories for more than a century.

Mention has already been made of the work of Faber and his associates at Mainz, Cologne, and the whole lower Rhine and Westphalia; and that of Canisius and his associates in Southern Germany, Austria, and Bohemia. In Poland the work of *Hosius* († 1579), begun in his college at Braunsberg (1565-1568), won back Poland from Protestantism, and for a while imperilled the Reformation in Sweden. In the north of Italy and in Switzerland *Carlo Borromeo* († 1584) established seminaries and schools, and even Sunday-schools, for children and adults, and destroyed Protestantism thereby in Northern Italy and several of the Cantons of Switzerland. The Protestantism of the Engadine was at one time well-nigh overthrown. *François de Sales* († 1622), bishop of Geneva,[1] worked powerfully in Savoy and French Switzerland; and even Geneva was in grave peril from the Catholic reaction.

The battle in France was a longer one. The Catholic Church in France was long under the control of the Gallican spirit, which was nationalistic in character, and really put the Church under the domination of the king rather than the pope, and kept the clergy in constant trouble by the conflict of the two jurisdictions. The University of Paris insisted upon its own historic privileges as the dictator of theology, and resisted the Jesuits and the Tridentine Seminaries with all their influences. This undoubtedly hampered the Catholic reform in France. It was not until Louis XIV. came under the influence of the Jesuits, and gave his authority and great power to the establishment of diocesan seminaries, that the intellectual strength of the Catholic reaction began to tell upon the French Protestants. Undoubtedly the Revocation of the Edict of Nantes (1685), and the severe persecution that followed, had much to do with the overthrow of Protestantism in France; but not so much as the Tridentine Seminaries, and a better educated Catholic clergy, and Catholic scholars, who succeeded by their superior theological ability in persuading multitudes of Protestants to return to the Mother Church. It is easy to attribute such cases to fear and self-interest; but in a multitude of instances such motives do not really explain the situation. The Jesuits in the seventeenth century had the potent help of the new foundation of the *Oratorians* (1575), the institution of St. Vincent de Paul (1631),

---

[1] *Vide* p. 151.

and the Sulpicians (1642), the great educators of modern France.

It may be interesting here to note the rules of Cardinal *Allen* for the Seminary at Douai, in which priests were trained for the English mission. These rules of the year 1580 make the study of the Bible of fundamental importance, and require Greek and Hebrew that the students may understand the Scriptures in the original texts. Church History was to be studied privately ; also important patristic works, especially Bede's, ' that it may be seen that the ancient Faith was Catholic.' The *Summa* of Thomas was to be taught by lecture and disputation. The doctrine of the Council of Trent and the Roman Catechism were to be studied privately. Morals and cases of conscience were to be discussed publicly. Great stress was laid upon practical studies, including Catechetics, Liturgics and Pastoral Theology. Four public exercises were required each week for drill in public speaking, comprising one practical and two doctrinal sermons, and one disputation on controverted questions of theology.[1] There was no such drill in any Protestant school of theological education.

12. *The Greek Church was compelled to consider the questions raised by the Reformation of the Western Church. Her position was defined by her theologians in three symbols. An abortive attempt at reform, led by Cyril Lucar, was productive in the field of theological scholarship.*

At the Reformation both Romanists and Protestants strove to win the support of the Greek Church, which eventually defined its position in three symbols : (1) *The Answer of Jeremiah*, (2) *The Confession of Mogilas*, and (3) *The Confession of Dositheus*. A movement toward reform was led by Cyril Lucar, a theologian of European reputation, who sought to introduce into the Greek Church certain of the characteristic doctrines of Calvinism.[2]

1. *Jeremiah*, patriarch of Constantinople († 1595), wrote in 1576 an answer to communications from the Lutheran theo-

---

[1] *Vide* Siebengärtner, *Schriften und Einrichtungen zur Bildung der Geistlichen*, pp. 119 *seq.*

[2] *Vide* Briggs, *Theological Symbolics*, pp. 200 *seq.*

logians *Andreæ* and *Crusius*, which was approved by the Synod
of Jerusalem in 1672. All of the distinctive doctrines of the
Protestant Reformation were rejected with the exception of the
institutional matters of communion in both kinds and the
marriage of priests.

2. *Petrus Mogilas* († 1647), metropolitan of Kieff, and father
of Russian orthodoxy, was trained in the University of Paris,
and chosen by Cyril Lucar as exarch of his see. Mogilas published editions of the Fathers and several Service Books, and is
an example of the great learning to be found among Russian
ecclesiastics.[1] His Confession of Faith, written in the form of
a Catechism, was revised and adopted by a provincial synod at
Kieff (1640), and again by a synod of Greeks and Russians at
Jassy (1643), under the influence of *Meletius Syriga*, metropolitan
of Nice, and was signed by the four eastern patriarchs. It thus
became the symbol of the entire Russo-Greek Church. It
defines the faith of the Greek Church against Protestantism on
the one hand and Romanism on the other, and is especially
directed against Cyril Lucar.

3. *Dositheus*, patriarch of Jerusalem (1699-1707), is called by
Meyer ' one of the most important figures of the modern Greek
Church.' His great work on the history of the patriarchs of
Jerusalem (1715) is ' the Greek counterpart to the Annals of
Baronius and the Magdeburg Centuries.' [2] The Confession of
Dositheus was adopted by the Synod of Jerusalem (1672), and
afterwards signed by sixty-eight bishops of the Greek and Russian
Churches. It is less complete and more polemic than the Con-
fession of Mogilas, but the doctrinal position is the same.

4. *Cyril Lucar* (1572-1638). ' the one brilliant star of his age ' [3]
in the East, was born in Crete, and studied at Alexandria, Venice
and Padua. He came under the influence of *Maximos Mar-
gunios*, an earnest advocate of the reunion of the Greek and
Roman Churches, and of several of the Protestant theologians.
In 1602 he was made patriarch of Alexandria, and, though
banished five times, was as often recalled. Finally he was chosen
patriarch of Constantinople (1620), and this position gave great
importance to the publication of his Confession of Faith (Latin,
1629 ; Greek, 1633). It was condemned, however, by several
provincial synods. According to Cyril, ' The authority of Holy
Scripture is far greater than that of the Church ; for it is a

---

[1] *Vide* Adeney, *The Greek and Eastern Churches*, pp. 411 *seq.*
[2] Meyer, ' Dositheus,' in *New Schaff-Herzog Encyclopedia.*
[3] Adeney, *Greek and Eastern Churches*, p. 320.

different thing to be taught by the Holy Spirit from being taught by man.   Man may through ignorance err and deceive, and be deceived.   But the Holy Spirit neither deceiveth, nor is deceived, nor is subject to error, but is infallible.'[1]   Cyril undertook the translation of the Bible into the vernacular.   It was he who presented to Charles I. of England the great *Codex Alexandrinus*. Through his recommendation the brilliant *Metrophanes Critopulus* received his training at Oxford.   Among Cyril's numerous followers were *Karyophylles*, the noted Calvinist, *Konopios*, translator of Calvin's *Institutes*, and *Kalliupolites*, translator of the Scriptures.   *Cornelius Haga*, Dutch ambassador to the Porte, declared in 1632 that there was no one among the many metropolitans then at Constantinople who was not prepared to sacrifice ' his person, his life and his goods for the defence of the patriarch and his Confession.'[2]   Yet the bitter enmity of the Jesuits finally secured his death by order of the sultan on a false charge of treason.

---

[1] *Vide* Adeney, *Greek and Eastern Churches*, p. 318.
[2] *Vide* Gieseler, v. p. 134, *n.* 34.

CHAPTER III

THE STUDY OF THEOLOGY IN THE SEVENTEENTH AND EIGHTEENTH CENTURIES

IN the Roman Catholic Church the Reformation was, to a great extent, a reform of education and a revival of theology. But in the Protestant world there was a serious decline in theological education, although there were revivals here and there, especially among the Calixtines of Germany and the Puritans of England. The successors of the Reformers reverted to the scholastic philosophy of Aristotle ; and Protestant Scholasticism became as barren, hopeless, and irreformable as the Mediæval. There was the same incessant strife of schools and parties over merely theoretic questions of theology. This is the period of the *Formula of Concord* (1576), the *Synod of Dort* (1619), and the *Zürich Consensus* (1549), and of the ecclesiasticism of Laud († 1645), but also of the retreat of Protestantism all along the line.

The universities of Germany sank so low that their situation seemed hopeless.[1] Even *Leibnitz* († 1716), the greatest scholar of his time, did not think of the revival of learning in connection with universities, but through the association of scholars apart from universities. He thought travel and intercourse with learned men and men of affairs of much more importance than a university education ; and so they were in his day. English historians do not give adequate consideration to the peril

---

[1] *Vide* Paulsen, *Geschichte des gelehrten Unterrichts auf den deutschen Schulen und Universitäten*, 1896², i. pp. 495 *seq.*, 511 *seq.* ; *German Universities*, p. 55 ; Döllinger, *Universities Past and Present*, pp. 11 *seq.*, 14.

of Protestantism in the sixteenth, and especially in the second half of the seventeenth century, from a theological point of view. The people of England realised it, as shown by the Guy Fawkes scare ; and ' no popery ' was branded into the very blood of the English people, and is there to-day. The clergy, Anglican and Nonconformist alike, realised it at the time ; and, notwithstanding the bitter conflicts in which they were engaged, they combined to save themselves from the greater evil of Rome by the British Revolution. I know of no more desperate literary battle, none more severe, comprehensive, and thorough, than that waged from 1687 to 1689 between Catholic and Protestant writers in England. If James II. had been an abler man and a wiser politician, it is quite possible that he might have become the Louis XIV. of England, and English Protestantism might have shared the fate of the French. Now it was the priests trained in the English Catholic seminary at Douai, France (transferred for a time to Rheims), at the English Seminary in Rome, and those in Spain and Portugal, that carried on this theological battle against the best scholars of the Church of England and the Nonconformists ; and from the scholar's point of view it cannot be said that the Protestant scholars had always the best of the argument. It was the sturdy Protestantism of Sweden that saved Protestantism in Northern Germany, and the sturdy Protestantism of Holland and Scotland that saved England, and that by success in war rather than by superiority in theological scholarship.

In the third quarter of the seventeenth century the Counter-Reformation was triumphant. In the last quarter of the century Protestantism organised a more sturdy and effectual resistance. In the eighteenth century Protestantism began to gain ground, and continued to do so all through the century. This was due to several influences, but, from the point of view of theological study, largely to the decline in efficiency of Roman Catholic education. The Jesuit Order had become wealthy and haughty, self-seeking and possessed of the evil spirits of domination and falsehood. This made them hated by the secular clergy and the regulars of the other orders. Their strife for wealth and political power made them a peril in civil politics, and gradually produced the universal feeling that they were a political menace. This brought about the banishment of the order from many countries, and at last its temporary abolition by the pope (1773). The worldly spirit of the order suppressed the religious and the intellectual spirit ; and the ability of its members in theological scholarship became weakened. Furthermore, the Jesuits refused to adapt themselves to the spirit of the age, and persisted in their ultra-conservative adherence to the older methods. Their Scholastic Theology had become per-verted into a newer Scholasticism that was worse in some respects, especially on the ethical side, than the corrupt Scholasticism that preceded the Reformation. The society thought more of making successful men of the world than of making pious priests and scholarly teachers. The *Ratio Studiorum* (1599) was still followed in the Jesuit schools, but in a pedantic, mechanical, traditional way. Ignatius had introduced the new learning of his age, and harmonised it with the old ; but the Jesuits of the eighteenth century were hostile to the new learning of their times. The order refused the science and philosophy and history which char-acterised the new learning of the eighteenth century. They insisted upon the absolute authority of the Aristotelian Philosophy and of the Scholastic Theology, and would allow no deviation from it.

In 1730-1731 the General Congregation of the Order decided against the allowance of liberty of opinion in philosophy, which had been requested by several provinces of the order, and resolved:

(1) Nothing is in contradiction with the Aristotelian philo-sophy, and all the phenomena of nature must be explained in accordance therewith.

(2) The philosophy of Aristotle must remain, according to the constitution and rules of the order, not only for logic and meta-physics, but also for physics, where the peripatetic doctrine of the nature and constitution of natural bodies must be maintained.[1]

---

[1] Pachtler, *Ratio Studiorum*, i. 104 ; *vide* Paulsen, *Geschichte des gelehrten Unterrichts*, ii. pp. 103 *seq.*

The Jesuit schools were thus made antagonistic to the new learning of the eighteenth century—that is, to natural science and the inductive methods of study, to the modern philosophy of Descartes, Locke and Leibnitz, as the Obscurants of Cologne had been opposed to the new learning of the sixteenth century. They also held fast to the supremacy of the Latin language in education, and resisted the growth of modern national literature. In other words, the Jesuits of the eighteenth century were formalists and pedants ; they retained the form of the rules of Ignatius and the other founders of the order, but they had altogether lost their spirit.

Thus inevitably theological education declined all over the Roman Catholic world, as it advanced through the Protestant world.

The eighteenth century was a bad century for religion everywhere. The reaction against the Scholastic Theology of Protestants and Catholics alike was so bitter, and the determination to get rid of its intolerable dogmatism so thorough, that Deism, Pantheism, Atheism and Rationalism took the place of the Christian religion to a considerable portion of the learned world. The inevitable result was the French Revolution, with all its serious consequences for education as well as for religion. It was Pietism which saved German and Dutch Protestantism, and Methodism that saved Anglo-Saxon Protestantism from the utter ruin into which Scholasticism and Ecclesiasticism had brought the Protestant Churches.

1. *France was the centre of theological learning for the Roman Catholic Church during the greater part of the seventeenth and eighteenth centuries ; and the Jesuits, Benedictines, and Oratorians produced the greatest number of eminent theologians.*

The *Jesuits* became noted especially for their work in the departments of Moral Theology and Canon Law.

Among the celebrated casuists of the order may be mentioned : (1) *Sanchez* († 1610), (2) *Suarez* († 1617), and (3) *Cardinal de Lugo*

(† 1660); among the canonists, (4) *Labbeus* († 1667), whose collection of conciliar decrees was completed by *Cossart*; and (5) *Harduin* († 1729), author of the *Conciliorum collectio regia maxima*. The Biblical scholars of the order included the popular exegete (6) *Cornelius a Lapide* (Van den Steen, † 1637), whose commentaries cover almost the whole Bible; and (7) *Menochius* († 1655), whose work, according to Kihn,[1] is too little known. Pre-eminent among the Jesuits of his day was (8) the cardinal, *Robert Bellarmine* († 1621), Biblical exegete, dogmatic theologian, and author of a catechism printed in many languages and many editions, of an epoch-making work, *De scriptoribus ecclesiasticis*, and of the famous *Disputationes de controversiis Christianæ fidei*. (9) *Petavius* († 1652) also brought honour to the order by his work as Biblical scholar, Church historian and dogmatic theologian. He greatly promoted the study of ecclesiastical Chronology, and won the title of 'Father of the History of Dogma.' The most notable work of the Society in the department of Church History was done by (10) *Sirmond* († 1651), in his editions of Church Writers; (11) *Maimbourg* († 1686), in his histories of schisms from the Roman Church, both Greek and Protestant; and (12) *Jan Bolland* († 1665), with whom began the publication of the *Acta Sanctorum*, continued under his name to the present time.[2]

Among the scholars trained by the Jesuits may be mentioned: (1) *Valesius* († 1676), noted for his editions of the early Church historians; (2) *Du Cange* († 1688), who made valuable contributions to the study of the Middle Ages, and published *Glossaria ad scriptores mediæ et infimæ ætatis*, both Greek and Latin; (3) *Baluze* († 1718), who carried on the work of Labbé and Cossart, and published *Capitularia Regum Francorum*, and other important historical works; (4) *Huetius* († 1721), editor of Origen's Commentaries; (5) *Febronius* (Von Hontheim, † 1790), author of the famous treatise *De statu ecclesiæ et legitima potestate Romani Pontificis*; (6) *Gerbert* († 1793), celebrated for his *Monumenta veteris liturgiæ Alemannicæ* and his works on sacred music.

The *Benedictine* Order rendered invaluable service to Historical Theology, especially through the labours of

---

[1] *Vide* Kihn, *Encyklopädie der Theologie*, p. 253.
[2] The 'Bollandists' are still far from the end of their great enterprise, although they have gone through the calendar as far as November. A new edition of their work has appeared in sixty-six volumes (Brussels, 1863-1911).

the *Congregatio Sancti Mauri,* which numbered over one
hundred and eighty cloisters, and had its centre in Paris,
at the Abbey Saint Germain des Prés.

The most distinguished of the scholars of Saint Maur were:
(1) *D'Achery* (Dacherius, † 1685), noted for his *Spicilegium veterum aliquot scriptorum*; (2) *Mabillon* († 1707), his collaborator
and successor as historian of the order, a pioneer in the preparation of those editions of the Fathers and Church Writers for
which his Congregation became famous, and author of works of
exceptional importance in the departments of Church History
and Liturgics, of an epoch-making work, *De re diplomatica* (1681),
by which was laid the foundation for Ecclesiastical Diplomatics,[1]
and of a treatise in defence of the study of theology in monasteries; (3) *Ruinart* († 1709), celebrated for his *Acta sincera
primorum martyrum*; (4) *Martianay* († 1717), who published an
edition of Jerome; (5) *Ruæus* (De la Rue, † 1736), editor of
Origen's works; (6) *Edmond Martène* († 1739), a pupil of D'Achery
and Mabillon, collaborator in several of the great enterprises of
his Congregation, and author of monumental works, including a
collection of ancient ecclesiastical rites and the famous *Veterum
scriptorum et monumentorum collectio amplissima*; (7) *Mont-
faucon* († 1741), editor of Origen's *Hexapla,* and of the works of
Chrysostom and Athanasius, whose many valuable contributions
to theology include a collection of the Greek Fathers and Church
Writers; (8) *Prudentius Maranus* († 1762), noted for his critical
editions of the Fathers, and for works on the divinity of Christ.
This Congregation also undertook the revision and continuation
of the *Gallia christiana,* and published the celebrated *Histoire
littéraire de la France, L'Art de vérifier les dates des faits historiques,*
and Le Nourry's *Apparatus ad bibliothecam maximam patrum
veterum.* Among the Church Historians of the Benedictine
Order should be mentioned: (9) the abbot, *Claude Fleury*
(† 1723), whose *Histoire ecclésiastique* (in twenty volumes) became
'almost a classic among the French, and supplanted all other
works of the kind';[2] and (10) *Remy Ceillier* († 1761), famous for
his *Histoire générale des auteurs sacrés et ecclésiastiques.* The
Benedictines could also boast of possessing in (11) *Augustin
Calmet* († 1757) the most notable Biblical exegete of the Roman
Catholic Church in the eighteenth century.

---

[1] *Vide* Schmitz-Kallenberg, 'Die Lehre von den Papsturkunden,' in
Grundriss der Geschichtswissenschaft, i. p. 174.
[2] Gieseler, v. p. 240.

The original *Congregatio Oratorii* was founded by *Philip of Neri* (1564).

Among its first members was (1) *Cæsar Baronius* († 1607), afterwards cardinal, who published over against the *Magdeburg Centuries* his *Annales ecclesiastici*,[1] enriched by the use of hitherto unknown documents from the Vatican archives and papal library, but criticised by Protestants as compiled *sine ullo judicio*.[2] The Congregation founded at Paris by *Pierre de Bérulle* (1611), under the same name, produced such scholars as (2) *Jean Morin* (Morinus, † 1656), Biblical scholar, and author of the celebrated *Commentarius de sacris ecclesiæ ordinationibus*; (3) *Thomassin* († 1695), who wrote the *Ancienne et nouvelle discipline de l'église*, and other important works; (4) *Richard Simon* († 1712), who applied historical criticism in a systematic manner to the study of the books of the Old Testament,[3] and also wrote on the Greek and Oriental Churches; (5) *Renaudot* († 1720), who prepared a collection of Oriental liturgies, and a history of the Patriarchs of Alexandria; (6) *Houbigant* († 1783), whose *Biblia Hebraica* offered a new recension of the text; and (7) *Massillon* († 1742), celebrated for the eloquence of his sermons. Sacred music was cultivated by this Congregation to a remarkable degree, and in the Oratory at Paris originated the first musical *Oratorio*.[4]

Theological scholarship was not confined to these three orders. The *Dominicans* could boast of

(1) *Goar* († 1653), author of the *Euchologium Græcorum* (1645, 1730); (2) *Combefis* († 1679), the Patristic scholar; and (3) *Natalis Alexander* († 1724), provincial of his order, who made important contributions to Dogmatics, Ethics and Church History.

Among the doctors and teachers of the *Sorbonne*, Paris, were:

(1) *Richer* (Richerius, † 1631), the celebrated canonist and defender of the liberties of the Gallican Church; (2) *Jean de Launoi* († 1678), an historical critic in the field of Hagiology; (3) *Cotelier* († 1686), the Patristic scholar; (4) *Bossuet* († 1704), the most learned, eloquent and influential bishop of France in

---

[1] *Vide* p. 113.
[2] So Scaliger, quoted by Heinrici, *Theologische Encyklopädie*, p. 190
[3] *Vide* Briggs, *Study of Holy Scripture*, pp. 274 *seq.*
[4] *Vide* Gieseler, v. p. 119, *n.* 5.

his day, chief composer of the famous Four Propositions of the Gallican Church (1682), and author of the *Histoire des variations des églises protestantes* and of many other important works; (5) *Du Pin* († 1719), the founder of Patrology as an independent theological discipline, whose many valuable works include a *Méthode pour étudier la théologie.*

The *Jansenists* also had their notable scholars :

(1) *Cornelius Jansen* († 1638), professor of theology at Louvain, and eventually bishop of Ypres, was distinguished as a Biblical exegete.   His *Augustinus*, the fruit of twenty-two years of toil, published posthumously (1640), excited bitter opposition from the Jesuits, and gave rise to the Jansenist Controversy.   (2) *Blaise Pascal* († 1662), a man of exceptional learning, in whom the scientific and the mystic tendencies were strangely combined, is now known chiefly for his *Pensées*, which rank as a religious classic, and for his *Lettres provinciales* (1656), which were universally read in their day, and exposed the errors of the Jesuits as teachers of morals in a ' masterpiece of satire.'   (3) *Le Nain de Tillemont* († 1698) is celebrated for his *Mémoires pour servir à l'histoire ecclésiastique des six premiers siècles.*   (4) *Arnauld* († 1694) and (5) *Nicole* († 1695), remarkable for their apologetic and polemic writings over against the Jesuits and the Reformed Churches. (6) *Paschasius Quesnel* († 1719), priest of the *Oratoire* at Paris, was driven from France as a Jansenist.   He prepared a French translation of the New Testament, accompanied by *Réflexions morales*, which was strongly approved by *De Noailles*, archbishop of Paris, and other leaders of the French Church, but was condemned by the papal bull *Unigenitus* in one hundred and one propositions.

Italy also had theologians of distinction, especially in the eighteenth century, among whom may be mentioned :

(1) *Leo Allatius* († 1669), ' the most celebrated of all the so-called Latinising Greeks ' ; [1]   (2) *Muratori* († 1750), who gave his name to the *Muratorian Canon*, and published many other hitherto unknown or inaccessible works, including *Liturgia Romana vetus* ;   (3) *Mansi* († 1769), archbishop of Lucca, whose great collection of conciliar decrees is now appearing in a new and enlarged edition ;   (4) *Ugolino* (c. 1750), author of *Thesaurus antiquitatum sacrarum* ;   (5-7) three celebrated members of the family *Assemani* : *Giuseppe Simone* († 1768), editor of the works of

---

[1] Gieseler, v. p. 249.

Ephræm Syrus, and author of *Bibliotheca Orientalis Clementino-Vaticana* ; his brother, *Giuseppe Aloysio* († 1782), who published among other monumental works a *Codex liturgicus ecclesiæ universæ* ; and their cousin, *Stefano Evodio* († 1784), whose works include *Acta sanctorum martyrum orientalium et occidentalium* ; (8) *Alfonso Maria di Liguori* († 1787), saint and doctor of the Church, founder of the Order of Redemptorists (1732), and noted for his *Theologia moralis*.

The leading *Mystics* of the period were :

(1) *François de Sales* († 1622), a pupil of the Jesuit *Possevin*, who has been canonised, and ranks as a doctor of the Church ; (2) *Molinos* († 1697), a Spanish priest, celebrated at Rome as preacher and confessor, whose *Guida spirituale* exerted extraordinary influence among both Catholics and Protestants, yet brought condemnation upon him through Jesuit influence ; and (3) *Fénelon* († 1715), instructor of princes, who sought to ' reconcile Quietism with orthodoxy.' [1]

2. *The Puritan movement in England was essentially a Biblical movement. The Puritans urged a more thorough study of the Scriptures, a catechetical instruction of the people, and effective preaching. In dogma they used the doctrine of the Covenant as a structural principle, over against the Scholastic method.*

The reformers were men of great intellectual and moral vigour. Their doctrines were the expression of their Christian life and experience. But they were succeeded by lesser men, who gave their energies to the construction of systems of dogma. These soon enveloped the principles of the Reformation in a cloud of speculation and established a Protestant Scholasticism, Ecclesiasticism, and Ritualism, which seemed to earnest men little better than that which the reformers had cast aside. Accordingly a second reformation arose in Great Britain in the form of Puritanism, which reaffirmed and sharpened the principles of the Reformation and advanced toward a holy doctrine, a holy discipline, and a holy life.[2]

[1] Gieseler, **v.** p. 174.   [2] *Vide* Briggs, *Church Unity*, pp. 317 *seq.*

Puritanism emphasised the fundamental religious principle of Protestantism, that the Bible is the chief medium of divine authority and grace, and laid down principles of interpretation, which wrought mightily during the seventeenth century in Great Britain, and produced exegetical works that ought to be the pride of the Anglo-Saxon Churches in all time. The Puritans laid stress upon practical exegesis, or the application of the Scriptures to the Christian life. The great majority of their writings are upon themes comprehended by the term *Practical Divinity*.[1]

The eminent scholars among the Puritans and the members of the Westminster Assembly were, for the most part, trained in the English universities.

Cambridge can boast of : (1) *Thomas Cartwright* († 1603), chief of the English Puritans, and the father of English Presbyterianism, who wrote a *Treatise of the Christian Religion* (1611, 1616), in which, like Vermigli and Hemmingsen, he arranged his material on the principle of the Law and the Gospel—an example followed by the Puritans generally ; (2) *William Perkins* († 1602), whose *Golden Chaine*, an attempt to work out the order of the divine decrees, stirred up controversy not only in England, but all over the Calvinistic world ; (3) *William Ames* († 1633), who carried the principle of the Covenant into Holland ; (4) *Herbert Palmer* († 1647), whose catechism became the basis of the *Westminster Larger Catechism*, and whose *Memorials of Godliness and Christianity* are equal, if not superior, to Jeremy Taylor's *Holy Living* ; (5) *William Gouge* († 1653), ' the father of the London divines, and the oracle of his time ' ; (6) *Stephen Marshall* († 1655), the most influential member of the Westminster Assembly in ecclesiastical affairs ; (7) *Edmund Calamy* († 1666), who with Marshall and others prepared the famous *Answer of Smectymnuus* to the *Humble Remonstrance* of Joseph Hall, which *Answer* became the platform of the Presbyterian as the *Remonstrance* was that of the Episcopal party ; (8) *Anthony Tuckney* († 1670), one of the most active members of the Westminster Assembly ; (9) *John Milton* († 1674), who for twenty years produced chiefly prose works on behalf of the Puritan cause ; (10) *John Lightfoot* († 1675), author

---

[1] *Vide* Briggs, *Theological Symbolics*, pp. 260 *seq.* ; *Study of Holy Scripture*, pp. 155, 467, 573, 651 *seq.*

of *Horæ Hebraicæ et Talmudicæ*, and important Biblical works ;
(11) *Matthew Poole* († 1679), the great Presbyterian critic of the
seventeenth century, whose masterpiece, the *Synopsis criticorum*,
is a monument of Biblical learning.[1]

The University of *Oxford* sent forth such scholars as : (1) *John
Reynolds* († 1607), one of the translators of King James' Version
of the Bible ; (2) *Nicholas Byfield* († 1622), whose *Principles, or
Pattern of Wholesome Words*, is a valuable compend of divinity ;
(3) *John Ball* († 1640), one of the fathers of Presbyterianism in
England, and the author of treatises on Faith and on the Covenant
of Grace of exceeding value ; (4) *Edward Leigh* († 1671), who
ranks among the best Biblical scholars of the century ; (5)
Edward Reynolds († 1676), one of the master spirits of the Westminster Assembly ; (6) *John Owen* († 1683), the polemic divine,
who gave to Puritan Theology a scholastic type which it did
not possess before ; (7) *John Durie* († 1689), the great peace-
maker, who tried to rally the Christians of his time on what he
called *Practical Theology* ; that is, such doctrines of Faith and
Morals as are of practical importance.[2]

Eminent among the Puritan leaders unconnected with
the English universities were :

(1) *Andrew Melville* († 1622), a pupil of Ramus and of Beza.
As reformer Melville led the battle against prelacy in Scotland ;
as a teacher at Glasgow and St. Andrews he ' led the revolt against
the mediæval method of studying Aristotle, and created a taste
for Greek letters.' [3]   His last years were spent in exile, teaching
theology at the Academy of Sedan.[4]   (2) *James Ussher* († 1656),
a pupil of *Travers* at Trinity College, Dublin, became eventually
archbishop of Armagh and primate of Ireland.   He drew up
the *Irish Articles of Religion*, and proposed a *Reduction of Episco-
pacy unto the Form of Synodical Government received in the
Ancient Church*.[5]   Ussher also wrote *Annales Veteris Testamenti*,
a monumental work on the Apostles' Creed, notable contributions

---

[1] *Vide* Briggs, articles on ' Cartwright,' ' Perkins,' Palmer,' ' Gouge,'
' Marshall,' ' Calamy,' ' Tuckney,' and ' Poole,' in *Schaff-Herzog Encyclopedia* ; *Study of Holy Scripture*, pp. 149, 459, 575 ; *American Presbyterianism*, pp. 41 *seq.*, 200.

[2] *Vide* Briggs, articles on 'Byfield' and ' Ball' in *Schaff-Herzog
Encyclopedia* ; also those on 'Durie', *ibid*. (1st edition), and in *Presbyterian
Review*, 1887, vol. viii. pp. 297 *seq.* ; *Study of Holy Scripture*, pp. 162,
225 *seq.*, 462 *seq.*

[3] Sandys, ii. p. 247.   [4] *Vide* p. 158.

[5] *Vide* Briggs, *American Presbyterianism*, Appendix II. pp. xvii *seq.*

to Church History, especially in the department of Patristics, and a Chronology of the Bible still in use. (3) *Samuel Rutherford* († 1661), the Scottish Covenanter, a graduate of Edinburgh University, was an able, though bitter, controversialist. (4) *John Bunyan* († 1688), the Baptist preacher and 'immortal dreamer,' set forth in his *Pilgrim's Progress* and *Holy War* the Puritan conception of human life as a battle with evil, and gave in this respect the most popular and best exposition of the ethical side of Puritanism. (5) *Richard Baxter* († 1691), one of the greatest of English theologians, acquired exceptional learning without a university education. He is now chiefly known as the author of the *Reformed Pastor, A Call to the Unconverted* and the *Saints' Everlasting Rest*, and is honoured by Churchmen and Nonconformists alike as one who 'in a stormy and divided age advocated unity and comprehension, pointing the way to everlasting rest.' [1]

The reviving influences of the Puritan movement were not confined to the Puritan party.

Among the notable theologians of the period were the *Cambridge* scholars : (1) *Brian Walton* († 1661), whose Polyglot Bible was the greatest critical achievement of the seventeenth century ; (2) *John Pearson* († 1686), author of a standard exposition of the Apostles' Creed, of *Vindiciæ epistolarum S. Ignatii*, and of other important critical works ; (3) *William Cave* († 1713), the eminent Patristic scholar ; also the great divines : (4) *Lancelot Andrewes* († 1626), now known chiefly through his *Private Devotions* ; (5) *George Herbert* († 1633), famous, not only for his sacred verse, but also for his treatise on the *Country Parson* ; (6) *John Cosin* († 1672), prelate and controversialist, who made a *Collection of Private Devotions in the Practice of the Ancient Church* ; (7) *Jeremy Taylor* († 1667), 'the Chrysostom of England,' author of *A Discourse of the Liberty of Prophesying*, a *Rule of Conscience*, the *Great Exemplar*, the *Worthy Communicant*, and *Rule and Exercises of Holy Living* and *of Holy Dying*.

Among the theologians of *Oxford* may be mentioned : (1) the poet and preacher, *John Donne* († 1631); (2) *William Chillingworth* († 1644), who, in his *Religion of Protestants*, declared the Bible to be 'that wherein they all agree, and which they all subscribe . . . as a perfect rule of their faith and actions ;' [2]

---

[1] *Vide* Briggs, article on 'Baxter' in *Schaff-Herzog Encyclopedia*; *American Presbyterianism*, pp. 44 *seq.*, 53.

[2] *Vide* article on 'Chillingworth' in *Schaff-Herzog Encyclopedia*.

(3) *John Hales* († 1656), 'the ever-memorable,' whose *Golden Remains* contain letters from the Synod of Dort; (4) *Henry Hammond* († 1660), who wrote his *Paraphrase and Annotations upon . . . the New Testament* in the spirit of Erasmus; (5) *Edward Pococke* († 1691), Oriental and Biblical scholar, who gathered in the East rich spoils of Arabic literature; (6) *John Mill* († 1707), noted for his critical edition of the New Testament; (7) *Joseph Bingham* († 1723), who wrote on Christian Antiquities; and (8) *Humphrey Prideaux* († 1724), who connected the Old and New Testaments with the history of the Jews and the neighbouring nations.

Mention must also be made of the founder of the Society of Friends, *George Fox* († 1691), who urged the following of the Inner Light; and of the apologist of that society, *Robert Barclay* († 1690), a theologian of exceptional learning and ability.

3. *In the Netherlands theological scholarship revived in the newly founded universities, the Arminian movement, and the Federal School of Theology. Among the Arminians of Holland, especially the scholars of Leyden, the Humanistic spirit found expression.*

William of Orange founded the *University of Leyden* in 1575, with Louis Cappell [1] as the first professor of theology. Ten years later the *University of Franecker* was established, to be followed in the next century by those of *Groningen* (1612), *Utrecht* (1636), and *Harderwyk* (1648). The University of Leyden 'became for Holland what Wittenberg had been to Germany, Geneva to Switzerland, and Saumur to France.' [2]

Among the great scholars that taught at Leyden were the theologians: (1) *Junius* (Du Jon, † 1602), a pupil of Calvin; (2) *Scaliger* (De la Scala, † 1609), 'the leading philologist of France,' who laid the foundations for the science of Chronology; (3) *Drusius* (Van den Driesche, † 1616), Biblical scholar and exegete; (4) *Arminius* († 1609), a pupil of *Lambertus Danœus* at Leyden, and of Beza and Grynæus at Geneva and Basel.

---

[1] *Vide* p. 158. [2] Lindsay, *History of the Reformation*, ii. p. 264.

Arminius became professor of theology at Leyden in 1603, and soon aroused the opposition of his colleague, *Gomarus*, by his interpretation of the Epistle to the Romans. He also came into conflict with *William Perkins* of Cambridge.[1] In the controversy which raged about him and his followers, Arminius attained such pre-eminence that his name was given to all subsequent forms of the milder Augustinianism in the Reformed Churches.[2]

Episcopius († 1643), professor at Leyden, and *Uytenbogœrt* († 1644), preacher at the Hague, were prominent among the Arminians. But the flower of the movement was (5) *Hugo Grotius* (1583-1645), the greatest scholar of his age, a pupil of Scaliger and of Uytenbogært, and a supporter of Barneveldt in his efforts to maintain peace in the Church. Grotius revived the Humanism of Erasmus, and in his Annotations on the Scriptures laid stress upon the historical interpretation. In this he was followed by the Arminians generally, and especially by *Clericus* (Le Clerc, † 1736). The numerous writings of Grotius include valuable theological works in the departments of Dogmatics, Irenics, Polemics, Church History, Liturgics, and Canon Law.

Important service to the study of theology was also rendered by the Arabic scholar, (6) *Erpenius* († 1624), and his celebrated pupils, *Louis Cappell*, the Younger,[3] and (7) *Louis de Dieu* († 1642); by (8) *Voss* († 1649), who became unpopular at Leyden because of his sympathy with the Remonstrants, and gave his last years to the University of Amsterdam (1632-1649); and by (9) *Rivetus*, the Huguenot († 1651), one of the chief Reformed divines of the Continent.

Among the *Anti-Remonstrants* may be mentioned: (10) *Jacob Revius* († 1658), Hebrew scholar and controversialist; and (11) *Voëtius* († 1676), professor at Utrecht, whose influence helped to establish a Protestant traditional orthodoxy in the Dutch schools.[4]

The Arminian movement, defeated by Dutch Scholasticism, passed over into England, and especially

---

[1] *Vide* p. 152.
[2] *Vide* Briggs, *Theological Symbolics*, pp. 211 *seq.*
[3] *Vide* p. 155.
[4] *Vide* Briggs, *Study of Holy Scripture*, p. 147.

into the Anglican Church, in the author of the London Polyglot, in *Hammond, Pococke, Whitby, Lowth,* and *John Taylor* of Norwich (who greatly influenced German Theology in its reform in the eighteenth century), and in Wesley took the form of Evangelical Arminianism.

The principle of the Covenant, passing over into Holland with the English Puritan *Ames,* gave birth to the Covenant Theology of *Cocceius* and *Witsius.*

Ames [1] became professor of theology at Franecker in 1622, and rector of the university four years later. Among his pupils was (12) *Cocceius* († 1669), the father of the Federal School in Holland, who was called to Franecker in 1636, and to Leyden in 1650. In addition to his famous *Summa doctrina de fœdere et testamento Dei* (1648, 1654), he made important contributions to Biblical Philology, Theology, and Exegesis, and to the departments of Dogmatics, Ethics, and Catechetics. Among the pupils of Cocceius was (13) *Vitringa* († 1722), professor at Franecker, celebrated for his commentaries, and his works on Sacred History and Chronology, and on Biblical and Practical Theology. (14) *Hermann Witsius* († 1708), Biblical theologian and leader of the Dutch Federal School, taught at the Universities of Franecker, Utrecht and Leyden, published a notable work, *De œconomia fœderum Dei cum hominibus,* treatises on the Apostles' Creed, the Lord's Prayer, the Christian Faith, the Character of a True Theologian, and important Biblical works.

The Covenant Theology of Cocceius and Witsius influenced German Pietism, but eventually combined with Scholasticism to form a new Scholasticism, especially in Scotland and America.

4. *The critical principle reasserted itself mightily in the French School of Saumur, and a freer type of Theology was there maintained.* [2]

There were in France, in the seventeenth century, six Protestant academies, all modelled after those of Strasburg and Geneva : namely, *Nîmes* (1561), irenic in

---

[1] *Vide* p. 152. Ames published his *Medulla theologica* in **1623** (English, 1642).
[2] *Vide* Briggs, *Study of Holy Scripture,* p. 222.

spirit; *Saumur* (1593), mildly Calvinistic and progressive; *Montauban* (1597) and *Sedan* (c. 1602), both Scholastic; *Orthez* (1566) and *Die* (c. 1596), both insignificant. The Academies of Saumur, Sedan and Montauban took an active part in theological controversy, and became centres of theological learning. The foreign element was always strong, especially in Saumur and Sedan; and Italy, Switzerland, Holland, Germany, and Scotland contributed to the faculties of the French Academies as well as to the student bodies. Scotland gave ' a Pleiades of distinguished men.' [1]

(I.) The Academy of *Nîmes* was originally a school of grammar and logic, civil and canon law, dating from the fourteenth century. Early in the sixteenth century it was transformed after the model of the School of the Three Languages [2] at Paris, and under the inspiration of the pedagogic principles of Sturm of Strasburg. In 1561 the Protestant consistory added to it a school of theology with four professors, one for Hebrew, one for Greek, one for philosophy, and one for doctrine. The only famous teacher of theology in this academy was *Pierre Viret*.[3]

(II.) The Academy of *Orthez* was founded in 1566 with professors of theology, Greek, Hebrew, philosophy, mathematics and music. *Viret* taught there in 1571, and *Lambert Daneau* in 1583-1593.

(III.) *Sedan* was organised as a College in 1579; the Academy proper was established in 1602. Among the famous teachers of theology at this institution were *Louis Cappell* (1576-1586), who came to Sedan from Leyden; [4] *Jacques Cappell* (1599-1624), a nephew of Louis; *Daniel Tilénus* (1600-1620), *Andrew Melville* [5] (1611-1620), and *Le Blanc de Beaulieu* (1644-1675). Philosophy was taught here by *John Cameron* (1602-1604) and by *Pierre Bayle* (1675-1681). Other illustrious names might be added. *Pierre du Moulin* (1621-1658), who had taught philosophy at Leyden, is said to have ' acquired at Sedan an influence equal to that which *Amyraut* enjoyed at Saumur.' [6]

(IV.) The School of *Montauban* was founded in 1597. One of

---

[1] Bourchenin, *Étude sur les Académies Protestantes en France au XVIᵉ et au XVIIᵉ Siècle*, 1882, p. 402.
[2] Le collège royal des trois langues.
[3] *Vide* p. 127.   [4] *Vide* p. 155.   [5] *Vide* p. 153.
[6] Bourchenin, *Les Académies protestantes en France*, pp. 428 *seq*.

its first professors of theology was *Daniel Chamier* (1612-1621). *John Cameron* taught there in 1624-1625, and *Jean Claude* in 1662-1666. Claude was 'regarded in his day as the soul of the Reformed party in France.'[1] In theology the school of Montauban mediated between those of Sedan and Saumur.

(V.) *Die* had a college in 1596, and an academy of theology *c.* 1604. *Daniel Chamier* presided there in 1607-1608 ; and *John Sharp* taught theology in 1607-1629.

(VI.) The Academy of *Saumur* was founded in 1593 by the great general, *Duplessis-Mornay,* and became the most famous of all the French academies. There were chairs of theology, Greek, Hebrew, and philosophy.

Saumur had several great divines : *John Cameron, Josué de la Place,* and *Amyraut,* theologians who taught mediate imputation and hypothetic universalism ; and *Ludovicus Cappellus,* the greatest Biblical critic of his age.

(1) *John Cameron* of Glasgow († 1625) taught theology at Saumur (1618-1622), and impressed his views upon his illustrious pupil, Amyraut. (2) *Moïse Amyraut* (Amyraldus, 1596-1664) was a teacher at Saumur for thirty-eight years. As early as the year 1634 he created great excitement by the publication of a *Traité de la prédestination.* His important work includes a System of Christian Morals (in six volumes). (3) *Placeus* (De La Place, 1596-1655) was also a follower of Cameron, and taught theology at Saumur for nearly a quarter of a century. In his *Disputatio de imputatione primi peccati Adami* (1655) he asserted the doctrine of *mediate imputation* as alone justifiable on moral grounds.[2] (4) *Louis Cappell,* the Younger (Cappellus, 1585-1658), nephew of the elder Louis and brother of Jacques, taught Hebrew and theology at Saumur for forty-four years, and became the most eminent Biblical scholar of his day. Falling back on the views of the Jewish scholar, *Elias Levita* († 1549), and of the Protestant reformers, Cappellus denied the verbal inspiration of the Massoretic Biblical text, showed that the Hebrew vowel points were not original, and that there were different readings of the text, and laid stress upon grammatical and historical exegesis. He was sustained by the French theologians generally, and by

---

1 Gieseler, **v.** p. 351.

2 *Vide* Briggs, *Theological Symbolics,* pp. 213 *seq.* ; also Placeus, *De statu hominis lapsi ante gratiam,* 1640.

the body of English critics. Cocceius first gave his name to the
public as author of the anonymous work, *Arcanum punctuationis
revelatum* (1624). This work remained unanswered and wrought
powerfully for nearly a quarter of a century, when the younger
Buxtorf undertook to maintain against Cappellus the traditional
Rabbinical position. The three universities of Sedan, Geneva,
and Leyden were roused to such opposition to Cappellus, that
they sought to prevent the publication of his great work, the
Critica sacra. It appeared, however, in 1650, and proved to be
the first of a series of corresponding productions.

These great scholars of Saumur taught large bodies
of students from many lands. In England the influence of this school was apparent among the Puritans,
especially in Calamy and Baxter, and became known
as *Baxterianism*, or the *New Theology*, and so passed
over to America as New School Theology, and in
England and Ireland attached itself to vital reforming
movements.[1] But the scholastic theologians of France,
Holland, and Switzerland bitterly opposed the School
of Saumur. These controversies greatly weakened
French Protestantism at a critical period.

Among the French theologians trained at Saumur and Sedan
were: (1) *Jacques Basnage* († 1723), fourth in a succession of
theologians of that surname, the author of many historical,
dogmatic and polemic works; and (2) *Jacques Abbadie* († 1727),
whose apologetic and ethical treatises were widely known.

In addition to these six academies there were two schools of
little or brief importance, the one at *Montpellier*, the other at
Orange. (VII.) *Montpellier Academy* was founded in 1596. In
1609 it possessed chairs of theology, Hebrew and Greek; but
by 1617 it had been absorbed in the school of Nîmes. *Isaac
Casaubon* († 1614), the great Humanist, whose learning almost
rivalled that of *Scaliger*, came from teaching Greek at Geneva
to help in building up the new school (1596-1599). His chief
contribution to theology was his edition of the Greek Testament.
Daniel Chamier († 1621) was active in the founding of this
academy; and *Thomas Dempster* taught philosophy there in
1605.

---

[1] *Vide* Briggs, *Study of Holy Scripture*, pp. 222 *seq.*; *Theological
Symbolics*, pp. 373 *seq.*

(VIII.) The School of *Orange* (c. 1573) had also a brief existence, and like those of Montpellier and Orthez, took no part in theological controversy. Indeed, the Academy of Orange was not attached to the French Churches by any administrative link.[1]

All of the French theological schools were short-lived. The last was suppressed by Louis xiv. in 1685.

5. *In England Francis Bacon became the father of Inductive Philosophy over against the Aristotelian, and greatly influenced all subsequent English thought, giving it an abiding bent towards empirical and experimental philosophy.*

This philosophy in its several forms undermined British Theology, and produced eventually the Deist movement.

The influence of Bacon († 1626) and the Inductive Philosophy was greatly promoted by the growth of Natural Philosophy, or the study of the Science of Nature by the experimental method, pursued on the Continent by *Copernicus* († 1543), *Kepler* († 1630), *Galileo* († 1642), and a host of followers ; and in England by *Napier* († 1617), *Harvey* († 1657), and others. These men built up the Natural Sciences, which continually pressed more and more into the universities and influenced students of theology, who were led thereby to make more of the realities of nature and of life. With that came increased attention to the principles of education and the building up of the science of education, especially through the labours of *Ratichius* (1571-1635) and *Comenius* (1592-1670). Amos Comenius, bishop of the Moravians, exerted extraordinary influence through his *Great Didactic* and other educational works. His principles were :

(1) *Omnia e principiis rerum immotis deriventur.*

---

[1] *Vide* Bourchenin, *Les Académies protestantes en France*, p. 396.

(2) *Nihil doceatur per autoritatem nudam, omnia per demonstrationem sensualem et rationalem.*

(3) *Nihil methodo analytica sola, synthetica potius omnia.*

All these efforts for reform aimed, as Paulsen shows,[1] at these things :

(1) The learning, not only of languages, but also of *realities* (mathematics, the natural sciences, history, geography).

(2) The learning of languages aright : not the language from grammar, but the grammar from language.

(3) The study of the modern languages.

(4) Study not by compulsion, but by rational methods : the use of the intelligence, rather than the rod.

In the course of the seventeenth century new philosophical theories came into the field to displace the Aristotelian and Platonic philosophies, in the works of *Hobbes, Descartes, Spinoza, Locke, Leibnitz,* and their associates. Deism arose in England, and sought to reduce Christianity to a religion of nature with the human reason as the sole authority. In the eighteenth century the movement was gradually overcome in Great Britain and driven to the Continent, where it ran riot in various forms of Rationalism. It should be said, however, that the Scholastic Theology did not recover the authority it had lost in the universities of England, but only in Scotland and among the English Nonconformists in part, so far as they were influenced by their training in the universities of Holland. The Church of England since the Reformation has always trained her clergy in Positive Theology, that is, in the Scriptures and the Creeds. No great system of theology has been produced since the Reformation in the Church of England.

(1) *Francis Bacon* (1561-1629) was trained at Cambridge, where he ' first fell into the dislike of the philosophy of Aristotle,

---

[1] *Vide* Paulsen, *Geschichte des gelehrten Unterrichts,* 2nd edition, i. pp. 469, 471 *seq.*

. . . being a philosophy only strong for disputations and contentions, but barren of the production of works for the benefit of the life of man.'[1] He described the Schoolmen as 'having sharp and strong wits, and abundance of leisure, and small variety of reading, but their wits being shut up in the cells of a few authors (chiefly Aristotle their dictator), . . . and knowing little history, either of nature or time (they) did, out of no great quantity of matter and infinite agitation of wit, open out unto us those laborious webs of learning, which are extant in their books.'[2] Bacon's great works include his *Novum organum*, *Advancement of Learning*, and famous *Essays*. He also wrote a Confession of Faith, and devotional works.

(2) *John Locke* (1632-1704), of Oxford, ' the originator of the empirical philosophy of the eighteenth century,'[3] and author of the famous *Essay on the Human Understanding*, published also *Letters on Toleration*, the *Reasonableness of Christianity*, treatises on Miracles and on Education, and Paraphrases on the great Pauline Epistles.

Among the opponents of Deism may be mentioned : (3) *Joseph Butler* (1692-1752), also an Oxford scholar and bishop of Durham, famous for his sermons and for his *Analogy of Religion, Natural and Revealed* (1736), which has been a universal text-book of Apologetics.[4]

6. *At Helmstädt the irenical school of Calixtus struggled with the scholastic spirit, and reverted from the scholastic method to the historical and Biblical methods.*[5]

The University of Helmstädt allowed its theological professors exceptional liberty in matters of doctrine. One of the Helmstädt theologians, (1) *George Calixtus* (1586-1656), became the chief irenic divine of the early seventeenth century.

The father of Calixtus, a pupil of Melanchthon, transmitted to him the theology of that Reformer. Some years of travel in other countries gave him a personal knowledge of both the

---

[1] Bacon, *Advancement of Learning*, ed. Aldis Wright, pref. p. vi. ; *vide* Sandys, ii. p. 338.

[2] *Vide* Sandys, ii. p. 339.

[3] *Vide* article on ' Locke,' in *New Schaff-Herzog Encyclopedia.*

[4] *Vide* Briggs, *Whither ?* p. 217.

[5] *Vide* Briggs, *Study of Holy Scripture*, pp. 147, 574 ; *Theological Symbolics*, pp. 9, 21.

Roman Catholic and the Reformed Churches. He began to seek a basis for reunion in the Christian consensus of the first five centuries. Serving as professor of theology at Helmstädt for over forty years (1614-1656), he exerted a widespread and powerful influence as an advocate of Christian Unity. He also did valuable work as a Biblical and dogmatic theologian, and to him is ascribed the founding of the discipline of Ethics in theology.

The irenic teaching of Calixtus excited great opposition in the so-called *Syncretistic Controversies.*

The University of *Helmstädt* supported Calixtus. Among his defenders was (2) *Hermann Conring* († 1681), who ' excelled in almost every department of human knowledge '[1] and published several irenic works. (3) *Molanus* († 1722), who worked with *Leibnitz* and *Spinola* for a reunion of Protestants and Catholics, and with *Leibnitz* and *Jablonski* for a union of the Lutherans with the Reformed, was one of the pupils of Calixtus. Prominent among his opponents was (4) *Calovius* of Wittenberg († 1686). Several of the theologians of Königsberg were classed as *Syncretists*, among them (5) *Grabe* († 1711), the patristic scholar, who published an edition of the Septuagint. (6) *Johann Gerhard* († 1637), regarded by his cotemporaries as the greatest theologian of the time, died before the controversy had fairly begun. His pupils at *Jena*, (7) *Glassius* († 1656), author of *Philologia sacra*, and (8) *Musæus* († 1681), a noted dogmatic theologian, maintained a mediating position. (9) *Martin Geier* of Leipzig († 1680) took no part in the conflict; but produced, according to Gieseler, ' the best commentaries on the books of the Old Testament which appeared during this period.'[2]

7. *The milder Calvinism and the critical spirit of the school of Saumur took refuge in Switzerland, and reappeared in the younger Turretin of Geneva, in Osterwald of Neuchâtel, and in Werenfels of Basel.*

In 1675 *Heidegger* of Zürich, with the co-operation of *Gernler* of Basel and *François Turretin* of Geneva, drew up the *Formula Consensus Helvetica* as a definition of Scholastic Calvinism over against the milder Calvinism of the school of Saumur. Under the influence of these

great divines the Formula was adopted by several of
the Cantons of Switzerland ; and its doctrines were
maintained by Scholastic Calvinists in other countries,
especially in Holland and Scotland ; but it had little
influence in Germany or England, and was overthrown
in Switzerland in the next generation, under the leadership of the younger Turretin.[1] The reaction may be
said to have begun even earlier, with *Peter Werenfels*
(† 1703), Gernler's successor at Basel,[2] whose son *Samuel*
(† 1740) co-operated with Turretin and Osterwald in
the Swiss revolt against Scholasticism.

(1) *Heidegger* of Zürich († 1698) made important contributions
to Dogmatics, Ethics, Church History, Biblical Theology, Symbolics, and Christian Institutions. (2) *François Turretin* (Tur-
rettini, † 1687) published an *Institutio theologiæ elencticæ*, which
was used as a text-book by Scottish and American Presbyterians till towards the close of last century, to the neglect
of the Westminster divines. His son, (3) *Jean Alphonse Turretin* († 1737), was the chief of those who secured the abolition
of the Helvetic Consensus in 1725. He corresponded with
Leibnitz, Frederick I. of Prussia, and Archbishop Wake of Canterbury, on behalf of Church Unity, and published dogmatic, irenic
and exegetical works. (4) *Benedict Pictet* († 1724) was a cousin
of the younger Turretin, and like him a liberal and irenic theologian. He produced important works on Christian Theology
and Ethics.

Among the other Swiss theologians of the period were : (5)
the Semitic scholar, *Johann Heinrich Hottinger* of Zürich († 1667),
and (6) his son, *Johann Jacob* († 1735), both of whom did notable
work in Church History ; (7) *John Buxtorf*, father († 1629) and
(8) son († 1664), who were influential in establishing a Protestant
traditional orthodoxy in the Swiss schools, and maintained the
divine origin and authority of the Massoretic vowel points and
accents, yet rendered valuable service by their Hebrew Concordance and other philological, Biblical and historical works ; and
(9) *Suicer* († 1684), author of the celebrated *Thesaurus ecclesi-
asticus*, and other lexicographal works.

---

[1] *Vide* Briggs, *Theological Symbolics*, pp. 213 *seq.* ; *Study of Holy
Scripture*, p. 225.
[2] *Vide* Dorner, *Geschichte der protestantischen Theologie*, p. 439, *n.* 1.

8. *The Cambridge Platonists revived the ethical type of Theology in England, and strove to give the human reason its proper place and function in matters of religion.*

The Cambridge Platonists were Puritan in origin and training. Predominantly rational and ethical, they were characterised also by the mystic spirit, especially in the case of *Henry More* († 1687). Like the school of Saumur in France and the school of Calixtus in Germany, this group of Cambridge scholars helped to prepare the way for a broad, comprehensive Church.[1] The leaders among them, with the exception of More, all belonged to the famous Puritan college *Emmanuel.* The most notable of these theologians were Whichcote and Cudworth.

(1) *Benjamin Whichcote* (1609-1683) exerted strong influence as a teacher, especially through the lectures which he gave at Trinity College on Sunday afternoons for twenty years. *Cudworth, More* and *John Smith* († 1652) were among his disciples. His writings were all issued posthumously, and include *Moral and Religious Aphorisms,* sermons, and a remarkable correspondence with Anthony Tuckney.[2] Whichcote declared : ' God hath set up two lights to enlighten us in our way : the light of reason, which is the light of His creation ; and the light of Scripture, which is after-revelation from Him. Let us make use of these two lights ; and suffer neither to be put out.' [3]

(2) *Ralph Cudworth* (1617-1688), the most celebrated philosopher of this school, was Regius Professor of Hebrew. He wrote on *The True Intellectual System of the Universe,* on *Eternal and Immutable Morality,* and on *Free Will.*

9. *Puritanism eventually gave birth to Pietism in Reformed and Lutheran Germany, producing the Biblical school of Bengel and the Moravians.*

Pietism was the salvation of Germany and Methodism of Great Britain. Pietism in Germany owed its origin to English Puritanism, which gave the impulse to

---

[1] *Vide* Briggs, *Study of Holy Scripture,* pp. 574 *seq.*
[2] *Vide* p. 152.
[3] *Vide* article on ' Whichcote,' in *New Schaff-Herzog Encyclopedia.*

Holland first, and then to the Reformed Churches of
the Rhine, until at length it reached Strasburg, and
moved first Spener, then Koelmann, and finally Zinzendorf. The Pietism of Germany and Holland, especially
that of the type of Zinzendorf, in turn greatly influenced
British Methodism.[1]

(1) *Philip Jacob Spener* (1635-1705), the father of German
Pietism, studied at Strasburg, Basel, Geneva and Tübingen, and
was influenced by the Puritan piety, especially of Baxter, and by
the French of *Jean de Labadie* († 1674), founder of a Quietistic
sect in Holland. Spener began to preach at Strasburg in 1663,
and three years later was called to Frankfort-on-the-Main, where
he organised the *Collegia pietatis* (1670) to promote the study of
the Bible and the practice of devotion. Similar circles were
formed in other cities, and the interest in Biblical study greatly
increased. Spener worked subsequently in Dresden, and finally,
from 1691, in Berlin, exerting great influence, especially through
his writings. The most important of these were the *Pia desi-
deria* (1675), *Geistliches Priesterthum, Theologische Bedenken,*
and the treatise *De impedimentis studii theologici.* Spener
emphasised the practical in theology. He and his followers
were of the mystic type; and they adopted many of the chief
features of Puritanism. The German Pietists laid stress upon
personal relations to God and experimental piety, in order to the
interpretation of Scripture. This was accompanied among the
best of them with true scholarship. In their study of theology
they discarded the scholastic method in favour of the historical
and Biblical methods. They did not form a separate denomination, but remain as a party in the Churches of Germany until the
present day.[2] However, they established a theological school
at Halle with *Francke* at its head.

(2) *August Hermann Francke* (1663-1727) was one of the
founders of the *Collegium philobiblicum* (1686), and of the
Collegia biblica (1689), at Leipzig. Through Spener's influence
he was called to the new university at Halle (1692) as professor
of Greek and the Oriental languages, and as pastor to a suburban
church. With the co-operation of his colleagues, *Breithaupt*
(† 1732) and *Anton* († 1730), he made Halle a great centre of

---

[1] *Vide* Briggs, *Study of Holy Scripture,* p. 574; *American Presbyterianism,* pp. 238 *seq.* ; *Theological Symbolics,* pp. 244 *seq.*
[2] *Vide* Briggs, *Study of Holy Scripture,* pp. 466 *seq.* ; *Theological
Symbolics,* pp. 9, 244.

Pietism. He founded the famous Orphan Asylum, the *Päda-gogium*, and other educational institutions, and made them training schools in Pedagogy and Pastoral Theology for the students of Halle. At his death more than 2200 children were under instruction, and 250 students were receiving practical training as teachers and pastors in these institutions. The most important of Francke's writings treat of Biblical Interpretation and Hermeneutics. The best exegete among the Pietists was (3) *Johann Albert Bengel* († 1752), 'the founder of New Testament criticism in the Lutheran Church,'[1] whose interpretation is a model of piety and accuracy. To his famous *Gnomon Novi Testamenti* he added other valuable Biblical works, and carried on the work of Mill in a critical text of the New Testament.

Pietism was carried into the Moravian Church by (4) *Nicolaus Ludwig Zinzendorf* (1700-1760), a disciple of Francke, trained at his *Pädagogium* in Halle. Zinzendorf received the exiles from Moravia on his estate at Herrnhut (1722), and reorganised them as the *Unitas Fratrum* with the *Ratio disciplinæ* of Bishop Comenius.[2] His writings comprise sermons, hymns, and various doctrinal and devotional works.

10. *The vital religion and ethical principles of Puritanism revived in Great Britain and her colonies in the form of Methodism, under the leadership of Wesley and Whitefield.*

Deism was overcome in Great Britain and her colonies by the vital religion and Christian experience of Methodism, a genuine development of British Christianity, yet strongly influenced by the Pietism of the Continent. Methodism was, indeed, an historical recompense for the influence of Puritanism upon Continental Christianity. The fathers of Methodism were *Wesley* and *White-field*, the one an Arminian, the other a Calvinist. It was their earnest desire and purpose to organise holy circles within the Church, after the example of German Pietism ; but intolerance compelled their followers for the most part to organise separate churches in England, Scotland, Ireland and America. The Church of England secession was made by Wesley and Whitefield, and

[1] Gieseler, v. p. 296.   [2] Briggs, *Theological Symbolics*, p. 244.

resolved itself into the Arminian branch of Wesley and the Calvinistic branch of Whitefield. The secession from the Church of Scotland was led by the *Erskines*, who, after suspension by that Church, organised an Associate Presbytery (1733). The American secession was in the New Side Presbyterians. The Congregationalists and the Baptists divided into parties ; but did not separate, because of their loose organisation and the difficulty of ecclesiastical division. There was, however, a considerable amount of disfellowship and conflict. A large number of Methodists remained in the older organisations, preferring limitation to separation. Still greater numbers were influenced more or less by the new movement, and the whole Christian body was enlivened and refreshed. Scholasticism and Deism were stayed, and gradually driven back all over the Anglo-Saxon world. Methodism, like Pietism, emphasised the Christian religious experience, laying more stress on vital and spiritual Christianity, and less on doctrinal and institutional Christianity ; although they cannot be said to have departed from the fundamental doctrines or historic institutions of Christianity.[1] Yet while Pietism succeeded in establishing its headquarters at the University of Halle, Methodism, forced out of the national Church, had to train its ministers in theological colleges and seminaries.

(1) *John Wesley* (1703-1791) was trained at Oxford University, and was one of the founders of the famous *Holy Club* (1729), whose members won the name of *Methodists* by ' the exact regularity of their lives and studies.' Wesley was strongly influenced by Thomas à Kempis, Jeremy Taylor, Luther, and his cotemporary, the mystic, *William Law* († 1761), author of the *Serious Call to a Devout and Holy Life, A Practical Treatise on Christian Perfection*, and other remarkable works. But it was chiefly through the Moravians that Wesley was guided to the adoption of those

---

[1] *Vide* Briggs, *Theological Symbolics*, p. 245.

principles and methods which have become the characteristic features of Methodism. In 1739, following the example of Whitefield, Wesley began the practice of preaching in the open air, which he continued for upwards of fifty years. In the same year the first society of Methodists was formed. The writings of Wesley include a *Plain Account of Christian Perfection, Notes on the New Testament*, a *Short History of Methodism*, sermons, journals, and doctrinal and practical tracts.

(2) *Charles Wesley* (1708-1788), brother and collaborator of John, has been called ' the poet of Methodism,' and is now known chiefly through his hymns.

(3) *George Whitefield* (1714-1770) was one of the members of the Holy Club at Oxford. He became known in Great Britain and her colonies in America as an evangelist and field preacher of wonderful power and success. He laid the foundations of a famous school at Kingswood, near Bristol ; and wrote *The Christian History ; or, A General Account of the Progress of the Gospel in England, Wales, Scotland, and America*, as well as sermons and autobiographical works.

(4) *Fletcher of Madeley* (De la Fléchère, † 1785), the chief theologian of the Wesleyans, was born on Lake Geneva, but entered the ministry of the Church of England, and became associated with John Wesley. He served as pastor at Madeley for nearly a quarter of a century, and was noted for his power in preaching and his moderation in controversy. He wrote the celebrated *Checks to Antinomianism* and a *Portrait of St. Paul, or the True Model for Christians and Pastors*.

Methodism began in America in the Dutch Reformed Church, under the ministry of (5) *Jacob Frelinghuysen*, a native of East Friesland and disciple of Koelmann, the Dutch Pietist. He became pastor of a church in Raritan, New Jersey (*c.* 1720), and laboured in that region for twenty-seven years. Through Frelinghuysen the Puritan spirit flowed with new vigour. Whitefield recognised in him ' a worthy old soldier of Jesus Christ,' ' the Beginner of the great Work, which I trust the Lord is carrying on in these parts.'[1] The representative Methodists among the Presbyterians were the *Tennents*, father and son. (6) *Gilbert Tennent* began his work at New Brunswick in 1726. His father, (7) *William* († 1746), opened a *Log College* at Neshaminy, Pennsylvania (after 1727), for the training of young men for the ministry, which proved of immense service to the cause of Christ, and was likened by Whitefield to ' the Schools of the old

---

[1] *Vide* Briggs, *American Presbyterianism*, pp. 239 *seq.*

Prophets.'[1] About the Tennents gathered a strong body of earnest, devout, and zealous ministers and laymen.

The great Congregational Methodist was *Jonathan Edwards*,[2] the father of modern British and American Theology—not so much in those metaphysical matters to which his name is so frequently attached, as in those characteristic doctrines of the Methodist movement, which he so successfully formulated and explained.[3]

11. *The American colonists founded colleges modelled after those of the British Universities, as residential colleges, where instruction in Theology was mingled with general education. The greatest theologians of America studied and taught in these institutions.*

The American colonists brought with them their ministers. At first there were more than were needed. But subsequently ministers could not be secured from the mother country in sufficient numbers, and educational institutions began to be organised.

The first college was that of *Harvard*, founded at Cambridge, Massachusetts (1636); the second, that of *William and Mary*, opened at Williamsburg, Virginia (1693); the third, *Yale College*, located at first in Saybrook (1701), but afterwards removed to New Haven, Connecticut (1718). The *Log College* of William Tennent[4] was the basis for the *College of New Jersey*, opened at Elizabethtown (1646), removed to Newark (1647), and finally established at *Princeton* (1757). *King's College*, founded in New York City by royal charter in 1754, was reorganised as *Columbia* after the Revolution (1787). *Rhode Island College* (opened in 1764) took the name of *Brown* in 1804. In 1749 the foundations of the *University of Pennsylvania* were laid at Philadelphia. *Dartmouth* was opened at Hanover, New Hampshire (1770), and *Williams* at Williamstown, Massachusetts (1793). *Cokesbury College* was organised by the Methodists at Abingdon, Maryland, in 1787, and removed to Baltimore in 1795, but was finally abandoned (1796) because of repeated losses by fire.

---

[1] *Vide* Briggs, *American Presbyterianism*, pp. 186 *seq.*, 240, 242, 304 *seq.*   [2] *Vide* p. 173.
[3] *Vide* Briggs, *American Presbyterianism*, p. 261.
[4] *Vide* p. 170.

The chief purpose of these colleges was to train a Christian ministry. Thus Palfrey says, with reference to Harvard :

'The course of study [at Harvard], adopted from the contemporaneous practice of the English Universities, consisted of Latin and Greek (in which some proficiency was required for admission) ; of logic, arithmetic, geometry, and physics ; and of Hebrew, Chaldee, Syriac, and divinity,—the forming of a learned ministry being a main object of the institution.' [1]

Woolsey writes with reference to Yale :

'In general it may be said that the system pursued by the earlier teachers rested upon logic and theology, and presupposed that the students would choose the clerical profession, rather than the offices of civic life. To this cause is to be ascribed the part which the study of Hebrew played for a considerable period.' [2]

Fisher also says of Yale :

'Its chief design was to furnish the churches with competent ministers of the Gospel. For a long time theological studies, including the Hebrew language, held a prominent place in the undergraduate course. The President was a teacher of Divinity, and the first professorship created was in that department.' [3]

The American colleges produced two great theologians : *Jonathan Dickinson* and *Jonathan Edwards*, who remain as the best exponents of the theology of the eighteenth century.[4]

(1) *Dickinson* (1688-1747), the great representative American Presbyterian of the Colonial period, was trained at Yale, took charge of several congregations in Elizabethtown, New Jersey, and the neighbourhood, and became the first president of the College of New Jersey. The charter for that college was obtained through his efforts, and it was opened at his house. No better man could have been found to lay the foundation of higher

---

[1] Palfrey, *History of New England*, 1860, ii. p. 48.
[2] Woolsey, *An Historical Discourse pronounced before the Graduates of Yale College*, 1850, p. 57.
[3] *Vide* Fisher, *A Discourse, Commemorative of the History of the Church of Christ in Yale College*, 1858, pp. 36 *seq.*
[4] *Vide* Briggs, *American Presbyterianism*, pp. 176 *seq.*, 216, 260 *seq.*, 306.

education for the Presbyterians in America. He was head and shoulders above his brethren in the ministry in intellectual and moral endowments, the recognised leader in all the crises of the Church. It is due chiefly to him that the Presbyterian Church in America was not split up into fragments, perpetuating the differences of Presbyterians in the mother countries of Great Britain, and the several parties in those countries.

(2) *Jonathan Edwards* (1703-1758) is the greatest divine America has yet produced. He found no equal in Great Britain in the eighteenth and nineteenth centuries. He was at once recognised as the teacher of the Calvinistic Methodists of Great Britain, and has become the master spirit in theology to the Presbyterian and Congregational world of the nineteenth century, in Scotland as well as in England and America. Through him the theology of the school of Saumur first came into prominence in America. Edwards studied at Yale, served as pastor to Congregational churches at Northampton and Stock-bridge, Massachusetts, and was made president of the College of New Jersey shortly before his death. Under his ministry occurred the *Great Awakening*, a series of revivals (1734-1735, 1740-1741) which spread through a great part of New England. The most notable writings of Edwards were his doctrinal sermons, his dissertations on the Nature of True Virtue, the Freedom of the Will, the Religious Affections, and Original Sin, and a History of Redemption. His pupils included such theologians as *Joseph Bellamy* († 1790), *Samuel Hopkins* († 1803), and his own son, the younger *Jonathan* († 1801).

In the middle of the eighteenth century there was a great theological battle about education for the ministry in the Presbyterian and Reformed Churches, which had much to do with the division between the Old Side and the New in the Presbyterian Church. A learned ministry and a devout ministry were put in antithesis in the struggle. Early in the following century it became evident that there must be provision for a more thorough training in theology.

12. *In the eighteenth century the Nonconformists of England began to establish public colleges for the training of their ministry.*

After the Restoration and the Act of Uniformity (1662),
the Nonconformists of England, excluded from the
English universities, could only train their ministers in
private academies, or send them to the universities of
other countries. There were, however, a number of
private academies conducted by eminent men in different
places all through the seventeenth century, where the
principles of Nonconformity were taught, and students
received excellent practical training and good discipline.
Some of the best of the students went for higher training
to the universities of the Continent.

The Nonconformist academies trained such theologians as :
(1) *Matthew Henry* († 1714), a pupil of Thomas Doolittle at
Islington, and author of *Expositions of the Old and New Testaments*, in which the Biblical exegesis of Puritanism attained on
the practical side its highest mark ; [1] (2) *Isaac Watts* († 1748),
student at the academy in Stoke Newington, called by Mont-
gomery ' the inventor of English hymns ' ; [2] (3) *John Taylor*
of Norwich († 1761), pupil of Thomas Dixon at Whitehaven,
disciple of *Samuel Clarke* [3] and the philosopher *Locke* († 1704),
and author of a Paraphrase on Romans, a Hebrew Concordance,
The Scriptural Doctrine of Original Sin, and other important
doctrinal works.

After the Revolution of 1688 the Nonconformists
began to plan for the training of their ministry in public
colleges. In the course of the eighteenth century a
number of such colleges were founded, including : [4]

(1) *Homerton College*, established in London (*c.* 1744) by the
combination of two earlier schools, the *Fund Academy* (*c.* 1695)
and the *Academy of the King's Head Society* (*c.* 1730). The first
teachers of theology in the *Fund Academy* included : *Thomas
Goodwin* (1696), son of the famous Thomas († 1680), leader of the
Independents in the Westminster Assembly ; *Isaac Chauncey*
(1701-1712), son of Charles († 1672), the second president of

---

[1] *Vide* Briggs, *Study of Holy Scripture*, p. 467.
[2] *Vide* Christlieb, ' Watts,' in *Schaff-Herzog Encyclopedia*, 1st ed.
[3] *Vide* p. 176.
[4] *Vide Calendar of the Congregational Colleges of England and Wales*,
1879, pp. 11 *seq.*

Harvard College ; and *Thomas Ridgley* (1712-1734), author of a *Body of Divinity*.

(2) *Coward College*, founded by the liberality of a London merchant in 1738, and under the instruction of *Philip Doddridge* until his death († 1751). Doddridge, a pupil of Samuel Clarke and John Jennings, published a *Family Expositor*, or practical commentary on the Bible, which was of great service to the churches.

(3) *Highbury College*, established in 1778 by an evangelical society to promote the evangelical movement. These three colleges were united in 1850 as (4) *New College*, which became the chief Congregational seminary of England.

(5) *Western College* was founded at Plymouth by the Congregational Fund Board (1752). (6) *Rotherham College* was established in Yorkshire (1756); (7) the *Countess of Huntingdon's College* at Cheshunt (1768) ; and (8) *Airedale College* at Bradford (1800).

A number of other Congregational colleges were founded in the nineteenth century, but all were of the same type. In the older academies the course was usually a mixed course of theology and philosophy, extending over four years ; in the colleges the course was one of five years, two in philosophy and three in theology.

The Presbyterian (Unitarian) Board founded *Carmarthen College* in 1697 ; the Congregational Fund Board *Brecon College* in 1757, after the separation from the Presbyterians. The Baptists established similar institutions ; so also the Wesleyans and other bodies.

All of these schools were of the same type, offering a preparatory philosophical course and a theological course—essentially the same type as the Tridentine Seminaries. These English Seminaries exerted upon the Nonconformists an influence similar to that of the Tridentine Seminaries upon the Roman Catholics.

There was a constant irritation between the men trained practically in the seminaries and the men trained theoretically in the universities. The ministers trained in the universities of Holland were either

Scholastics, or advocates of the Covenant Theology. Those trained in the Scottish universities were either Scholastics, or men influenced by the Free Thought of the eighteenth century.

Early in that century the Nonconformists of Britain began to be agitated by the spirit of inquiry that was already active in the Church of England in *William Whiston* († 1752), *Samuel Clarke* († 1729), and others. *Thomas Emlyn* († 1743), a Presbyterian minister of Dublin, was the first to advocate Semi-Arianism. He was removed from his associate ministry in 1702. *James Pierce* of Exeter adopted similar opinions from Clarke and Whiston (*c.* 1717). The ministers of Exeter appealed to London for advice. The London ministers debated the matter for a long time. In 1719 they divided on the subject of subscription. The majority were opposed to subscription. The minority separated and subscribed to the first of the *Articles of Religion* of the Church of England, and to the fifth and sixth Questions of the *Westminster Shorter Catechism*. The Presbyterians were chiefly non-subscribers ; [1] the Congregationalists chiefly subscribers.[2] This division resulted in the gradual departure of the English Presbyterians from the Westminster Faith until the whole body became Unitarian. The Congregationalists, however, remained orthodox, and to a great extent reactionary.

The same conflict arose in Scotland over the case of *John Simson* († 1740), professor of divinity in the University of Glasgow, who sought to reconcile Christianity with modern thought within the sphere of historical Christianity, but was regarded as compromised in an anti-trinitarian direction, and so warned by the General Assembly in 1717.[3] His views continued to excite the Church of Scotland until his final suspension in 1729.

Steadily but surely the universities of Scotland, as well as those of England, came into the hands of representatives of Free Thought, who were named *Moderates* ; and these maintained their supremacy into the nineteenth century. The Scholastics, who at first had succeeded in driving out the men of piety, the *narrow men*, as they were called, under the leadership

[1] Fifty non-subscribers to twenty-six subscribers and nine neutrals.
[2] Twenty-three subscribers to seven non-subscribers and five neutrals.
[3] *Vide* Briggs, *Theological Symbolics*, p. 243.

of the Erskines, were at last themselves overcome by Moderatism.

13. *The revival of the study of Theology took place gradually in Germany during the eighteenth century by the introduction of the new learning, especially as based on the inductive method and the inductive sciences, and under the influence of the Universities of Halle and Göttingen.*

The older universities resisted the movement so long as they could. Some of them became extinct ; others were removed and united to newer foundations ; others gradually adopted the new methods. The first modern university was that of *Halle*, which was founded in 1694, under the same influences as those which produced the *Academy of Sciences* in Berlin (1700), by the instrumentality of Leibnitz and his associates. The university of *Halle* gained its character under the influence of the two scholars who were its chief teachers at the beginning : *Thomasius* († 1728), a jurist, rationalistic in tendency ; and *Francke*,[1] a theologian and a Pietist. Both were opposed to the scholastic methods and slavish imitation of the classic writers which generally prevailed, and they were united against these tendencies. But they also represented other opposing tendencies that soon came into conflict. This conflict came to a head in connection with the philosopher, *Christian Wolff* († 1754), whose more pronounced Rationalism brought him into trouble. He was expelled from the University of Halle (1723), but was called to Marburg, and his influence constantly increased. In 1740 he was recalled to Halle in triumph, and the victory finally won for freedom of scholarship. Upon that principle the University of *Göttingen* was founded in 1734. These two institutions now became the leading universities of Germany, and so remained throughout the eighteenth century.

[1] *Vide* p. 167.

At *Halle* the theological professors reverted from the Scholastic Theology to the Positive Theology. They devoted themselves to the study of the Scriptures in the original languages, to the study of the Lutheran symbolical books, and to the practice of piety.

Among the theologians of *Halle* were : (1) *Johann Heinrich Michaelis* († 1738), the Hebrew scholar ; (2) his nephew, collaborator and successor at Halle, *Christian Benedict Michaelis* († 1764) ; (3) *Baumgarten*, who taught at Halle from 1730 until his death in 1757, and exerted great influence through his works on Church History and Doctrine ; his disciple (4) *Semler* († 1791), a Biblical scholar, and the channel through which the historical method of interpretation made its way into Lutheran Germany.[1] Through these theologians Halle became distinguished for Biblical and symbolical scholarship.

The first great theological teacher of *Göttingen* was (1) *Mosheim* († 1755), formerly of Helmstädt, a scholar of encyclopædic learning and a preacher of great eloquence, who contributed important works to almost all the departments of theology, and made Church History a new discipline. He was followed by (2) *Johann David Michaelis* († 1791), son of *Christian Benedict*, who produced Biblical works of great value ; (3) *Eichhorn* († 1827), the father of the Higher Criticism, who carried its methods into the entire Old Testament with the hand of a master, and laid the foundation of views that have been maintained ever since.[2] These men made Göttingen a great seat of Biblical and historical scholarship.

Leipzig also became an important centre of Biblical study through the labours of *Ernesti* († 1781), the chief of the new era of Biblical interpretation in Germany. Essentially a philologist rather than a theologian, he began at the foundation of interpretation, grammatical exegesis, and placed it in such a position before the world that it has ever since maintained its fundamental importance.[3]

In Austria and Southern Germany also the new methods gradually conquered the old in the Catholic universities, greatly to the mortification of the Jesuits, who were driven by degrees from one institution after

---

[1] *Vide* Briggs, *Study of Holy Scripture*, p. 470.
[2] *Vide* Briggs, *ibid.*, pp. 279 *seq.*   [3] *Vide* Briggs, *ibid.*, p. 469.

another, and from one country after another, until the
order was suppressed by the pope (1773), and its
influence was reduced to a minimum. So at the close
of the eighteenth century Roman Catholic and Protestant scholars were more at one than they had been
since the Reformation ;[1] and, it may be added, than
they have been since that time. But the enlightened
rulers of Austria and Bavaria, however much they
improved the universities, did great mischief by the
destruction of the Catholic seminaries, or the merging
of the smaller in larger seminaries, thereby destroying
their character and making them poor copies of the
universities. In Protestant Germany, however, and
so it may be said in Holland and Switzerland, the
development was more normal. The chief result of the
reformation of the universities was the deliverance of
theological instruction from bondage to the Church and
to the State, and the establishment of the principle of
freedom of scholarship.

14. *The revival of the study of Theology extended all
along the line of theological scholarship, and resulted in
new theological learning, the opening up of numerous
new fields of theological study, and a zealous and enthusi-
astic pursuit of these, in which all countries began to take
part.*

The gain may be said to have been in these four
particulars :

(1) Freedom of instruction, over against limitation by authority.

(2) The new philosophy of Wolff and Kant, based on Cosmology and Physics, over against Aristotle.

(3) The new Humanism, in place of the imitative study of
the Classics : a critical historical study.

(4) The use of the modern languages in place of Latin.[2]

---

[1] *Vide* Paulsen, *Gesch. des gelehrten Unterrichts*, ii. p. 123.

[2] Paulsen, ii. p. 145.

Several new theological disciplines were opened up, especially at Halle.

I. The discipline of *Theological Encyclopædia* was first established by *Mursinna* [1] of Halle (1764).

II. The foundations for the discipline of *Symbolics* were laid by *Baumgarten* [2] of Halle (1750) ; and *G. J. Planck* [3] united *Symbolics* with *Polemics* (1796) in a broader scheme. [4]

III. In *Biblical Study* the gain may be given with more detail :

A. The Text. In England *John Mill* issued a critical edition of the New Testament (1707), and was assailed by unthinking men, who preferred pious ignorance to a correct text of the New Testament ; but he was sturdily defended by the great Cambridge scholar, *Richard Bentley* († 1742), the father of the Higher Criticism in England. Bishop *Lowth* († 1787) called the attention of scholars to the necessity of emending the Massoretic text of the Old Testament, and discerned and set forth the principles of Hebrew poetry (1753-1778). *Kennicott* († 1783) collated a large number of Hebrew manuscripts for his monumental work on the state of the printed Hebrew text of the Old Testament, with various readings (1753-1780). On the Continent the work of Mill was continued by *Bengel* (1725-1734), *Wetstein* (1751-1752), and *Griesbach* (1785-1793). Lowth's work was carried on in Germany especially by *Michaelis* of Göttingen (1770) and by *Koppe* (1779-1780). [5]

B. The Higher Criticism. *Astruc*, a French physician, discovered the several documents of the Pentateuch in 1753. His work was taken to Germany by *Jerusalem* (1762). *Eichhorn* of Göttingen came independently to the same conclusion in 1779. The poet *Herder* († 1803) first caught the Oriental spirit in his *Geist der hebräischen Poesie* (1782-1783). All these results were combined by *Eichhorn* (1780) in the discipline of *Higher Criticism.* [6]

---

[1] *Vide* Mursinna, *Primæ lineæ encyclopædiæ theologicæ.*
[2] *Vide* Baumgarten, *Kurz Begriff der theologischen Streitigkeiten.*
[3] *Vide* Planck, *Abriss einer historischen und vergleichenden Darstellung der dogmatischen Systeme unserer verschiedenen christlichen Hauptpartheyen.*
[4] *Vide* Briggs, *Theological Symbolics,* pp. 24 *seq.*
[5] *Vide* Briggs, *Study of Holy Scripture,* pp. 226 *seq.*
[6] *Vide* Briggs, *ibid.,* pp. 278 *seq.*

C. Biblical Interpretation. *Ernesti* of Leipzig applied to the Bible the principles employed in the interpretation of the ancient classics (1761). *Semler* of Halle urged the importance of historical interpretation (1760-1769). These scholars laid the foundations of the grammatico-historical school of Biblical study.[1]

D. Biblical History was studied in England by *Prideaux* (1716-1718), *Shuckford* (1727-1728), *Stackhouse* (1732), and *Paley* (1790); in France by *Basnage* (1704-1706) and *Calmet* (1722); in Holland by *Reland* (1704-1708) and *Spannheim* (*Opera,* 1701-1703); in Switzerland by *Hess* (1768-1788); in Germany by *Waehner* (1701-1703), *Buddeus* (1715-1718), and especially by *Michaelis* (1769-1775).[2]

E. Biblical Theology. The foundations of this discipline were first laid by *Gabler* of Jena in 1787. There was, however, preparatory work done by *Zachariä* of Halle, and Göttingen (1771-1775), on the Pietistic side. *Ammon* also published works on Biblical Theology from the Rationalistic side (1792-1801).[3]

IV. *Church History* before *Mosheim* had been the handmaid of Polemic Theology. The great polemic histories were the Protestant *Magdeburger Centurien,*[4] and the reply of the Roman Catholic *Baronius* in his *Annales ecclesiastici,*[5] continued by *Raynaldus, Theiner,* and others. The British historical writers, like *Ussher* and *Bingham,*[6] were chiefly interested in antiquities and institutions. *Calixtus* had vainly tried to infuse a more irenic spirit and objective method. *Mosheim* was the first to give Church History its position as an independent, strictly objective, historical discipline in his *Institutiones historiæ ecclesiasticæ* (1755). And so there began a detailed and thorough research into various fields of historical investigation, which gradually resulted in the outlining of many sub-departments of Church History. *Schröck,* a pupil of Mosheim, wrote a very elaborate Church History in forty-five volumes (1768-1812), in

---

[1] *Vide* Briggs, *Study of Holy Scripture,* pp. 469 *seq.*
[2] *Vide* Briggs, *ibid.,* pp. 490 *seq.*
[3] *Vide* Briggs, *ibid.,* pp. 575 *seq.*
[4] 13 vols., 1559-1574.   [5] 12 vols., 1588-1607.
[6] *Vide* pp. 153-155.

which he adopted the division of Church History into periods, instead of the older division into centuries. It is valuable for its information as to sources; but, as Schaff remarks, 'Nobody ever read it through except the author and proof reader.'[1] The principles of Mosheim were followed by *C. W. F. Walch*, also of Göttingen († 1784), who established the discipline of the *History of Doctrine* and other branches of Church History, such as the *History of the Popes, of the Sects*, and so on. All came into play, and each department was thoroughly searched by the investigations. The *History of Christian Literature* received especial attention from such scholars as *Fabricius* († 1736), *J. C. Wolf* († 1739), *Pfaff* († 1760), and *J. G. Walch* († 1775).

V. *Dogmatics* was delivered from bondage to the scholastic method of the Aristotelian philosophy. The ancient conflict between Positive Theology and Philosophical Theology was renewed. In the Roman Catholic seminaries and universities Positive Theology remained a comprehensive system, including both the Bible and the Fathers; but in Protestant universities Biblical Theology set forth the Theology of the Bible, and Symbolical Theology that of the Symbols of the Church. Over against these in the Catholic seminaries was the Scholastic Theology in a more chaste form. In Protestant universities the system of theology was constructed on the basis of the various systems of philosophy as these arose from time to time: at first the Pietistic over against the Rational of the school of Wolff; then the Kantian, which appeared at the close of the period.

VI. *Practical Theology.* More attention was given to the scholarly or scientific side of this department of theology; and it was elaborated in Theological Encyclopædia into a number of logically defined, separate departments, which were studied by scholars in purely

---

[1] Schaff, *Theological Propædeutics*, p. 300.

scholarly interests; as, for instance, *Catechetics, Liturgics, Church Law*, and the *History of Preaching*. The older system of disputation and declamation gradually disappeared from the universities. In place of these there was established at Göttingen for the first time a *Predigerseminar*, for practical exercise in preaching and teaching.[1]

[1] The theological *Seminar* of the university for the purpose of training in theological investigation belongs to a later time, and began in the schools of philology and philosophy (*vide* p. 187).

CHAPTER IV

THE STUDY OF THEOLOGY IN THE NINETEENTH CENTURY

THE eighteenth century closed with the storms of the French Revolution and the wars of Napoleon, which continued into the second decade of the nineteenth century. With these were also associated the American Revolution and the establishment of the United States of America. The wars of Napoleon wrought havoc all over Europe, and resulted in the destruction of a large number of universities and the establishment of new ones. The old universities were regarded as scholastic, pedantic, and reactionary by the statesmen of Europe.

Five Protestant universities either died or were closed up: those of *Erfurt, Helmstädt, Rinteln, Duisburg,* and *Altdorf.* Two others, those of *Wittenberg* and *Frankfort-on-the-Oder,* were combined with other universities; Wittenberg with *Halle* (1815), and Frankfort with *Breslau* (1811).

Ten Catholic institutions perished; and one, that of *Ingolstadt,* was eventually absorbed by the new university at *Munich.* Those that perished were: *Cologne, Mayence, Trèves, Paderborn, Fulda, Bamberg, Dillingen, Linz, Salzburg,* and *Olmütz*; among them some of the most famous schools of olden times.

Several new universities were established: those of

Berlin (1810), *Breslau* (1811), and *Bonn* (1818), by
Prussia ; and that of *Munich* (1826), by Bavaria.

1. *The new universities took the lead in the educational
movements of the nineteenth century. But they received
their impulse, not only from the new spirit of the revolutionary epoch, but also from the scholars of the older universities, especially those of Halle, Göttingen, and Königsberg.*

At *Halle* the new theological learning was chiefly
practical Biblical scholarship ; at *Göttingen* it bore fruit
in the fields of Church History and Biblical Criticism.
Königsberg produced the first in a series of great philosophers—*Kant*, followed by *Fichte* († 1814), *Hegel* († 1831),
Schelling († 1854), and their associates and successors—
who undermined and well-nigh destroyed the ancient
philosophical forms in which Christian doctrine had
been framed.[1]

Immanuel Kant (1724-1804) was trained at Königsberg, and
taught philosophy and other subjects there for over forty years
(1755-1796). Among his great works may be mentioned his
Kritik der reinen Vernunft (1781, 1787), *Kritik der praktischen
Vernunft* (1788), *Die Religion innerhalb der Grenzen der blossen
Vernunft* (1793), and *Die Metaphysik der Sitten* (1797). Kant
insisted upon a religion in accordance with the practical reason—
a religion of morality, and upon an ethical interpretation of
Scripture and history. His views produced a profound impression at the close of the eighteenth and the beginning of the
nineteenth century ; and several prominent theologians adopted
his principles, among them : *Tieftrunk*[2] of Halle (1791-1795) ;
Ammon[3] of Göttingen and Erlangen (1797) ; *Stäudlin*,[4] also of
Göttingen (1800) ; and *J. W. Schmid*[5] of Jena (1797). But, as
Gieseler states, ' the philosophy of Kant did not permanently
maintain this influence in theology.'[6] It was not his philo-

---

[1] *Vide* Briggs, *Theological Symbolics*, p. 245.
[2] *Vide* Tieftrunk, *Censur des christlichen protestantischen Lehrbegriffs.*
[3] *Vide* Ammon, *Entwurf einer wissenschaftlich-practischen Theologie.*
[4] *Vide* Stäudlin, *Dogmatik und Dogmengeschichte.*
[5] *Vide* J. W. Schmid, *Ueber christliche Religion.*
[6] Gieseler, v. p. 323.

sophic principles that prevailed; but his critical method of investigation, which became characteristic of the age.

2. *The University of Berlin became the great theological centre of Germany; and a series of great teachers of Theology and Philosophy, as well as of all other branches of learning, has continued there all through the century and until the present time.*

Schleiermacher was raised up to be the father of the modern German evangelical theology. He began to build the structure of modern theology in the true mystic spirit on the religious feeling, apprehending Jesus Christ as Saviour. A series of intellectual giants carried on his work, such as *Neander, Tholuck, Rothe, Müller,* and *I. A. Dorner.* These led German Theology back to the position of the Protestant reformers.[1]

Friedrich Schleiermacher (1768-1834), the great reformer of theology at the beginning of the nineteenth century, studied at Halle, and in 1793 began to teach and to preach at Berlin. After more than a decade he went to teach in the University of Halle, and in 1806 was made full professor there. It was not long, however, before he returned to Berlin, where he became one of the first professors in the new university (1810), and dean of the theological faculty. Schleiermacher combined the critical method with evangelical piety. He reorganised theological study, the discipline of *Encyclopædia*, the system of theology, and enriched all branches of theological learning. His many influential writings include: *Reden über die Religion, Kurze Darstellung des theologischen Studiums,* and *Christlicher Glaube nach den Grundsätzen der evangelischen Kirche.*

3. *Berlin was sustained by the newer universities of Bonn and Breslau, and also by those of the previous century, Halle and Göttingen; and gradually all of the universities adopted the newer methods of theological study.*

These methods were: (1) *Theological investigation*: research over the whole field of theology. This was promoted, not only by the stimulation, through *lectures,*

---

[1] *Vide* Briggs, *Study of Holy Scripture*, p. 158.

of professors who themselves were engaged in research, but also by the establishment of *Seminars* for the special training of the more advanced students.

The earliest *Seminar* was one in Philology, established at Halle, by F. A. Wolf, in 1787. Such a Seminar was opened at Berlin in 1812 ; one for Natural Science was founded at Bonn in 1825 ; and an historical Seminar at Königsberg in 1832. In the theological Seminar conducted by I. A. Dorner at Berlin, that great scholar is said to have ' developed his highest qualities as a teacher of youth.' [1]

(2) *A comprehensive training*, by a large number of professors (ordinary and extraordinary professors, and licentiates), covering the whole field of theology ; and in several kinds of courses (ordinary, private, and most private).

The number of full professors in the theological faculty of the German university at the present time is usually five ; but some universities have a larger faculty, and those of Berlin and Bonn number ten. The number of *Ausserordentliche Professoren* and of *Privatdozenten* varies. The department of theology is usually divided into 5 sections, embracing the *Old* and *New Testaments, Church History, Systematic* and *Practical Theology*. The course may be extended from three to five or more years, and divided between several universities. Training for the practical work of the ministry must be sought at a *Predigerseminar*, or in service as pastor's assistant.[2]

4. *The revival of the study of Theology was not confined to Germany, but extended into other countries. It was generally characterised by the spirit of free theological investigation, and led to the organisation of a large number of new theological disciplines, such as Biblical Theology, Symbolics, Irenics, and Theological Encyclopædia. Among Roman Catholics it became a revival of Positive Theology and of Patristic.*

[1] Simon, ' Isaac August Dorner,' in *Presbyterian Review*, October 1887, vol. viii. p. 587.
[2] For further details *vide* W. A. Brown, *Theological Education*, in Monroe's *Cyclopedia of Education*, v. pp. 589 *seq*.

Great Britain and America, yes, France, Holland, Switzerland and the Scandinavian countries, were dependent upon German Theology all through the nineteenth century. The reason for this dependence was that German scholars ranged over the entire field of theology with freedom of scholarship both to investigate and to write and teach. But British and American Theology had its own peculiar principles and methods, and its own work to perform. In the latter part of the century the tide of thought, which has ebbed and flowed between Great Britain and the Continent several times since the Reformation, began to turn, and to set strongly in our direction.[1]

It is impossible to cover the entire field of modern theological study in a few pages. Only a few of the most important achievements of the nineteenth century can be referred to here.

5. *Theological Encyclopædia, first established as a theological discipline by Mursinna of Halle,[2] was reorganised by Schleiermacher, and further developed by other scholars.*

Schleiermacher, in his *Kurze Darstellung des theologischen Studiums* (1811, 1830), reorganised the discipline of Theological Encyclopædia, and gave to it a more thorough exposition.

He was followed by a large number of scholars, such as: *Rosenkranz* (1831); *Hagenbach* (1833); *Harless* (1837); *Pelt* (1843); *Lange* (1877); *Hofmann* (1879) and *Rothe* (1880) in posthumous works; *Räbiger* (1880); *Heinrici* (1893).[3] Among Roman Catholic scholars may be mentioned *Klee* (1832); *Staudenmaier* (1834, 1840); *Wirtmüller* (1874); and *Kihn* (1892). The chief German works now in use are those of

---

[1] *Vide* Briggs, *Study of Holy Scripture*, p. 158.
[2] *Vide* p. 180.
[3] August Dorner's *Grundriss der Encyklopädie der Theologie* appeared in 1901.

Hagenbach and *Kihn*.[1] Less attention has been given to the
subject in other countries. I may refer, however, to the works
of *Kienlen* (1842), and *Martin* (1883), for France; those of
Clarisse (1832), *Hofstede de Groot* and *Pareau* (1851), and *Kuyper*
(1894; English, 1898), for Holland; those of *Hannah* (1875),
Drummond (1884), and *Cave* (1886, 1896), for Great Britain;
those of *M'Clintock* (1873), *Crooks* and *Hurst* (on the basis of
Hagenbach, 1884, 1894), and *Schaff* (1892-1893), for the United
States.[2]

6. *There was a great revival of Biblical study in the
latter part of the nineteenth century, and Biblical scholarship assumed the importance that it had in the sixteenth
and seventeenth centuries.*

In the latter part of the eighteenth century and the
first half of the nineteenth century Biblical studies were
neglected. But in the second half of the latter century
there was a great change, and Biblical studies came to
the front.[3] Important work was done in many departments:

(1) *The Biblical Languages*.[4] The *Hebrew* language was studied
especially by *Gesenius* of Halle and *Rödiger* of Berlin. Their
work was reproduced by *Edward Robinson* in the United States
and by *Davidson* in Great Britain, and was carried on in the
New Hebrew Lexicon (1906) by *Francis Brown, S. R. Driver*, and
C. A. Briggs. The study of Hebrew grammar was greatly
advanced in Germany by *Gesenius, Hupfeld* and *Kautzsch* of
Halle, *Böttcher* of Dresden, *Ewald* of Göttingen, *Stade* of Giessen,
and *König* of Bonn; in Great Britain, chiefly by *Davidson* and
Driver; in the United States by *Nordheimer, Green*, and *Harper*.
The *Greek* language was studied especially by *Winer* and
Buttmann for grammar; and for lexicography by *Grimm*, whose

---

[1] Hagenbach, *Encyklopädie und Methodologie der theologischen Wissenschaften*, 1833, 1884[10,11], ed. Kautzsch; 1889[12], ed. Reischle; Kihn,
Encyklopädie und Methodologie der Theologie, 1892.

[2] In the latter part of the century encyclopædic works on theology
began to be issued in serial form. Of these the *International Theological
Library* (1891- —), founded and edited by Dr. Briggs, is an example.

[3] *Vide* Briggs, 'Study of the English Bible,' in *Presbyterian Review*, **x.**
pp. 295 *seq.*

[4] *Vide* Briggs, *Study of Holy Scripture*, pp. 42 *seq.*

work was reproduced in the United States by *Edward Robinson* of New York, and *Thayer* of Cambridge, Massachusetts.

(2) The *Textual Criticism* [1] of the Old Testament has been carried on chiefly in recent times in Germany, through the texts of *Baer* and *Delitzsch*, and, still more recently, of *Kittel*, and by the work of *Hermann Strack* of Berlin. In England, *Davidson* did important work as a forerunner. But Ginsburg's *Massora* is the greatest achievement since the Reformation in that line, and his Hebrew Bible has great merit. The *Polychrome Bible*, edited by *Haupt* of Baltimore, and published in parts, began to appear in 1894, many scholars on both sides of the Atlantic taking part in the work. The text of particular books was studied by *Wellhausen, Baethgen, Cornill, S. R. Driver, Klostermann, Beer*, and others. In New Testament Criticism there was a succession of great critics: in Germany, *Scholz* (1830-1836), *Lachmann* (1831-1850), *Tischendorf, Gregory, Gebhardt, Weiss*, and *Blass*; in England, *Tregelles* (1857-1872), *Scrivener, Westcott, Hort, Rendel Harris*, and others; in the United States, *Ezra Abbot* of Harvard.[2]

(3) The *Biblical Versions* have been studied especially in Germany by *Lagarde* (Bötticher) of Göttingen, and *Nestle* of Maulbronn; in Italy by *Ceriani* of Milan; in England by *Swete* of Cambridge, *Wordsworth, Brooke, M'Lean*, and others.

(4) The *Higher Criticism*,[3] established by *Eichhorn* of Göttingen in 1780, has had a long development and a terrific struggle. In the several stages of progress three hypotheses were unfolded: *I. The Documentary Hypothesis* of Eichhorn (over against the *Fragmentary Hypothesis* of Geddes, 1792, and Vater, 1805), adopted among others by *Edward Robinson*; *II. The Genetic Hypothesis* of *De Wette*, followed by *Gesenius, Bleek, Ewald, Knobel, Hupfeld*, and others; battled with by *Hengstenberg, Hävernick* and *Keil* in Germany; adopted by *Samuel Davidson, Dean Stanley*, and, in a measure, by *Perowne*. *III. The Development Hypothesis* of Reuss (1833), *Vatke, Graf, Wellhausen, Colenso, Kalisch*, and most modern scholars.

The Higher Criticism of the New Testament is involved in that of the Old, but the Old Testament has been the battleground.

---

[1] Briggs, *Study of Holy Scripture*, pp. 226 *seq.*
[2] [The work of Dr. Briggs in this department includes the planning of the *International Critical Commentary* (1895-—), its editorship in conjunction with S. R. Driver and A. Plummer, and his own contribution to the series.]
[3] *Vide* Briggs, *Study of Holy Scripture*, pp. 282 *seq.*; also *Higher Criticism of the Hexateuch*, 1893, 1897.

The conflict resulted in the *Robertson Smith* case in Great Britain, the *Briggs* case in the United States, the *Loisy* case in France and Italy.[1]

(5) *Historical Criticism.*[2] In this department four hypotheses have been advanced : *I. The Mythical Hypothesis* of *G. L. Baur* (1820) for the Old Testament, and of *Strauss* (1835) for the New; overcome by *Ullmann, Neander,* and others. *II. The Legendary Hypothesis,* set forth in Renan's *Life of Jesus* (1863), rejected by *Keim, Weiss, Beyschlag, Wendt* and others. *III. The Development Hypothesis,* applied by *F. C. Baur* to the New Testament, by *Vatke* to the Old Testament, under the influence of the Hegelian philosophy ; overcome by *Neander, Dorner, Lechler, Weiss* and others. *IV. The Hypothesis of the School of Ritschl,* according to which Catholic Christianity is rather Greek and Roman than Jewish ; and, in the Old Testament, the Persian and Babylonian religions dominate the Israelitish.

(6) *Contemporaneous History.* The earliest writer in this department is *Schneckenburger* of Bern, whose *Neutestamentliche Zeitgeschichte* appeared in 1862. He was followed by *Hausrath* (1868-1874), *Schürer, Holtzmann, Porter,* and others, for the New Testament. This department was not organised for the Old Testament, although *Bertheau* paved the way (1842). But a large amount of preparatory work was done, especially in the study of the archæology and the history of the other Oriental nations, by *Schrader, George Smith, Lenormant, Robertson Smith, Francis Brown, Ebers, Erman, Baudissin, Baethgen, Tiele, M'Curdy,* and others.

(7) To *Biblical Archæology* contributions of value were made by *Ewald* (1844), *Saalschütz* (1855-1856), *Keil, Benzinger, Nowack,* and other scholars.

(8) *Biblical Geography* was greatly advanced in the nineteenth century. *Reland* had summed up all previous knowledge of Palestine, and laid the foundations of the discipline in 1714 ; but the father of modern Biblical Geography is *Edward Robinson,* who made a personal investigation of the greater part of the Holy Land in two expeditions (1837, 1852), and published the results in three monumental volumes (1838-1860). An important systematic work was written by *Carl Ritter* (1848-1855). The work of Robinson was followed up by *Tobler, De Saulcy,*

---

[1] [For these and other cases *vide* Briggs, *Study of Holy Scripture,* pp 286 *seq.* ; for the Briggs case, *vide The Case against Professor Briggs'* 1892, 1893 ; *The Defence of Professor Briggs,* 1893.]

[2] *Vide* Briggs, *Study of Holy Scripture,* pp. 491 *seq.* ; also *Biblical History,* 1890 ; *New Light on the Life of Jesus,* 1904.

Sepp, Guérin, Stanley, Tristram, Merrill, Wetzstein, Palmer, Arnaud, Thomson, and *Trumbull.* A new impulse was given to the study of Biblical Geography by the Palestine Exploration Societies, established in England, the United States, and Germany, by their journals, maps, and other publications. Valuable contributions were made towards the close of the century by *Socin, George Adam Smith, Ramsay,* and *Gautier.*

(9) *Biblical Chronology* was studied by *Wieseler* (1843), *Caspari* (1869), *Niebuhr* (1896), and others.

(10) *Biblical Theology,*[1] first organised as a discipline by Gabler (1787), had a rich development in Germany, but only a slight one outside of Germany. *Schmid* first gave to this department its proper place in Theological Encyclopædia. [The first to write upon this subject in the United States, so far as known, was the author,[2] who published an Inaugural Address upon *Biblical Theology* in 1870.[3] At that time] the chief works were posthumous : those of *Schmid* (for the New Testament), and of *Oehler* (for the Old Testament), both of the University of *Tübingen.* The most important works of the century published since that time are those of *Ewald* (1871-1876), *Kuenen, Riehm* and *Dillmann* (both posthumous), *Smend, Wendt,* and *Holtzmann,* in Germany ; *Toy* and *Stevens,* in America ; *Duff* and *Davidson,* in Great Britain.

7. *The nineteenth century was characterised by historical investigation over a very extensive field.*

The great historians of the nineteenth century were chiefly Germans :

(1) *Neander* of Berlin († 1850) made an epoch in Church History. His *General History of the Christian Religion and Church* [4] extends to the Council of Basel (1430). It is comprehensive in method, not only dividing by periods, but in each period dividing again by departments. This method, while advantageous for

---

[1] *Vide* Briggs, *Study of Holy Scripture,* pp. 569 *seq.*

[2] [Dr. Briggs was also the first in the United States to attempt a complete course of lectures upon Biblical Theology, and held the first professorship on the subject from 1890-1904, publishing works on the theology of both Testaments: *Messianic Prophecy* (1886, 1902[9]), *Messiah of the Gospels* (1894), *Messiah of the Apostles* (1895), *The Incarnation of the Lord* (1902), *The Ethical Teaching of Jesus* (1904).]

[3] Briggs, 'Biblical Theology,' in *American Presbyterian Review,* 1870, pp. 105 *seq.,* 293 *seq.* ; *Presbyterian Review,* 1882, vol. iii. pp. 503 *seq.*

[4] Neander, *Allgemeine Geschichte der christlichen Religion und Kirche,* 1825-1852, 1863-1865[4]; English, 1847-1852, 1882.

thoroughness of treatment, involves considerable repetition; and the unity of the movement of history is lost in details.

(2) *Gieseler* of Bonn († 1854), afterwards of Göttingen, used the same method as that of Neander. His Church History [1] has a brief comprehensive text, and is rich in footnotes, giving the original sources.

(3) *F. C. Baur* of Tübingen († 1860) wrote a Church History,[2] both critical and philosophical, under the influence of the Hegelian philosophy, and with a profound insight into historical development. These are the three great Church historians of the middle of the last century.

There were many minor historians at this period, such as the Protestants, *Niedner, Hagenbach* and *Hase* in Germany, *Robertson* in England, *Chastel* in Geneva; and the Roman Catholics, *Moehler* and *Döllinger*, both of whom were the peers of the Protestant writers of the time.

The chief historians in the latter part of the century were: (4) *Philip Schaff* († 1893), of the school of Neander, who thus characterised his own work: ' It is written from the Anglo-German and Anglo-American standpoint, and brings the past in living contact with the present.' [3] Schaff's work is irenic, comprehensive, discursive, boiling over with suggestions about all sorts of things loosely connected with his theme. This is its chief fault.

(5) *Adolf Harnack* of Berlin has not written a general Church History, but deals only with special themes; and in treating of these he writes under the domination of the philosophy of *Ritschl*. His principal work is his History of Christian Doctrine.[4] His greatest service, however, has been in the field of early Christian Literature, and his most valuable contribution to Theology is his history of that Literature.

(6) *Karl Müller* of Breslau and Tübingen produced in his Church History (1892-1902) a judicious work.

(7) *Loofs* of Halle published invaluable *Grundlinien der Kirchengeschichte* (1901).

(8) *Fisher* of Yale wrote a *History of the Christian Church* in

---

[1] Gieseler, *Lehrbuch der Kirchengeschichte*, 1824-1857; the last part issued posthumously by Redepenning in 2 vols., 1855-1857; English translations by Davidson and Hull, revised by H. B. Smith and Stearns, 5 vols., 1857-1880.

[2] Baur's *History* was published in 5 volumes under different titles (several posthumously), 1853-1863.

[3] Schaff, *Theological Propædeutics*, p. 303.

[4] *Vide* p. 196.

1888 ; and (9) *Hurst* published one in two volumes, 1897-1900. Both produced also several lesser historical works.

(10) *Duchesne* of Rome is the great Roman Catholic historian. His monumental work is now in progress (1905- ; English, 1909-). Three volumes have appeared, reaching to the close of the fifth century. Duchesne has written many monographs, the chief of which is his *Origins of Christian Worship* (1889), which has appeared in several editions and has been translated (English, 1902). Duchesne has many disciples, who, like *Batiffol* and *Turmel*, have written valuable monographs.

Church History has been divided into a large number of departments and sub-departments. One may say that all things have been put into the frame of Church History. It is impossible here to do more than mention some of the departments in which important work has been done.

I. *The Study of the Sources*: (1) *Diplomatics*. The work of *Mabillon* (1681) was carried on by *Jaffé* (1851), *Wattenbach*, *Delisle*, and others. (2) *Christian Archæology, Inscriptions, Monuments*, especially the Catacombs, and *Christian Art*. The work of *De Rossi* on Inscriptions (1861-1888), the Catacombs (1864-1877), etc., was continued by *Garrucci, Marucchi, Wilpert*, and others. *Piper* published valuable works on Monumental Theology (1867) and the Mythology of Christian Art (1847-1851). Many books were printed on Christian Art, including the learned works of Lübke, Schultze, Kraus, and others, and the popular works of Mrs. Jameson. Dictionaries of Christian Antiquity and Archæology were issued by *Martigny* (1865), *Kraus* (1880-1886), *Smith* and *Cheetham*; Manuals on Archæology by *Augusti* (1836-1837), *Bennett* (1888), and others ; and sources were collected by *Augusti* (1817-1831), *Binterim* (1825-1837), and a multitude of other scholars.

(3) *Geography* was studied by *Wiltsch* (1846), *Spruner, Grundemann, Werner*, and others.

(4) *Chronology* by *Grotefend* (1819-1844), *Piper* (1841), *Brinkmeier, Brockmann, Latrie*, and others. Chronological Tables were published by *H. B. Smith* (1860), *Kraus* and *Weingarten*.

(5) *Statistics* were studied by *Stäudlin* (1804), *Augusti* (1837-1838), *Wiltsch*, and others.

(6) *Christian Literature* attracted great attention ; and important work was done (*a*) for the *Patristic Period* by *Harnack, Von Gebhardt, Zahn, Lipsius, Lightfoot, Müller, Kihn, Barden-*

hewer, Krüger, Robinson, McGiffert, and many other scholars; (*b*) for the *Middle Ages* by *Gass, Krumbacher, Ebert, Denifle, Ehrle, Potthast,* and others; (*c*) for the *Modern Age* by *Ersch* (1822), *Danz* (1843), *Winer, Darling, Hurst, Gla, Hurter,* and others.[1] Collections of the works of the Fathers, Reformers, and other famous Christian writers appeared in great numbers.

(7) *The History of Church Councils* was studied by *Hefele, Hergenröther, Richter, Bright, Haddan, Stubbs,* and many others. *Richter, Froude,* and others also wrote on special Councils.

(8) The *Saints* and their lives were studied by the Bollandists in their great *Acta Sanctorum* and in the *Analecta Bollandiana*; and also by *Le Blant, Pitra, Egli, Baring-Gould, O'Hanlon, Newman,* and many more. *Piper* published an *Evangelical Calendar* (1850-1871), which was translated in part by *H. M. M'Cracken* as *Lives of the Leaders of Our Church Universal* (1879). Lives of special Saints were also written, like that of St. Francis by *Paul Sabatier,* and that of St. Catherine of Genoa by *Baron Von Hügel.*

(9) *Christian Biography* received many valuable contributions. *Nitzsch* and *Hagenbach* edited the lives of the Fathers of the Lutheran and Reformed Churches. *Brook* and others followed the illustrious example of *Neal* in the preceding century, and studied the lives of the Puritans. *Smith* and *Wace* published a valuable *Dictionary of Christian Biography* (1877-1887). Many series of biographies appeared, and numerous important monographs.

II. *Special Sections of Church History* were studied, such as

(1) *The History of Institutions.* (a) *Worship.* This department attracted such scholars as *Wordsworth, Cabrol,* and *Duchesne.* Collections of Liturgies were made by *Neale, Hammond, Daniel, Littledale, Swainson,* and others. (b) *Government.* On this subject important works were published by *Richter, Sohm, Von Schulte, Hergenröther,* and others. (c) *Canon Law* was studied by *Walther, Von Schulte, Dodd, Fulton,* and others. New editions of the *Corpus juris canonici* were issued by *Richter* (1834-1839) and by Friedberg (1880-1882). (d) *The Papacy* and its history were studied by *Von Ranke* (1834-1839), *Nielson, Pastor, Creighton,* and others; *Particular Popes* by *Law, Roscoe,* and others. *Mirbt* published the Sources, and *Duchesne* prepared an

---

[1] *Vide* also the works on *Theological Encyclopædia* already referred to (pp. 188 f.).

edition of the *Liber Pontificalis*. (e) *The Monastic Orders* received special attention from *Montalembert* (1860-1867), *Heimbucher*, and others.

(2) *The History of Doctrines and Dogmas*. *Neander* and *Baur* wrote histories of doctrine, and also monographs on the history of special doctrines. Baur's works on Gnosticism and on the Trinity are especially noteworthy ; so also are *Julius Müller's* Doctrine of Sin, and above all, *Dorner's* History of the Doctrine of the Person of Christ, the greatest of all monographs of the kind. Dorner also wrote a History of Protestant Theology (1867). *Harnack's* History of Doctrine appeared in major (1886-1890) and minor (1889) editions ; so also that of *Seeberg* (1895-1898, and 1901). *Loofs* published *Leitfaden zum Studium der Dogmengeschichte* (1889, 1906) ; and *G. P. Fisher*, a *History of Christian Doctrine* (1896). The chief Roman Catholic writer on the subject is *Schwane*, whose work was issued in four volumes (1862-1890).

(3) *The History of Christian Life and Morals* was studied by *Uhlhorn*, *Brace*, and others, and valuable monographs were published.

III. *Parts of Church History*, or the *History of Particular Churches*, or of *Special Periods*. A large number of historians devoted their attention to some special part of Church History. Thus *Milman* wrote the History of Latin Christianity ; *Neale* and *Stanley*, the History of Eastern Christianity ; *Friedrich, Hauck*, and others, the Church History of Germany ; *Reuterdahl*, that of Sweden ; *Bright, Stubbs, Hore, Plummer*, and others, that of England ; *Hetherington, Cunningham, Stephen*, and others, that of Scotland ; *Lanigan* and *Killen*, that of Ireland, etc. ; *Hanbury, Dexter*, and others studied the History of Congregationalism ; *Hetherington* and *Mitchell*, that of the Westminster Assembly.[1] Each denomination and every important epoch had its own historians. Several serials were issued, such as the *American Church History Series*, the *Epochs of Church*

[1] [To the study of church history Dr. Briggs contributed a volume on *American Presbyterianism*, 1885, and numerous articles in the *Encyclopædia Britannica*, the *Presbyterian Review*, *Magazine of American History*, and other periodicals.]

History, the *National Churches*, etc. The History of the
Early Church received especial attention from *Neander,
Döllinger, Farrar, Pressensé, Lechler, Wordsworth, Blunt,
Bright, Fisher, McGiffert, Duchesne,* and many others ;
the Mediæval Period from *Hardwick, Moeller, Trench,
Stubbs, Schmidt,* and others ; the Reformation from
Merle D'Aubigné, Hagenbach, Hardwick, Häusser, Fisher,
and others. These are but examples of the numerous
specialists at work in the field of Church History during
the century.

8. *There arose in the course of the century a series of
great systematic theologians, who aimed at a complete
system of Theology, built upon Philosophy and Science,
Bible and History, Church and Creed.*[1]

The older divisions of *Doctrinal Theology* were :
Positive Theology and *Scholastic Theology,* and *Faith*
and *Morals.* These divisions are still retained in the
Roman Catholic Church. In the Protestant Churches,
however, *Positive Theology* has been resolved into
Biblical Theology and *Symbolical Theology.* These are
variously classified. If the main purpose is dogma, they
may be classified as *Biblical Dogmatics* and *Symbolical
Dogmatics* ; if history, as the *History of Doctrine in the
Bible* and the *History of Symbols.* But really both
disciplines have become so comprehensive that we
must classify *Biblical Theology* with the Biblical Department, and *Symbolics* under another head as *Comparative
Theology,* to be considered later on. The usual Protestant
divisions of *Systematic Theology* are *Apologetics, Dogmatics,* and *Ethics.* The division which I have used is
rather *Religion, Faith,* and *Morals.*

1. Under the head of *Religion,* the union and communion of man with God, unfolds the *Philosophy of
Religion,* and the statement and defence of the Christian

---

[1] *Vide* Briggs, *Church Unity*, pp. 331 *seq.*

Religion, or *Apologetic* proper. The recent study of the Ethnic Religions has greatly extended this field, so that it now includes the study of the origin and history of every particular religion and a *Comparative Study of Religion*. These departments of Theology are in their infancy, and must be considered under another head. The older term of *Natural Theology* has gone out of use, and the discipline is now included under the larger term of *Philosophy of Religion*.

2. The *Faith* of the Church as defined in the Bible is *Biblical Dogmatics* ; as defined in the Creeds is *Symbolical Dogmatics* ; as defined by the consent of the Fathers it is *Patristic Dogmatics* ; as defined by the Scholastics it is *Scholastic Dogmatics*. The division of the Church into denominations gave rise to a large number of denominational dogmatics ; those of the Greek Church, the Roman Catholic, the Lutheran, Reformed, Anglican, Methodist, Presbyterian, etc. But most modern divines construct their dogmatics on certain philosophical principles ; and so we have various speculative systems, representing different schools of philosophy and theology.

The chief Roman Catholic systems of the century were those of *Perrone*, a Jesuit (in nine volumes, 1835-1843) ; *Scheeben* (1892) ; *Bilot*, and *Janssen*, a Scholastic. The chief Lutheran systems were those of *Hase*,[1] *Schmid, Twesten, Martensen, Philippi, Thomasius, Luthardt, Kahnis*. The chief writers among the Hegelians were *Marheinecke, Strauss, Biedermann, Pfleiderer* ; among the Mediators, *Müller, Tholuck, Ullmann, Rothe, I. A. Dorner* ; among the Ritschlians, *Ritschl* (1870-1874), *Kaftan*, and *Herrmann*. The Ritschlians exclude Mystic and Metaphysic, and make their *Werturtheilen* the subjective test of all theology. The Neo-Kantians recognise only the earlier Luther, not the later one ; and only that in the New Testament which is commended as of real value. The chief Reformed systems of the Continent were those of *Schweizer* (1844-1856), *Heppe*, and *Ebrard*. The Anglican Church has had practically none since Ussher, except that of *Beveridge* (1710-1711, 1828).

---

[1] Hase, *Hutterus redivivus*, 1829, 1883[12].

The Scottish Presbyterians have had those of *Hill, Dick, Chalmers,* and *Cunningham;* the American Presbyterians those of *Charles* and *A. A. Hodge, Shedd,* and *H. B. Smith.* Among the German Reformed theologians may be mentioned *Gerhart;* among the Wesleyans, *Watson, Pope, Raymond, Miley;* among the American Episcopalians, *Buel;* among the Baptists, *Strong* and *Clarke.*

3. *Christian Ethics,* the third division of Dogmatics, was kept as a separate field in the Roman Catholic Church from the Middle Ages onward, but has only been cultivated by Protestants since the last century. It used to be taught in connection with Philosophical Ethics under the head of *Moral Philosophy.*

Among the chief writers of the century in this department may be mentioned the Protestants, *Neander, Rothe, Gass, Wuttke, I. A. Dorner, Martensen,* and *Newman Smythe;* and the Roman Catholics, *Sailer, Scavini, Hirscher, Klee, Lehmkuhl,* and *Schwane.*

9. *Comparative Theology has risen above all the differences of religious denominations into that higher unity in which they all agree, and endeavours to consider their differences in religion, doctrine, and institution from an irenic point of view.*[1]

1. The *Science of Religion,* as we have seen,[2] has branched out into a large number of different departments, giving the history of every particular religion, and a comparative study of them all. This field of study supplies the first part of *Comparative Theology,* or *Comparative Religion.* The older study of the Ethnic Religions was polemic; the present is historic and pragmatic. There is a tendency towards irenic, as illustrated in the work of *Charles Cuthbert Hall, George W. Knox,* and others. Each religion has to be studied by itself, and then the comparison has to be made between them. If Christianity is the *universal* religion, then the

---

[1] *Vide* Briggs, 'Ideal of the Study of Theology'; Address at *Dedication of the New Buildings of the Union Theological Seminary, New York, 1910,* pp. 133 *seq.*
[2] *Vide* p. 198.

theologian must recognise, with Clement of Alexandria,
that the Philosophy of the Greeks was, in its way, as
truly a preparation for Christianity as the Law of the
Hebrews ; and that the practice of ancient Israel in
taking up into the Old Covenant religion elements of
good, especially from the Babylonian and Persian
religions, and the practice of the ancient Church in
appropriating from the Greek, Roman, and Oriental
religions, is the true and wise course for modern Christianity to adopt, by enlarging this theory and practice,
so as to comprehend all of the religions of the world.

2. The discipline of *Symbolics*,[1] first established by
Planck of Göttingen (1796), has had a long development.

On the basis of the work of Planck, *Marheinecke*
published the first *Christliche Symbolik* (1810), and
Winer his useful comparative study (1824). Möhler
then came into the field with his *Symbolik* (1832, 1889[10]),
which fixed the terminology of the discipline. His work
was followed by those of *F. C. Baur* (1834), *Nitzsch*
(1835), *Hase* (1862, 1894[6]), *Neander* (1863), and others.
Of the writers whose works appeared towards the close
of the century, *H. Schmidt* (1890), *E. F. K. Müller*
(1896), and *Kattenbusch* (1892) may be mentioned.
Many works were written on special subjects, like those
of *Caspari* and *Kattenbusch* on the Apostles' Creed,
and of *Plitt* (1867-1873) on the *Augustana*.

Collections of Symbols were made by *Schaff* for all the Churches
(1877, 1890[5]); by *Niemeyer* (1840) for the Reformed Church; by
Hase (1827, 1845[3]) and *J. T. Müller* (1847-1848, 1890[7]) for the
Lutheran ; by *Streitwolf* and *Klener* (1836-1838), and *Denzinger*
(1854, 1911[11]) for the Roman Catholic ; by *Kimmel* and *Weissen-
born* (1843-1850) for the Greek Church.

Polemics, which had been an important theological
discipline in the preceding century, became discredited,

---

[1] [The latest published works of Dr. Briggs are his contributions to
this department, *The Fundamental Christian Faith*, 1913, and *Theological
Symbolics*, 1914.]

and in modern theology has been well-nigh abandoned. *Irenics* is the newest section of *Symbolics*, yet it has already an extensive literature. It has been most fruitful on the Continent of Europe, where it originated.[1] Irenics is the resultant of all the previous theological disciplines, and puts the copestone upon them all. It studies the concord of Christendom, and on that basis shows the true unity of the Church of Christ ; and it studies the discord, in order, if possible, to dissolve the differences and reconcile them in a higher unity, and in all to promote peace and harmony between all religious bodies.[2]

10. *The field of Practical Theology has also greatly expanded, and many valuable works were produced in this department before the close of the century.*

It is impossible here to do more than give the names of some of the sub-departments, in which important work was accomplished. (1) In the Department of *Religion* may be mentioned *Worship*, especially *Liturgics* and *Hymnology*, the *Sacraments*, *Pastoral Care* and *Pastoral Medicine*. (2) The Department of *Faith* now includes, with *Homiletics* and *Catechetics*, *Sunday Schools*, *Social Clubs*, etc. ; (3) the Department of *Morals*, *Church Government*, *Law* and *Discipline*. In the field of *Missions* (city, country, and foreign) a great advance has been made.

Among the comprehensive works on this branch of theology may be mentioned those written by the Protestants : *Nitzsch, Harms, Van Oosterzee, Von Zezschwitz, Achelis, Krauss,* and *Vaucher* ; and by the Roman Catholics : *Sailer, Hinterberger,* and *Graf.*

---

[1] *Vide* Briggs, *Theological Symbolics*, pp. 16 *seq.* ; 'Symbolics and Irenics,' in *Church Quarterly Review*, 1912, vol. lxxiv., No. 148, pp. 364 *seq.*

[2] [Dr. Briggs worked on the problems of Irenics for nearly thirty years, and published some of the results of his study in his volume on *Church Unity*, 1909.]

11. *The modern universities, like those of the Middle Ages, train theological scholars, but do not train ministers for the Church of Christ. The theological seminaries train ministers, but make no adequate provision for the higher studies of Theology.*

1. The universities of *Germany* have failed to provide the training necessary to an evangelical ministry. The *Predigerseminar* supplies the need only in part ; and the service of pastor's assistant (for two years or more), while necessary and valuable, also fails to accomplish the purpose, because in the university the bent of the student's mind becomes so fixed upon speculative and merely theoretic theology, that it is difficult for him afterwards to become practical. It is well known that the working ministry of Germany has long been dissatisfied with the theological teaching of the universities, and is constantly urging for reform. It is certain that, if these Protestant clergy had their way, the teaching in the universities would be transformed, and the Hegelians and the Ritschlians alike would be banished. But the State stands in the way. The German universities of the nineteenth century and the present one are in exactly the same position as the universities of the Middle Ages. Their methods are excellent for a scientific study of theology, but ineffective for the training of a Christian ministry.

2. Germany was dependent upon *Great Britain* for almost all the practical reforms and religious movements that arose among her people during the past century. And yet in the British universities also the training was altogether inadequate, so far as theology was concerned. These great institutions produced notable scholars ; but they did not supply the training necessary for the ministry of the Church. However, comparatively few of the students, even of those intending to enter the Christian ministry in the Anglican Church, attended the

university courses in theology. The Church of England was obliged to organise Diocesan Seminaries in order to provide the churches with ministers.[1] The Non-conformists were excluded from the universities until recent years. They were obliged to train their ministers in their private colleges ; and yet they have succeeded, notwithstanding all their disadvantages, in winning fully one half of the English people to the various branches of Nonconformity. In Scotland the universities have theological faculties, but with only four professors—a number altogether inadequate to do the work of modern theology. The Free Church with its three colleges, and the United Presbyterian with one (now united with the others in the reunion of those churches), have had more professors, longer courses, and a more thorough appropriation of modern methods and modern departments of theology ; and they have educated a ministry which, in spite of every disadvantage, has won nearly half of the Scottish people to their side.

3. The *French* and *Swiss* Protestants followed the methods of the British nonconforming bodies in their theological seminaries. The universities of Switzerland followed the same course as those of other countries. In *France* two seminaries were established for Protestants by Napoleon (1802) : the one at *Strasburg* for Lutherans, the other at *Geneva* for the Reformed. After the re-attachment of Geneva to Switzerland a new faculty of theology was established at *Montauban* (1808-1810) in connection with the academy of Toulouse. The Protestant faculty of theology at *Strasburg* was transferred to *Paris* in 1877, and became a mixed faculty, representing both the Lutheran and the Reformed Churches.

Towards the close of the century (1896) this Seminary became an organic part of the University of Paris. Two years later

---

[1] There are now twenty-nine theological colleges affiliated with the Church of England (W. A. Brown, *Cyclopedia of Education*, v. p. 592).

one of its professors described it as a ' mixed school . . . holding
a conciliatory attitude toward the parties contending in our
churches,' and as ' holding ground intermediate between the
conservatism of the Montauban Faculty and the rationalistic
bent of the Geneva Faculty.' [1]

In French *Switzerland* the Free Churches separated
from the State and established Free Seminaries in
Geneva, *Lausanne*, and *Neuchâtel*, which have since
educated the Evangelical clergy for French Switzerland
and France.

Baird, writing in 1880, describes the Free Church seminaries
as having a preparatory course or courses, covering from one
to three years, followed by a three years' course of theology
proper. Hebrew, as well as Greek and Latin, was studied in the
preparatory course. In Geneva the number of hours per week
in the Free Church Seminary was thirty ; in the State institution, twenty-one. In all the Seminaries one-third of the time
(8-10 hours weekly) was devoted to Biblical Exegesis, and
divided about equally between the two Testaments.[2]

4. After the disasters of the French Revolution and
the wars of Napoleon, the *Roman Church* devoted itself
to the revival of theological education. For that
purpose it undertook the restoration of the diocesan
seminary and improvement in the training of the priesthood. To this end the Jesuit Order was restored in
1814 ; their college in Rome revived, and put under
their control. The College of the Propaganda was
re-established, as also the Roman Seminary and the
College of Noble Ecclesiastics. The Jesuit Order
reassumed its position at the head of theological education, sustained by the other orders, especially the
Sulpicians in France. The newer learning was only
moderately employed in the seminaries. These reverted

---

[1] Bonet-Maury, 'The Protestant Faculty of Theology of the Paris
University,' in *New World*, 1898, vol. vii., No. 25, p. 128.
[2] *Vide* Baird, 'Notes on Theological Education in the Reformed
Churches of France and French Switzerland,' in *Presbyterian Review*,
1880, vol. i. pp. 85 *seq.*

to a modified Scholasticism, building essentially on
Thomas Aquinas. They have been successful in
reviving in the Roman Catholic Church theological
learning as well as a trained priesthood; but their
general attitude has been reactionary as regards modern
methods. So far as the Catholic universities are concerned, the Catholic Church has patronised them in
Germany [1] and Austria, and has tried so far as possible
to influence and control professors and students; but
only in small measure have they succeeded. The Old
Catholics of 1870 and the Modernists of to-day in
Germany have chiefly gone forth from the universities.
The Council of the Vatican (1870) urged the importance
of higher universities; not of the grade of the German
universities, but of a higher order, to which the best
scholars of the seminaries might resort for the highest
possible theological education. Such institutions were
established at Rome, in Belgium, and in the capital of
the United States. The Catholic Church has long aimed
at one in Ireland; and would undertake to establish
them in other countries, if it were practicable. This
highest theological education, for the training of specialists in Canon Law, Scholastic Theology, and Liturgics,
and also to make great preachers and evangelists, is in
advance of all theological education in the Protestant
world. Protestants also should establish and build up
graduate schools for the study of the highest branches
of theology, both scientific and practical. Otherwise
the future will be disastrous to Protestantism. The
present pope (Pius X.) [2] has undertaken to carry out a
long and carefully prepared scheme for the reformation of seminaries, especially in Italy. The diocesan

[1] Four of the twenty-one universities of Germany have in their
Theological Faculties Roman Catholics only; four have both Catholics
and Protestants; thirteen are wholly Protestant (vide W. A. Brown, in
Monroe's Cyclopedia of Education, v. p. 589).
[2] This was written in March 1913.

seminary is an excellent institution in a large diocese, but a very inefficient institution in a small diocese. In Italy the number of diocesan seminaries was considerably over two hundred. Consolidation was necessary, and is now in course of accomplishment. Furthermore, there is a reform in theological study, in accordance with the study in the best French, English, and American seminaries.

For entrance to the seminary, preparatory study in the lesser seminaries, in the Gymnasium and Lyceum, is required (essentially that of the grammar school and the academy) ; then comes an introductory year in the seminary for the special study of Philosophy. The scheme assigns to the introductory year : *Biblical Greek*, the *Introduction to Church History*, the *True Religion, Theodicy, Cosmology*, the *History of Philosophy*, and *Natural Law* ; to the four years of theology proper : *Greek, Hebrew, Biblical Introduction* and *Exegesis, Church History, Dogmatics, Morals, Pastoral Theology, Liturgics, Canon Law, Patristic, Archæology, Sacred Art*, and *Sacred Eloquence*. The study extends over five years of nine months each, or forty-five months, with seventeen hours of lectures weekly for the first year, and twenty hours weekly for the other four years ; that is, nearly double the amount of time required in some of the leading Protestant institutions. The apportionment of time is also different, the hours being so distributed among the four great departments, that where three are assigned to *Church History*, four are devoted to *Exegetical Theology*, six to *Doctrinal*, and seven to *Practical Theology*.[1]

5. The *Greek Church* in Russia provides for the training of its priests diocesan seminaries, and for the training of teachers and missionaries four theological schools, located at *St. Petersburg, Moscow, Kief*, and *Kazan*. Outside of Russia the Greek clergy receive their training under theological faculties in the universities of *Athens, Bucharest*, and *Czernowitz*, in the seminaries at *Constantinople, Jerusalem, Belgrade, Zara* (Dalmatia),

[1] Vide *Riforma degli Studi nei Seminari in Italia. Lettera e Programma della S. Congr. de' Vescovi e Regolari* (Supplemento agli *Acta Pontificia*, Ottobre 1907) ; Roma 1907.

Hermannstadt and *Karlowitz*, or in smaller seminaries of a lower grade.[1]

There are signs of a revival of the study of theology in the Greek Church.   According to Adeney,

' There is a remarkable development of scholarship among the higher ecclesiastics.   Learning was never allowed to die out in the leading monastic centres ; but hitherto this has been patristic learning without the least recognition of critical scholarship. Now the criticism of the West is breaking into the mind of the East.   Students from the Greek Church are now to be found in German universities.   The result is that the studies of Berlin, and Heidelberg, and Strasburg are being transplanted to Constantinople and Athens.   Already these studies have borne fruit, and the Greek Church is coming forward with its contributions to Historical Theology. [An]other movement . . . of a more popular character . . . consists of the formation of societies for Biblical study.   These societies are quite unecclesiastical in form, and are chiefly maintained by laymen. . . . The movement is spreading rapidly. . . . Meanwhile the need of schools for the clergy is being pressed.' [2]

6. Theological seminaries had their chief development among Protestants in *America*.[3]   Early in the nineteenth century it became evident that there must be more thorough training in theology, and theological seminaries began to be established after the method of the Roman Church.

The earliest of these was founded by the Congregationalists at *Andover* in 1808.   The Dutch Reformed Church established its seminary at *New Brunswick*, New Jersey, in 1810.   The Presbyterians opened one at *Princeton* (1812).   In the years 1816-1819 the Divinity School at *Harvard* was established as a school distinct from the college.   About the same time the Congregational Seminary of *Bangor*, Maine, was founded.   The *General Theological Seminary* was opened by the Protestant Episcopalians in New York City in 1819.   In the following year *Auburn* was founded by the Presbyterians, and *Hamilton* (now *Colgate*) by the

---

[1] *Vide* W. A. Brown, *Cyclopedia of Education*, **v.** p. 589.

[2] Adeney, *The Greek and Eastern Churches*, pp. 337 *seq.*

[3] *Vide* Briggs, 'Theological Education and its Needs,' in *The Forum*, 1892, vol. xii. pp. 634 *seq.*

Baptists. In 1822 the Divinity School at *New Haven* was separated from the college. Three years later *Newton* was founded by the Baptists. In Pennsylvania, the German Reformed opened a seminary at *Lancaster* (1825), and the Lutherans at *Gettysburg* (1826). *Western Seminary* was established by the Presbyterians at Allegheny in 1827, and *Lane* at Cincinnati in 1832. *Hartford Seminary* was founded in 1834, and *Oberlin* in 1835, both by the Congregationalists. *Union Theological Seminary* was established in New York City in 1836. These seminaries devoted themselves to the study of theology in a three years' course, which has never been modified until the present day.

Early in the century there was another struggle [1] among the Presbyterians as to ministerial education, resulting in the separation of the Cumberland Presbyterians (1810), who insisted upon having a godly ministry, and upon accepting godly men as candidates, even if they could not, under the circumstances of a new country, be sufficiently educated.

The Methodists and Baptists were from the very beginning more intent upon an efficient ministry than upon an educated one.

The first Methodist college of any permanency after that of Cokesbury [2] was opened at *Middletown* (1831). The Methodists, however, trained their ministry at conference seminaries. The *Biblical Institute* was organised at Concord, New Hampshire, in 1847 ; but was subsequently removed to Boston (1867), and attached to the *Boston University*. The *Garrett Biblical Institute* at Evanston, Illinois (1854), was adopted as the theological department of *North-Western University*. *Drew* was organised in 1867.

The Baptists and other bodies also gradually organised colleges and seminaries, all being of the same general type.

12. *The Theological Seminary and the University are in mutual need of each other. Theology needs all the light*

---

[1] *Vide* p. 173.   [2] *Vide* p. 171.

that every department of science can give. The University in all its departments leads up to Theology, and cannot gain completeness in any of them without Theology. In recent years there has been a movement to bring the Theological Seminary into closer relation with the University.

Great advantages arose from the organisation of theological seminaries as separate institutions. Theological education made rapid strides forward. The ministry as a class received a higher professional education than they could have had otherwise. Vital piety was developed, as it could not have been in the universities, where the provisions necessary for its development are not so easily made. The study of theology in the university tends to become merely intellectual and scholastic. But if there are perils in the study of theology in the universities, there are perils just as great in the isolation of theologians in the theological seminaries. The tendency of the seminary is to assume a special type of doctrine and to manifest a peculiar type of piety. Both alike are injurious, the one to the scholar's quest for Truth, the other to the Christian's life in God. The theological seminary, by shutting itself off from university life, became limited and cramped. Its students were alienated from their fellow-students in the other professions, and cut off from the progress made in the other departments of learning. But theology has begun to burst through these limitations, and is reaching out in all directions and demanding the larger, freer life of the university. It has unfolded into a great number of studies, overlapping and entwined with those in the other departments of human learning. This expansion makes it impracticable any longer to conduct the study of theology apart from the universities. On the other hand, all the departments of the university are so interrelated to theology that they cannot do their full work without theology. If a way can be found to combine the advantages of an independent theological school with the advantages of a university connection, we may hope to enter upon a new era of theological education, in which the hostility between Science and Religion, Philosophy and Theology, will pass away, and Theology itself expand with the appropriation of fresh material from all departments of human investigation.[1]

In recent years seminaries not attached to universities have been making connections with universities.

In Great Britain, *Mansfield* and *Manchester Colleges* have been affiliated with *Oxford University*, *Cheshunt* with *Cambridge*, *King's College*, the *Highbury School of Divinity*, *New College*, and *Hackney* with *London University*. Other denominational colleges have been brought into connection with the universities of *Wales*, *Manchester*, *Leeds* and *Bristol*. The movement is leading to further experiments in Canada and Australia.[2] It was begun in New York in the *Union Theological Seminary* a few years ago (1890), when an arrangement was made with *Columbia*, into which the *General Theological Seminary* and *New York University* subsequently came, by which the students of the seminaries were enabled to attend courses in the universities. The *Episcopal Divinity School* at Cambridge has entered into friendly relations with *Harvard*, and the *Philadelphia Divinity School* with the *University of Pennsylvania*. *Andover Seminary*, removing to Cambridge (1908), has been affiliated with both *Harvard University* and the *Divinity School*. The *Baptist Seminary* at Chicago has become the theological department of *Chicago University*.

---

[1] *Vide* Briggs, 'Theological Education and its Needs,' in *The Forum*, 1892, vol. xii. pp. 638 *seq.*; 'Ideal of the Study of Theology,' in *Dedication of Union Theological Seminary*, pp. 121 *seq.*; 'The Scope of Theology,' in *American Journal of Theology*, 1897, vol. i. pp. 38 *seq.*

[2] *Vide* W. A. Brown, *Cyclopedia of Education*, v. pp. 593 *seq.*

13. *The field of Theology is now so vast that it is impossible to cover it in three years. Graduate schools are needed, in which the study of Theology may be carried on to the highest degree of excellence and with the most comprehensive thoroughness.*

Theological education is very far from its ideal. The field of study has become so vast that it is no longer possible for the theological student to acquire an adequate knowledge of theology in a three years' course. Some of the seminaries are now offering graduate courses. But the study of theology is still very defective in the great majority of the theological schools, and is still far from perfection in those most richly endowed and manned. Theology, like law and medicine, can no longer do its work without the graduate school, where the choicest men may give from two to four additional years to the more comprehensive and difficult branches of study.[1] The age of irenics has come—an age whose supreme conception of God is love, whose highest estimation of Christ is love, whose ideal of Christian perfection is love. The great fields of study that invite the modern student of theology are *Christian Ethics*, *Christian Sociology*, *Christian Eschatology*, and *Christian Irenics*. Upon these studies of the graduate school of theology to a great extent depends the future of Christianity throughout the world.[2]

14. *The study of Theology is the highest, the most comprehensive, the most difficult, and the most important of*

[1] Union Theological Seminary was the first to establish a graduate department, with graduate professors and courses leading to a doctorate of theology. This action, and that which brought the seminary into connection with the New York universities, were a partial fulfilment of ideals long cherished and worked for by Dr. Briggs, who gave his last years as a teacher of theology to building up a graduate school.

[2] *Vide* Briggs, *The Forum*, vol. xii. pp. 638 *seq.*; *Dedication of the New Buildings of the Union Theological Seminary*, pp. 120 *seq.*; *American Journal of Theology*, vol. viii. pp. 433 *seq.*, 450 *seq.*

all studies ; for it is the study of God, and of all things in
their relations to God.

Theology can have no other final aim than God
Himself, communion with God, knowledge of God, and
the service of God. Upon theology more than upon
any other study the future of humanity depends. It
is a study which brings into fellowship with prophets
and apostles, with all the saints, with Jesus Christ, and
with God the Heavenly Father. It is a study which
calls forth all that is best within a man—his moral and
religious, as well as his intellectual powers. It is a
study which, in all its parts, may be animate with love
to God and love to mankind. It is a study which
men may share with angels and the spirits of the blessed.
It is a study which knows no end. Other studies will
pass away with the decay of the body and departure from
this world ; but the study of theology, begun in this
world, will go on for ever, richer, fuller, and more glorious,
in any and every world, in any and every dispensation,
in which God may place us through all the ages of
eternity.

BIBLIOGRAPHY

THE HISTORY OF THEOLOGICAL EDUCATION

Drane, A. T. *Christian Schools and Scholars, or Sketches of Education from the Christian Era to the Council of Trent.* 1867, 1881, 1910.

Graves, F. P. *A History of Education before the Middle Ages.* 1909.

Graves. *A History of Education during the Middle Ages and the Transition to Modern Times.* 1910.

Kraus, F. X. *Über das Studium der Theologie sonst und jetzt.* 1890².

Sandys, J. E. *A History of Classical Scholarship.* 3 vols. 1903-1908.

Siebengärtner, M. *Schriften und Einrichtungen zur Bildung der Geistlichen.* 1902.

Theiner, A. *Geschichte der geistlichen Bildungsanstalten.* 1835.

SCHOOLS OF THE EARLY CHURCH

Bigg, C. *The Christian Platonists of Alexandria.* 1886.

Chabot, J. B. *L'École de Nisibe.* 1896.

Duval, R. *Histoire politique, religieuse et littéraire d'Édesse.* 1892.

Guericke, H. E. F. *De schola quae Alexandriæ floruit catechetica.* 1824-1825.

Hergenröther, P. *Die antiochenische Schule.* 1866.

Kihn, H. *Die Bedeutung der antiochenischen Schule auf dem exegetischen Gebiete, nebst einer Abhandlung über die ältesten christlichen Schulen, besonders zu Antiochia, Edessa und Nisibis.* 1865-1866.

Kihn. *Theodor von Mopsuestia und Junilius Africanus als Exegeten.* 1880.

Kingsley, C. *Alexandria and her Schools.* 1854.

MATTER, J.   *Essai historique sur l'école d'Alexandrie.*   2 vols. 1820.

MOORE, G. F.   'The Theological School at Nisibis,' in *Studies in the History of Religions.*   1912.

SEITZ, K.   *Die Schule von Gaza.*   1892.

VACHEROT, E.   *Histoire critique de l'école d'Alexandrie.*   3 vols. 1846-1851.

THE PALATINE, CATHEDRAL, AND MONASTIC SCHOOLS

BOURRET, J. C. E.   *L'École chrétienne de Séville, sous la monarchie des Visigoths.*   1855.

CLERVAL, A.   *Les écoles de Chartres au moyen âge, du Ve au XVIe siècle.*

COOPER-MARSDIN, A.   *The School of Lérins.*

HEALY, J.   *Insula sanctorum et doctorum, or Ireland's Ancient Schools and Scholars.*   1890.

DOUAIS, C.   *Essai sur l'Organisation des Études dans l'Ordre des Frères Prêcheurs au 13e et au 14e Siècle.*   1884.

KAUFMANN, G.   'Rhetorenschulen und Klosterschulen in Gallien während des V. und VI. Jahrhunderts,' in *Historisches Taschenbuch.*   1869.

MAÎTRE, L.   *Les écoles épiscopales et monastiques de l'Occident (768-1180).*   1866.

MICHAUD, E.   *Guillaume de Champaux et les écoles de Paris au XIIe siècle.*   1867.

MULLINGER, J. B.   *The Schools of Charles the Great, and the Restoration of Education in the Ninth Century.*   1877, 1911.

ROBERT, G.   *Les écoles et l'enseignement de la théologie pendant la première moitié du XIIe siècle.*   1909.

SPECHT, F. A.   *Geschichte des Unterrichtswesens in Deutschland von den ältesten Zeiten bis zur Mitte des XIII. Jahrhunderts.*   1885.

THE UNIVERSITY OF PARIS AND THE GREAT SCHOLASTICS

DENIFLE, H.   *Die Entstehung der Universitäten des Mittelalters bis 400.*   1885.

DENIFLE.   *Les Universités françaises au moyen âge.*   1892.

FERET, P. *La Faculté de théologie de Paris et ses docteurs les plus célèbres.* 11 vols. 1894-1910.

HUGO OF ST. VICTOR († 1141). *Didascalion.*

POOLE, R. L. *Illustrations of the History of Medieval Thought in the Departments of Theology and Ecclesiastical Politics.* 1884.

RASHDALL, H. *The Universities of Europe in the Middle Ages.* Vol. i. (Paris), 1895.

THE UNIVERSITIES OF ENGLAND AND THE BRITISH SCHOLASTICS

BRODRICK, G. C. *A History of the University of Oxford.* [1887.]

HUBER, V. A. *The English Universities* (an abridged translation), ed. F. W. Newman. 2 vols., 1843.

MULLINGER, J. B. *History of the University of Cambridge.* 2 vols., 1873-1883 ; 3 vols., 1911.

PARKER, J. *The Early History of Oxford.* Oxford Historical Society Publications, vol. iii., 1885.

RASHDALL, H. *The Universities of Europe in the Middle Ages.* Vol. ii. Part ii. ('English Universities'), 1895.

THE UNIVERSITIES OF GERMANY, BOHEMIA, AND GERMAN SWITZERLAND

ANDREAE, J. *Oratio de studio sacrarum litterarum.* 1576.

ASCHLBACH, J. *Geschichte der Wiener Universität im ersten Jahrhundert ihres Bestehens.* 2 vols. 1865-1877.

BAUCH, G. *Die Universität Erfurt im Zeitalter des Frühhumanismus.* 1904.

BÖK, A. F. *Geschichte der . . . Universität zu Tübingen.* 1774.

BRIEGER, T. *Die theologischen Promotionen auf der Universität Leipzig, 1428-1539.* 1890.

HÖFLER, C. A. C. *Magister Johannes Hus und der Abzug der deutschen Professoren und Studenten aus Prag, 1409.* 1864.

KAMPSCHULTE, F. W. *Die Universität Erfurt in ihrem Verhältnis zum Humanismus und der Reformation.* 2 vols. 1858-1860.

KAUFMANN, G. *Geschichte der deutschen Universitäten.* 2 vols. 1888-1896.

KOSEGARTEN, J. G. L.   *Geschichte der Universität Greifswald.*
1857.

MEINERS, C.   *Geschichte der Entstehung und Entwickelung der
hohen Schulen unseres Erdteils.*   4 vols.   1802-1805.

MUTHER, T.   *Aus dem Universitäts- und Gelehrtenleben im
Zeitalter der Reformation.*   1866.

PAULSEN, F.   *The German Universities* (translated from the
German edition of 1902).   1906.

PAULSEN.   *Geschichte des gelehrten Unterrichts auf den deutschen
Schulen und Universitäten vom Ausgang des Mittelalters bis
zur Gegenwart.*   2 vols.   1896.

PRANTL, C. v.   *Geschichte der Ludwig-Maximilians-Universität
in Ingolstadt, Landshut, München.*   2 vols.   1872.

STÖCKER.   *Die theologische Fakultät in Heidelberg, 1386-1886.*
1886.

THORBECKE, A.   *Die älteste Zeit der Universität Heidelberg,
1386-1449.*   1886.

VISCHER, W.   *Geschichte der Universität Basel von der Gründung
1460 bis zur Reformation 1529.*   1860.

THE INFLUENCE OF THE REFORMERS ON THEO-
LOGICAL EDUCATION IN GERMANY AND GERMAN
SWITZERLAND

ANDREAE, J.   *Oratio de instauratione studii theologici in academia
Witebergensi.*   1577.

BRÜSTLEIN, J.   *Luthers Einfluss auf das Volksschulwesen und
den Religionsunterricht.*   1852.

GREVING, K. M. N. J.   *Johann Eck als junger Gelehrter.*   1906.

HEPPE, H.   *Philipp Melanchthon, der Lehrer Deutschlands.*   1860.

KOCH, L.   *Philipp Melanchthon's Schola Privata.*   1859.

LUTHER, M.   *Methodus studii theologici interprete Hieronymo
Wellero . . . cura I. G. Iochii.*   1726.

LUTHER.   *Regulæ de theologiæ studio recte instituendo,* ed. F.
Delitzsch.   1842.

LUTHER.   *Anweisung zum rechten Studium der Theologie . . .
von Hieron. Weller.*   1727, 1881.

MELANCHTHON, P.   *Brevis discendæ theologiæ ratio.*   1530.

PAINTER, F. V. N.   *Luther on Education.*   1889.

PLANCK, A. *Melanchthon, Præceptor Germaniæ.* 1860.

PORTA, C. *Pastorale Lutheri.* 1582, 1842.

RÜCKERT, O. *Zwingli's Ideen zur Erziehung und Bildung.* 1900.

WELLER, H. *Consilium de studio theologiæ rite instituendo ac feliciter continuando modoque recte disponendi et habendi conciones.* 1561, 1565, 1569, 1614, 1617.

WELLER. *Ratio formandi studii theologici.* 1563.

WOODWARD, W. A. *Desiderius Erasmus concerning the Aim and Method of Education.* 1904.

THE SCHOOL OF CALVIN AT GENEVA AND THE FRENCH ACADEMIES

AUZIÈRE, L. *Essai historique sur les facultés de théologie de Saumur et de Sedan.* 1836.

BAIRD, H. M. 'Notes on Theological Education in the Reformed Churches of France and French Switzerland,' in *Presbyterian Review*, January 1880, vol. i. pp. 85 *seq.*

BORGEAUD, C. *Histoire de l'Université de Genève.* 2 vols. 1900-1909.

BOURCHENIN, D. *Étude sur les académies protestantes en France au XVIe et au XVIIe siècle.* 1882.

COLANI, T. *L'éducation protestante.* 1858.

FÉLICE, P. DE. *Les Protestants d'autrefois.* 4 vols. 1897-1902.

JESUIT THEOLOGICAL EDUCATION

CAMBILHON, J. *Relatio de studiis Iesuitarum abstrusioribus.* 1608.

GRETZER, J. *Relatio de studiis Iesuitarum abstrusioribus.* 1609.

HUGHES, T. *Loyola and the Educational System of the Jesuits.* 1892, 1907.

IGNACIO DE LOYOLA. *Epistolæ et instructiones,* ed. Matriti, 1903 : *v. Monumenta Ignatiana,* Series I., tom. 1. 1908.

PACHTLER, G. M. *Ratio studiorum et institutiones scholasticæ Societatis Iesu; v. Monumenta Germaniæ Pædagogica.* Vols. ii., v., ix., xvi. 1887-1894.

STEINHUBER, A. *Geschichte des Kollegium Germanikum-Hungarikum in Rom.* 2 vols. 1893-1894, 1906.

ROMAN CATHOLIC SEMINARIES OF THE COUNCIL
OF TRENT

BELLESHEIM, A. *Wilhelm Cardinal Allen und die englischen Seminare auf dem Festlande.* 1885.

BORROMEO, C. *Pastorum instructiones.* 1586, 1701.

DANCOISNE, L. *Histoire des établissements religieux britanniques fondés à Douai avant la révolution française.* 1880.

GERARD, J. *Stonyhurst College, Its Life beyond the Seas, 1592-1794, and on English soil, 1794-1894.* 1894.

HOGAN, J. B. *Clerical Studies.* 1898.

LETOURNEAU, G. *Histoire du Séminaire d'Angers.* 3 vols. 1893-1895.

THEINER, A. *Il Seminario ecclesiastico.* 1834.

THEINER. *Geschichte der geistlichen Bildungsanstalten.* 1835.

THEMISTOR, G. *Die Bildung und Erziehung der Geistlichen nach katholischen Grundsätzen.* 1884.

ZSCHOKKE, H. *Die theologischen Studien und Anstalten der katholischen Kirche in Oesterreich.* 1894.

ZWICKENPFLUG, R. *Die Bildung der Geistlichen.* 4 vols. 1844.

INDEX TO VOL. II